Introducing Sociology

INTRODUCING SOCIOLOGY:

A Critical Perspective

Murray Knuttila

OXFORD
UNIVERSITY PRESS

OXFORD
UNIVERSITY PRESS

70 Wynford Drive, Don Mills, Ontario M3C 1J9

Oxford   New York
Athens   Auckland   Bangkok   Bombay
Calcutta   Cape Town   Dar es Salaam   Delhi
Florence   Hong Kong   Istanbul   Karachi
Kuala Lumpur   Madras   Madrid   Melbourne
Mexico City   Nairobi   Paris   Singapore
Taipei   Tokyo   Toronto

and associated companies in
Berlin   Ibadan

Oxford is a trademark of Oxford University Press

Canadian Cataloguing in Publication Data

Knuttila, Kenneth Murray
  Introducing sociology : a critical perspective

Rev. ed. of: Sociology revisited: basic concepts and
perspectives.
Includes bibliographical references and index.
ISBN 0-19-541207-9

1. Sociology.   I. Title.   II. Title: Sociology revisited:
basic concepts and perspectives.

HM51.K68   1996   301   C95-932546-8

This book is printed on permanent (acid-free) paper   .

Printed in Canada

CONTENTS

*For my mother, Allie,
and the memory of my father,
Charles Knuttila*

PREFACE

A great deal of the material in this volume was first presented in an earlier edition titled *Sociology Revisited: Basic Concepts and Perspectives*. While much of the material remains unchanged, much of it has been quite radically reorganized, and with the addition of several new chapters a new title was deemed appropriate. The new title is meant to suggest a *double entente* because the reader is asked to be critical of sociology while working toward the development of a critical sociology.

No single brief volume can possibly introduce any social science discipline; nevertheless, it is hoped that the material presented here will allow the reader to begin to grasp some of the essential features of sociological thought. The book is organized into three major sections. In Part I the reader encounters the basic concepts employed by sociologists in their efforts to understand human beings and our behaviour. Part II provides a critical overview of key developments in sociological theory, suggesting that recent feminist critiques have placed in question the entire agenda of previous theoretical work. The reader is encouraged to think systematically about the nature of sex and gender relations and to use the capacities of social theories to address these key issues as a benchmark when examining and evaluating these theories. In Part III an effort is made to illustrate the nature of sociological analysis by outlining some of the ways sociologists look at specific issues such as social inequality, the polity, deviance, and familial relations.

The overarching, unifying theme of each section is "the promise" of the sociological imagination. We must accept the underlying logic of the work of C.W. Mills and attempt to ensure that sociological thought, analysis, and theory contribute to fulfilling the potential of the discipline by facilitating a greater degree of self-understanding.

PART I

The Sociological Perspective and the Basic Language of Sociology

The first task a newcomer to a discipline faces is to become familiar with the basic language, concepts, assumptions, and premises that the discipline uses and embraces. The first five chapters of this book introduce the reader to the basic language, concepts, assumptions, and premises that sociologists use in their approach to analysing and understanding the social behaviour of Homo sapiens.

A simple yet important assumption informs all of the material presented in this volume, namely, that we are interested in and capable of understanding better ourselves, our behaviour and character, and the behaviour and character of others. C.W. Mills referred to the capacity to understand ourselves and our behaviour sociologically as the "sociological imagination." The first chapter introduces the discipline of sociology, examines how it is different from other disciplines, and explores the notion of the sociological imagination.

In Chapter 2 we begin to encounter the key elements of the sociological approach to understanding humans and their social behaviours when we learn that it is more appropriate to understand humans as cultural, as opposed to instinctual, creatures. Chapter 3 moves from the study of culture to an analysis of human society. When sociologists analyse human society, that is, resolve it into its component parts, they conclude that it can be understood to be composed of institutions, roles, statuses, values, norms, groups, and so on. These concepts represent the core language of the discipline. Chapter 4 connects the individual to the social structure by examining the importance of social learning, in sociology known as "socialization," for human development. In many ways Chapter 4 presents *the* core idea of the sociological perspective, specifically that our character, personality, and behaviour have been, and constantly are, radically influenced by our social environment and experiences. The last chapter in Part I presents

11

several alternate explanations of the processes by which human personality and character develop. Chapter 5 challenges the reader to consider alternate theories of socialization and personality formation with an eye to synthesizing insights from a variety of perspectives to better account for this complex process.

1

UNDERSTANDING HUMAN BEHAVIOUR

In a far-off country, terrorists plant a bomb that destroys a jumbo jet and ends the lives of 250 people who most likely know little or nothing about the cause they are dying for. At precisely the same moment in a city in another part of the world, rescue workers risk their lives to remove children from a burning building. Nearby, lovers in a city park hold hands and promise to treasure each other forever. Across town yet another woman is admitted to hospital after being battered by her spouse.

In a number of geographically scattered locations, families celebrate special events by feasting on different delicacies: food as diverse as raw sea urchins, sheep brains, spicy lentil soup, and partly cooked calf rump. Some of the celebrants eat with their fingers, others use long, thin, wooden sticks, and still others use silver utensils. In a Western city, two youths impulsively decide to rob a convenience store, while across town two other young people are considering the clothes they'll wear the next morning, on their first day of university classes.

After a wedding meal in one country, the loud burp of a guest causes considerable embarrassment among those present; in another part of the world a dinner guest's burp is ignored, understood as a compliment and an indication that the meal was thoroughly satisfying.

For students interested in understanding human behaviour, these snippets of human conduct raise important questions. What is terrorism? Why are terrorists willing to kill and injure people who have no direct connection to their particular grievances? What makes humans risk their lives for others? What is the role of romantic love in society? Why are women the most common victims of domestic violence in our society? What kinds of foods are considered tasty, and what kinds are unpalatable? What modes of conduct are appropriate during and after the consumption of food? Why do some people attend university while others do not? Why do some people commit acts defined as criminal while others do not? What is a criminal act? Above all else, perhaps, why do human beings exhibit so many and so diverse kinds of behaviour?

To answer questions like these we must be prepared and able to think systematically about human behaviour, about what is going on and why we behave and act in certain ways. And when we begin to consider the actions and behaviour of ourselves and others, we quickly realize that we are dealing with subject matter that is incredibly complex and wide-ranging.

We find out that all aspects of human behaviour, even the seemingly most trivial and unimportant events, are part of complex social processes that occur within complicated sets of social structures, rules, and conventions. To engage in this task, to explore this apparently formidable terrain of human behaviour and actions, we clearly need to use a wide variety of intellectual tools.

The social sciences aim to provide those tools necessary for understanding behaviour and existence. We use the plural form, social sciences, because different social science disciplines take different approaches, or use different tools, to answer the same questions. Anthropologists, psychologists, geographers, economists, political scientists, historians, sociologists tend to focus on different aspects of human social existence. Given the complexities of the subject matter, this is undoubtedly a necessary and desirable situation. No one discipline is capable of providing all the insights necessary for an understanding of the many and varied dimensions of human life. Indeed, each discipline is itself also broken down into subfields – it is next to impossible for any one person to cover any one particular field in its entirety.

Science as a Way of Knowing

Although the various social sciences approach the study of human behaviour differently, they all have at least one thing in common: they make an effort to be scientific. Used in this context, *scientific* refers to an approach to knowledge production that is systematic and based on specified principles and methods.

There are a number of possible responses to the simple questions "Why is that happening?" and "How do you know that?" You could cite an authority as your source – a special book, a special person, or even an oracle. The essence of this way of knowing is the total acceptance of the authority as an unquestioned source of knowledge. What you know is defined by the particular authority, and you have complete trust in that authority. Less common these days as a source of knowing is the experience of revelation, in which some unusual and even mystical occasion or phenomenon provides a certain knowledge. History is full of instances of individuals who claim to know something because of an experience that brings about a revelation.

We more often say we know things just because it is "plain old common sense." Indeed, much of what we call knowledge in our society is based on common sense, defined by one dictionary as "sound practical judgment that is independent of specialized knowledge or training." It reflects a kind of "normal native intelligence." Common sense might tell us that we should wear a hat when we go out into a cold rain. It tells us to lock our doors when we go out at night. It might warn us that it is wise not to "burn the candle at both ends." These bits of advice seem valid enough. But at one time common sense also told Europeans that the Earth was flat.

M.H. Walizer and P.L. Wienir (1978) note that common-sense knowledge is often presented in the form of old sayings. The problem is, some of those sayings – such as "opposites attract" and "birds of a feather stick together" or "he who hesitates is lost" and "look before you leap" – can directly contradict one another. Although common-sense knowledge is pervasive, it often forms an obstacle to systematic social analysis and investigation because of its inconsistencies and inaccuracies.

In Western society we have come to downplay both the authoritative and the mystical ways of knowing. Instead we rely on *science*, a way of knowing and a way of producing knowledge based on a number of basic assumptions or premises – even though these assumptions and premises are not often explicitly spelled out by scientists themselves in their work. First, the scientific method assumes that an external objective world exists outside of and apart from the human individual who is attempting to understand that world. Second, it assumes that we can secure information, knowledge, and an understanding of the world by collecting data through experimentation or observation. Scientists refer to this as empirical data. Third, the practice of science assumes that there is order and regularity in the world – that there is *causality*. Conditions, phenomena, or events are not created or do not just happen randomly and accidentally; rather, they are caused, and by following proper scientific procedures we can come to know and understand these causes.

While there are continuing debates about how to turn empirical data into knowledge and understanding, the practitioners in most scientific disciplines tend to agree that the production of knowledge requires the use of both empirical data and human reason. Scientists use both inductive and deductive thinking to produce knowledge about the world. *Inductive* thinking moves from the particular to the general, meaning that a general claim or statement is made after studying individual or particular instances of some phenomenon. *Deductive* thinking moves from the general to the particular. A conclusion about some particular phenomenon is deduced or drawn on the basis of some established general premise or law. In either case, scientists use knowledge grounded in empirical reality to provide a basis for making generalized statements about that world.

Building on these assumptions, the scientific approach specifies a series of steps or procedures that guide practitioners in their search for knowledge and understanding. The first step involves the selection of a problem, which becomes the centre of the investigation. Since science seeks to answer questions about both what is happening and why things happen, the second step involves the adoption or elaboration of a theory or explanatory framework. The explanation adopted may or may not be correct, so it must be tested and proved through empirical research. After scientists conduct research and analyse the data, they draw conclusions, which seek to provide answers to the initial problem. What is important about this method of knowing is its demands for empirical confirmation and verification of all statements that claim to represent knowledge in a field. If all contentions are not supported by proof and evidence, the knowledge is not accepted as scientific.

The data and evidence required in various disciplines can be different, so each discipline has its own procedures and methods for gathering data. The one common requirement is that the practitioners in the area recognize the methods used for gathering data as legitimate, and that other scientists are able to repeat them – which is referred to as replication. A part of learning about a given discipline is learning about the modes of inquiry and the standards of evidence characteristic of that discipline.

Sociology and the Social Sciences

In their efforts to understand human behaviour social scientists have developed a diversity of disciplines, of which sociology is only one. By focusing on different aspects of human social existence and behaviour, each discipline in its own way contributes to the project of understanding human behaviour.

Anthropology
There is a common misconception that anthropology and anthropologists are only interested in the study of pre-industrial or non-

industrial societies. Indeed, much of the classical literature in anthropology does focus on non-industrial societies or what the practitioners often referred to as "primitive societies" – thus revealing their own biased sense of cultural or racial superiority. But the discipline is also interested in the modern world. Anthropology is the study of human development and culture in a comparative and systematic manner, with an interest in the physical and cultural structures and development of the human species. The discipline is divided into several branches, with physical anthropology addressing the physical development of the human species and its relationship to the physical environment. Social or cultural anthropology concerns itself with the history, origin, characteristics, and structures of contemporary and past cultures. Linguistics and the study of human communication are also important parts of the anthropological enterprise, along with the study and recovery of physical artifacts, which is also the mandate of archeology.

Economics

The study of material production, consumption, and distribution is the purview of economics. Economics is usually defined as the study of the production, distribution, exchange, and consumption of various goods and services. Because economists deal with a large number of issues, from local pricing structures to patterns of international trade, the discipline is commonly divided into macroeconomics and microeconomics. Macroeconomics focuses on the study of the "big picture" or the aggregate level, looking at the larger patterns of production, consumption, savings, and investment at the national and international levels as well as looking at the impact of government actions and policies. Microeconomics concerns itself with economic activity and associated behaviour at the level of individual decision-making units and with associated theories of production, consumption, and distribution.

Geography

The human animal exists in an intimate relationship with the physical environment of the earth. Geography concentrates on the study of the earth's physical properties and characteristics and the relationship of these properties and characteristics to the human species, with recent studies ranging from the relationship between time and space to the development of urban areas. Geography is "located" somewhat between the social and natural sciences; at some universities it is considered a natural science and at others it is a social science. Like other disciplines there are internal specializations, with the key ones being physical and cultural (or human) geography. In an era of increasingly serious environmental crisis, geography's study of the relationship between the physical environment and the human species has become particularly important.

History

The importance of learning from the past has been a part of the common-sense knowledge of virtually every human society. In the university setting the discipline of history plays an important role because history is, by definition, the study of human and social development through the ages. When historians study the past record of human social development they do so with an eye to determining if there are patterns and regularities or if the events that occurred were unique parts of a larger and longer process.

Political Science

Political science is the social science whose mandate is perhaps most clearly understood by the average person, although most non-specialists do not fully understand the entire gamut of concerns that political scientists address. In focusing on the organization, structure, operation, and administration of the polity, including the operation of the government, political scientists are most often deeply concerned with the history and development of these institutions. While political scientists who appear on television to give commentary on elections and constitutional matters are undoubtedly interested in political parties and voting, they are also likely to be concerned with theories of political power and government and with the comparative study of all aspects of decision-making at the political and social levels.

Psychology

If political scientists tend to get the most media exposure on television news, psychologists are more often portrayed in the movies or on television dramas. As a discipline psychology focuses on the study of the mind, the personality, individual behaviour, and various mental processes. Psychologists tend to concentrate or specialize in various subfields or areas of specialization within the discipline, ranging from behavioural and experimental through clinical and social. Key areas of concern in the behavioural field include learning, intelligence, emotions, thinking, memory, and perception, while applied psychology is concerned with the diagnosis and treatment of personality, learning, and other disorders.

Sociology as the Study of Structure and Agency

How and where does sociology fit into this array of social sciences?

The term "sociology" appears to have been coined by the French thinker Auguste Comte around 1830. The two stems of the word are *socius*, Latin for "companion," and *logos*, Greek for "the study of," which together give us "the study of companionship" as a literal definition. But in its development as a discipline sociology has come to mean much more than this. The standard dictionary and introductory textbook definitions of sociology tend to refer to it as the scientific and systematic study of human society; but this short and general definition is of limited value, because it could just as easily apply to most of the other social science disciplines. Even if we extend the definition to include the scientific study of both human society and human behaviour, it is still not clear precisely what ground the discipline covers and how it is different from the other social sciences.

In their sociology dictionary, Nicholas Abercrombie, Stephen Hill, and Bryan S. Turner provide the basis for a useful definition of sociology by suggesting that sociology is not only the "study of the basis of social membership" – a translation of its literal meaning – but also "the analysis of the structure of social relationships as constituted by social interaction" (1988: 232). This very general definition is a useful point of departure for understanding just how the sociological enterprise is different from the other social sciences and how it contributes to the main goal of understanding human behaviour and action.

When Auguste Comte first used the term "sociology" he was trying to explain his own grandiose project. Comte was, somewhat immodestly, attempting to establish a new discipline that would represent nothing less than the crowning achievement of Western intellectual development. He was going to provide an approach to human affairs that would assist the establishment of an orderly social world. Such a discipline would have to address an enormous range of social issues. Few sociologists have ever attempted to develop an approach as grand as the one envisioned by Comte, although the discipline of sociology does tend to provide a broader and more holistic approach to human social existence than most of the other disciplines. Sociologists sometimes annoy their colleagues in other disciplines by borrowing ideas, concepts, data, and theories in the attempt to understand the entire social structure and the relationship of the individual to that social structure.

In a real sense sociology is differentiated from the other social sciences by its insistence that we need to understand the "larger picture" of how human beings are shaped and moulded by society and how humans in turn are a part of the process by which society is *produced* and also *reproduced* through labour power, both in the outside workplace and in the family and domestic labour. While sociologists recognize the importance of the work of the other social scientists, they would argue that the distinct areas covered by those other disciplines tell only part of the story. If we are to understand human behaviour and action, the insights of all the disciplines must be brought to bear and focused on the entire social structure. This holistic, comprehensive focus on social structure is one of sociology's tasks. But sociologists are also interested in studying people as individuals and the relationship of individuals to the larger society. All the various social science disciplines address this issue, but only one of them – sociology – makes it an essential component of its agenda or general project.

Sociology attempts to understand how the structures and processes of the social system influence human development, action, and behaviour. In addition, sociology also seeks to understand how social structures and processes themselves do not necessarily exist on their own but rather emerge out of the actions and behaviour of individuals. Sociology studies how people, acting both as individuals and together, influence and have an impact on the society. Sociologists believe that the holistic approach is the basis of improved self-understanding, and that self-understanding should be an essential objective of the social sciences.

Sociology can be defined, then, as the systematic analysis and investigation of how human beings, as social agents, produce their social structures, and how human beings are produced – and reproduced – by those structures.

To accomplish this task sociology engages in the systematic and scientific investigation of social structures, social relationships, and social interactions.

The Sociological Imagination and Its "Promise"

For many sociologists the essential mandate of modern sociology comes not from Comte but from an American sociologist, C. Wright Mills. He is perhaps best known for his books *White Collar* (1951) and *The Power Elite* (1956). A third book, *The Sociological Imagination* (1959), is also still widely read and remains one of the most important books in the discipline, in part because of the project it lays out for sociology and all the social sciences.

In the first chapter of *The Sociological Imagination*, "The Promise,"

Mills argues that the development of the ability or intellectual capacity that he calls the sociological imagination is essential for all citizens of modern complex societies. For Mills, the sociological imagination is an intellectual capacity, an ability or quality of mind – a kind of thinking that is essential if we want to begin to understand ourselves, our behaviour, and the behaviour of others around us, near and far.

Mills uses several different phrases to explain the concept, including "the quality of mind essential to grasp the interplay of man and society, of biography and history, of self and world." Elsewhere he notes, "The sociological imagination enables us to grasp history and biography and the relations between the two within society." He also states that the sociological imagination promises "an understanding of the intimate realities of ourselves in connection with larger social realities," an ability that if developed will allow human reason "to play a greater role in human affairs" (1959: 4, 6, 15).

The desire to understand ourselves should not be seen as something new. Indeed, the search for self-understanding has always been a part of what makes the human animal distinct. As our world seems to get more and more complex and confusing the task seems to become more difficult, yet an understanding of the structures and processes of society seems more important than ever.

Biography and History
According to Mills, the key to self-understanding is to grapple with the distinction between biography and history. Each of us has an individual biography or life story, and each of these individual biographies is set or located in a larger social and historical context. Each and every one of us was born into, grew up and developed in, and currently exists in a society that itself is part of an emerging and continuing historical process. We cannot understand much about our individual lives without locating ourselves in society and in the historical processes that have shaped, structured, and moulded that society. As Mills points out, although we may not always realize it the larger developments that take place in society and history have a direct impact on all of us as individuals.

For example, with the outbreak of war a person's entire life can change even if that individual has nothing to do with the causes of the war and is opposed to war. When an economic depression sets in, an entire family's way of life can change, due entirely to forces and factors beyond the members' immediate control. A new tax law has an impact on the country's whole economy, leading to lost jobs or new jobs and dramatic changes in the lives of many citizens. If a student receives failing grades at school, the tendency might be simply to think of the failure as a personal problem – the student didn't work hard enough or isn't intelligent enough. But perhaps the grades are really the product of having to work at two part-time jobs to pay for the university course or help out the folks back home. This factor would place the school performance in a new light. Similarly, a woman who experiences sexual harassment must be able to understand that the root cause of her problem is not to be found in her behaviour, demeanour, or dress, but rather in the social dynamics of a patriarchal and sexist society.

Simple as they are, these examples illustrate Mills's point, namely that our individual lives are not lived in a vacuum; rather, they unfold within a complex system of social structures, processes, and events. The situating of our lives in this larger context is an essential prerequisite for understanding ourselves, and this situating process is the task of the sociological imagination. The first step in the development of the sociological imagination is therefore to grasp the intimate connection between your own life and the historically developing society around about you.

The Three Vital Questions

The ability to connect our lives and our individual biographies with the larger social structures around us is just the first step in developing the sociological imagination. It should lead us to pose fundamental questions about ourselves and our society. Mills argues that a person's capacity for self-understanding, that is, the sociological imagination, is not complete without the capacity to ask and answer three different but essential kinds of questions (1959: 6-7):

1. What are the structures of my society like? How is my society organized and how does it operate? How is it similar to and different from other societies?
2. Where does my society fit into the broader picture of human history? How does the history of my society influence its current organization? What are the most important aspects of the current historical epoch? Where does my society seem to be going?
3. How do the structures of my society and the historical period of which I am a part influence me and those around me? What social and historical forces have shaped and molded my character and personality?

If individuals understand that their personal life stories, their biographies, are intimately tied to the history and development – as well as the current state – of their society, and if those individuals are able to ask and answer Mills's three types of questions, then they are well on the road to developing their sociological imaginations. The promise of the sociological imagination is quite simple – with a little thought and intellectual effort we can develop an understanding of ourselves and those around us. Such an understanding is the first step in ensuring that our lives are lived to their fullest and that we do indeed possess a degree of control over our destinies.

Developing the Sociological Perspective

For beginning students the subject matter of sociology often appears to be quite ordinary, mundane, and everyday. Certainly, sociologists do deal with many issues and processes that are a routine part of our everyday lives. Students in their first sociology course already know something about, have read about, thought about, or at least hold opinions about many of the issues and topics normally covered in the course. In some instances students just beginning to study society might even consider themselves experts in a given area, such as politics or religion, because they have been politically active for years or gone to church all their life.

In sociology, however, we tend to adopt an approach and a perspective that are different from those we use in our everyday lives. The sociological approach is different, in part because it looks at all social issues and processes in a deliberate, systematic, and holistic manner, with an eye to understanding their larger significance and role for society, as well as their impact on individuals and their development. A systematic investigation of what we thought was a simple issue about which we knew nearly everything can produce startling results. Being familiar with something at the level of "common sense" does not, it turns out, necessarily mean that you are an expert – or even that what you think you know is in fact correct. When there are fundamental differences between what we "know" at the levels of common sense and scientific knowledge, and when these differences result in a fundamental questioning of what we "know," the result is often controversial – as most students will quickly discover.

Sociologists maintain that even though we think we know everything about some phenomenon, we can still be wrong and our supposed "knowledge" can be flawed. What is required if we are to understand our complex social behaviours, they argue, is systematic thinking and research coupled with analytical perspectives. Usually the approach adopted in sociology is to do that work within a particular subfield.

The Subfields of Sociology

Like all of the disciplines in the social sciences, sociology is subdivided into fields or areas of specialization. For example, most economists wouldn't dream of studying all aspects of the production, distribution, and consumption of goods and services, and not many historians try to focus on all aspects of human history. Likewise, political scientists usually don't concentrate on every aspect of the polity and the political process. The complexity of human social structures and existence makes it nearly – if not completely – impossible for a practitioner in any field to be an expert or a specialist in all areas.

To understand the basic organization of the discipline it is necessary first to understand the basis of what is commonly called the sociological perspective. For simplicity's sake the *sociological perspective* can be summarized as the argument that the human animal is unique because it cannot exist, develop, or be understood outside of the context of human society. The society into which we are born and within which we develop and exist exercises a profound influence on our characters, personalities, behaviours, and whole beings. Understanding the overall structures, development, and processes of our society is the point of departure for self-understanding.

But human society is so complex and complicated that most of us cannot grasp its operation in its entirety. As a result sociologists have come to specialize in the study and analysis of particular aspects of society. The following partial list illustrates some of the areas of specialization, or subfields, that characterize modern sociology.

- Sex and gender roles
- Crime and criminology
- Health and medicine
- Education
- Religion
- Social stratification
- Class analysis
- Social movements and collective behaviour
- Industrial relations
- Ethnic group dynamics
- Power and domination
- The polity and the political process
- Sports and leisure
- Population and demography
- Art in society
- Mass media
- Social change

- Theories of society
- Research and the data-gathering process
- Urban development and structures
- Rural development and structures
- Knowledge
- Work
- Development and underdevelopment
- Family and household
- War and revolution
- Deviance and social problems
- The aging process

In essence, what sociologists do is investigate and study many different, and often quite particular, aspects of the social process.

Getting On with Sociological Analysis

Within the approach I am presenting here, sociology is not so much a specific body of knowledge as a mode of thinking. We must be confident that we can untangle and understand the complexities of our social existence, made up as it is of a web of interactions and relationships influenced by, among other factors, class, gender, race, nation, age, culture, religion, and locale or region. Although the task is difficult, we must be prepared to undertake the necessary research and thought to facilitate clarification and understanding.

In the pages that follow you will be encouraged to subject both your social existence and the discipline of sociology to a critical examination. In so doing you must be prepared to place both what you think you know and what sociologists and others have claimed they know under careful scrutiny. As I hope will soon become apparent, the existing approaches in sociology often seem ill-equipped and unable to account for life in the 1990s. If this is the case, the criticisms of thinkers influenced by important new approaches such as feminism must be acknowledged, and their insights must be incorporated into a reassessment of how we practise our craft as sociologists.

Throughout this book you will be asked to be critical of what you already know – or think you know. You will be expected to examine and re-examine, to be analytical and critical, and not to accept what you think you know until you have systematically investigated and examined the phenomenon you are interested in. The book emphasizes the centrality of systematic critical thought because the capacity to engage in such a process is one of the defining characteristics of the human species. If we are to realize our potentials and better ourselves and our species we must use our intelligence in a constructive manner; and using our intelligence constructively requires that we know how to think, how to engage in research, and how to arrive at satisfactory conclusions.

As we undertake these activities, we must also realize that the results of our intellectual efforts and the conclusions we reach may not be agreeable to everyone. The process of producing knowledge that is predicated on critical thought has always produced controversy, and even discord. Isn't it true that to live life fully and to make it worth living, you must examine it fully and understand it to the best of your abilities?

Terms and Concepts

Science – a way of knowing or producing knowledge that emphasizes the role of both empirical data and theoretically informed explanation. While scientists insist that all claims to knowledge must be supported by empirical data, they are also aware of empirical data being intimately connected to theoretical frameworks. They use theoretical frameworks and perspectives to order and make sense out of empirical data; thus the data never simply "speak for themselves," but must be interpreted.

Sociology – the systematic study, analysis, interpretation, and explanation of how human beings are produced by the social structures within which they develop and exist, and of how human beings in turn produce these social structures. Sociology adopts a holistic approach to the study of humans and society, freely incorporating insights, ideas, and perspectives from a variety of other disciplines.

The sociological imagination – a term that C.W. Mills coined to explain what he sees as the essential task of the social sciences: to facilitate self-understanding. Mills argues that if we are to understand ourselves in particular, and human behaviour in general, we must be able to locate our life stories, our biographies, within the context of our society and its larger historical context. Understanding the interconnection or intersection of biography and history is the first step in self-understanding. To develop the intellectual capacity or quality of mind we call the sociological imagination, Mills argues that we must be able to understand how society impacts on us, how society is structured and works, and how society changes and develops.

2

HOMO SAPIENS:
BIOLOGY AND CULTURE

If the general objective of the discipline of sociology is to help bring about a greater degree of self-understanding and to help us understand the behaviours, character, and actions of other humans, how or where do we begin the task? A useful point of departure is to consider first our prime subject matter – human beings – as biological creatures.

For social scientists, this raises elementary questions. First, are there essential characteristics of the human animal, or Homo sapiens, that are unique and that differentiate us from other species? And if there are, what are they and what do we know about them?

One reason for beginning by considering the biological side of human beings and human behaviour is the prevalence and popularity of arguments that offer simplistic biologically based explanations for complex human behaviours. Some social scientists argue that everything from our eating habits to our sexual conduct, apparent natural competitiveness, and war and male dominance can be explained in terms of biological imperatives. Among the better known efforts in this regard is the work of Robert Ardrey, who argues that although humans have undergone an impressive evolutionary process, we have not lost our instinctual propensity to be violent, aggressive, and competitive (Ardrey, 1961). In a similar vein, Desmond Morris explains a lot of human behaviour, including the penchant for aggressive and domineering behaviour that humans exhibit, by reference to "the accumulated genetic legacy of his (*sic*) whole evolutionary past" (1969: 9). Others, including Konrad Lorenz (1966) and Lionel Tiger (1969, 1972), have also argued that much human behaviour is genetically transmitted and therefore we are biologically predestined to act and behave in certain ways.

On the other side of the ledger, many scholars have developed systematic critiques of the works of those cited above. Joan Cook's *In*

Defense of Homo Sapiens (1976) was among the first. More recently, researchers, including R.C. Lewontin (1991) and Lewontin, Steven Rose, and Leon Kamin (1985), have argued that the re-emergence during the last decade of biologically based explanations for many complex social processes and structures must be understood as part of a larger political agenda. This political agenda seems geared to maintaining the status quo, as it maintains that there is nothing we can do to redress structural inequities such as sexism, racism, and class domination since they are deemed to be genetic in origin, and therefore they must be accepted as natural and inevitable (see Caplan, 1978).

Most sociologists and many other social scientists reject these simplistic arguments in favour of more complex arguments that draw on the cultural and social characteristics of Homo sapiens to explain our behaviour, while still recognizing the biological foundation of much of human conduct.

Physiological Needs and Drives

Although social scientists are well known for their ability to disagree on almost everything, there is one point they can all accept: that human beings are biological organisms; and that as such they have basic physiological or biological *needs*. The *Harper Collins Dictionary of Sociology* refers to a need as "the basic requirements necessary to sustain human life" (Jary and Jary, 1991: 325). The most obvious of our physiological needs are our nutritional or dietary needs. We all require a certain basic amount of food and nourishment if we are to survive physically. We also have a physiological need for liquid intake. In addition, the continued long-term survival of our species is dependent on sexual activity that leads to biological reproduction.

Associated with such physiological needs are what are commonly referred to as *drives*. Whereas a physiological need refers to the basic requirements of survival, such as food, oxygen, or sleep, a drive refers to what Gordon Marshall calls the "energizing forces" that direct an organism to try and provide for the requirements of life, that is, to meet needs (Gordon, 1994: 133). A drive is the internal impulse produced by the need. Drives motivate individuals to activity to reduce the tension or dissatisfaction produced by the need. The need for food manifests itself in the drive we commonly refer to as hunger. The need for liquid appears in what we refer to as thirst, and sexual tension produces the sex drive.

Our individual and species survival clearly depends on meeting our basic needs and dealing with our basic drives. In this regard human beings are no different than other non-human life forms. Your cat, dog, budgie, or boa constrictor must also satisfy its basic physical needs for food and liquids if it is to survive. Human beings are different, however, because of how we deal with our needs and drives. Because the objective of sociological analysis is to assist in understanding human behaviour, the key issue is not the existence of basic needs and drives – we can assume they exist – but the modes of social conduct or behaviour through which humans meet their needs and deal with their drives.

Instincts

Most non-human animals seem to have been genetically equipped with the ability to deal with their basic needs and drives, and as a result their conduct and behaviour seem automatic. They "come naturally." This is because the conduct and behaviour of many non-human animal life forms tend to be governed by instinct.

The concept of instinct is subject to much controversy, debate, and confusion. One author refers to instinct as "one of the most ideological concepts science ever operated with" (Heller, 1979: 5). The definition adopted here is a hybrid or composite drawn from a variety of sources in biology and the social sciences and incorporating the basic features of many common definitions. (See, for example, Case and Stiers, 1971; Torrance, 1979; Heller, 1979; Nagle, 1984; Johnson, 1969.)

Behaviour or actions can be considered instinctual if they are:

- relatively complex
- unlearned, genetically transmitted, innate, inborn
- species-wide, invariant among members of a species or common to all members of a species
- manifest full-blown the first time the required level of maturity has been reached and the triggering stimuli are present in the environment.

In addition, an action, behaviour, or mode of conduct is instinctual if a member of a species can be reared without contact with other members of its species and it still exhibits the behaviour in question the first time the animal is presented with the necessary "triggering" stimulus.

Imagine, for instance, that a sociologist skilled in the delicate art of securing research grants is able to convince a funding agency to support an international study of rat behaviour. After securing the grant the researcher's first step is a trip around the world to collect rat specimens from each continent. After returning our researcher sets up an experiment. He places each of the rats, one by one, in a corner of a confined area like a cage or room and then thrusts his hand forward in a sudden manner at the rodent. If performed boldly, the action forms a stimulus that registers in the rat's brain and central nervous system as a threat. The result is that the researcher observes a common response from the rats regardless of their country or continent of origin. Each and every rat rears up and fights to defend itself.

If we were to take blood tests from people who had just been startled, we would find high levels of adrenalin, but the mere presence of this hormone in the human bloodstream does not elicit or produce any particular behavioural patterns. There is no evidence that humans are preprogrammed to respond to actions or situations we might perceive as threatening or to behaviour that appears aggressive. Indeed, it is apparent that what we interpret to be aggression or aggressive behaviour is itself something we learn and thus cannot be instinctual. In rats, when we observe a species-wide, invariant, and unlearned response, the concept of instinct is appropriate. In the case of humans, the responses to fear or apparent aggression seem to be diverse, different, and unpredictable; therefore, they are by definition not instinctual.

Let us consider a more specific example of instinctual behaviour. James Torrance (1979: 79) describes two instinctual behaviours of the stickleback fish, one relating to defence of its territory, the other to its reproductive behaviour. During its breeding period the male stickleback will attack an object if its underside is red, even if the object does not bear a shape that resembles a stickleback fish. The red colouring is significant because a male stickleback's belly becomes red prior to mating. The research related to this phenomenon indicates that the colour red acts as a releaser or stimulus for the male's fighting behaviour, and this fighting behaviour is elicited or released by the simple presence of the colour red on the underside of an object. Experiments further demonstrate that a stickleback fish lacking red on its underbelly does not elicit the fighting behaviour in males, while any object with the appropriate shade of red does. This indicates that the colour red is the stimulus for this instinctual behaviour.

If all members of a species respond with an identical complex behaviour to some stimulus we can conclude that the behaviour in question is instinctual. Within the realm of human conduct, it is difficult to provide a similar instance, of a specific colour eliciting or stimulating a specific unlearned pattern of behaviour. There is no evidence that the human response to various colours is genetically programmed and species-wide. There are, it is true, a variety of different cultural responses to colours and combinations of colours, as in the pride a nationalist might feel for the flag, but these are behaviours and responses that are not instinctual but rather cultural and learned.

Reproductive behaviour is often very complex, not to mention fascinating and interesting to observe, and provides a rich source of data for the study of instincts and behaviour. In his work, Torrance describes the complex patterns of behaviour that both the male and female stickleback fish engage in as the females lay and the males fertilize eggs. The mating ritual involves a series of complex moves, manoeuvres, and dances all repeated in an identical fashion each time the fish mate. The mating behaviour of many birds, such as the whooping crane's dance, is equally complex, elaborate, and interesting. Perhaps the most significant aspect of these behaviour patterns, especially after you watch them several times, is their similarity among a given species. The elaborate mating dance of the whooping crane is repeated, for example, in a virtually identical manner by each and every whooping crane attempting to entice a partner to reproduce. Similarly, the dances or movements of the stickleback fish partners display an amazing degree of consistency. Indeed, one could argue that if you have seen one sexually aroused whooping crane or stickleback fish you have "seen them all," in that all sexually aroused members of those species exhibit virtually identical behavioural patterns.

Again, the challenge is to ascertain the extent to which humans exhibit species-wide, invariant complex behavioural patterns in their efforts to secure a compatible sexual partner. Are there standard or similar behavioural patterns, even in our own culture, that characterize the actions of a sexually stimulated human? I have often challenged students to investigate the behaviour of their fellow humans in search of a sexual partner, perhaps at a dance or at the local university pub, to determine the extent to which there are invariant or common patterns. After several hours of systematic observation, the students conclude that the "moves," actions, and countermoves of individuals of both sexes differ radically and are truly different, diverse, and varied, not similar and invariant.

If we consider, on the one hand, the behaviour of various animals in acquiring and dealing with food, a similar pattern emerges. The hunting patterns of animals such as weasels and wolves display amazing similarities, as do the food-gathering techniques of animals such as squirrels. These similarities are explained by the fact that such complex behaviours are unlearned, genetically transmitted, and species-wide; that is, they are instinctual. On the other hand, are there actions that characterize the behaviour of all humans as they attempt to acquire, prepare, or consume food? Indeed, there is perhaps no aspect of human existence that is more varied than our eating behaviour. The diversity of human conduct becomes more apparent if we begin with a simple consideration of what it is that we will accept as satisfaction for our basic nutritional requirements.

What sources of protein will we accept and will we be able to consume? Will we eat fish? If the answer is yes, then what species of fish do we find acceptable? Will we eat our fish cooked or raw? Will we eat the meat of the common domesticated hog? Are we able to tolerate the concept of eating the meat of a cow? What range of rodents do we find palatable? Are members of the trusty canine species legitimate objects of culinary interest? We could ask these questions about a whole range of other potential food sources, including insects, and get no consistent answer across the planet. This fact makes it possible to suggest that, when it comes to acquiring, preparing, and consuming food, human beings do not seem to be any more instinctively governed than we are in our sexual behaviour.

There is also an important distinction to be made between instinct and *reflex*. Human beings exhibit a number of reflex-based actions and reactions, such as the blinking of the eye, the movement of the leg when a specific point below the knee is tapped, sneezing when foreign objects invade the nose, and throwing out our arms when we lose our balance. Such behaviours are too simple to be considered the same as the more complex behaviour defined as instinct.

It is also important to differentiate instinct and reflex from other basic voluntary actions and involuntary physical or metabolic processes. Actions such as those involved in breathing, swallowing, digestion, the circulation of blood, and the internal production of bodily wastes are involuntary metabolic processes and not complex behaviours. In his overview of the role of reflexes in human conduct, Thomas Williams (1972: 29-30) suggests that there are three levels of reflexes: the superficial, the deep, and the visceral. Superficial reflexes refer to such actions as eye blinking, and a deep reflex involves actions like the movement of the leg when an area below the knee is tapped. Visceral reflexes are related to processes such as digestion.

The central question is: how important are instincts and reflexes in influencing the overall repertoire of human conduct? The sociological answer to this question is, "Not very important." Sociologists maintain that humans are not well endowed with instincts and are therefore willing to make the controversial claim that little of our complex social behaviour can be explained in instinctual terms. But although our biological makeup may not have endowed us well in terms of instinctual behaviours that solve our needs and problems, we do have a unique set of physiological characteristics and features that have allowed us to develop solutions.

Human Physiology

Although sociologists tend to maintain that instincts are not particularly important factors in influencing human conduct, they do recognize that much of what we do and how we go about living our lives has a biological component. An argument could be made that we have a number of unique physiological characteristics that have allowed us to survive as a species. (See, for instance, the excellent summary of much of the literature relating to this debate in Robert Endleman's "Reflections on the Human Revolution," 1977.)

Although numerous efforts have been made to catalogue the precise, unique physiological characteristics of human beings (see, for example, Schusky and Culbert, 1967), according to the classic work of Arnold M. Rose (1956: 96) humans possess nine important anatomical or physical characteristics:

1. erect posture
2. prehensile hands
3. forward vision
4. large and complex brain
5. complex voice mechanism
6. greater dependency in infancy and slow maturation
7. flexibility of needs and drives
8. constant sex drive
9. longevity

These biological features have clearly allowed human beings to survive and prosper. What is unique about our species is the extent to which we have used these traits to systematically develop ways of meeting our needs, solving our problems, and dealing with our drives. Although we may lack a significant instinctual basis for the complex behaviour required to survive and prosper as a species, we have survived and prospered because of our tremendous capacities for creativity, innovation, and the development of solutions to problems that confront us. These capacities are predicated on our unique biological traits and characteristics.

Posture and Hands

In addition to allowing us to survey our immediate environment, our nearly perfect upright or erect posture has freed two of our appendages, our arms. Since we do not need our arms for simple locomotion they have been made available for a variety of other uses, including tool manipulation. Our prehensile hands, with highly movable fingers and opposable thumbs, have in turn allowed us to become proficient at the construction and use of tools.

Take a moment to think about your hands, and especially your thumbs, and how vital they are to your various daily routines. You might prove this point to yourself by not using your thumb for a day. Try taping your fingers together with your thumb across your palm and see just how hard simple everyday tasks become. Clearly, our hands, with their fingers and opposable thumbs, are an important asset in our efforts to survive.

Vision

Our forward vision, though not as keen under some circumstances as in many other creatures, does allow us to perceive the world in a three-dimensional array of many colours. The capacity for three-dimensional vision is important for a creature that also engages in the systematic development of tools to assist its efforts to solve basic problems and meet basic needs.

Large and Complex Brain

Without our large and complex brain, the other listed attributes might not be as important. Indeed, one could argue that none of the other features would have been as decisive if they were not coupled to our huge and complex brain. The human brain is one of the most complex organs within all of the animal kingdom. Its size and degree of complexity, plus the highly developed cerebral cortex, make it unique among animal life forms.

First, our brain gives us the capacity for "creative intelligence," the simple ability to think, reason, and generally "figure things out." In addition, our brain gives us the capacity to remember and recall what we "figured out" and how we acted to solve some problem. As a result, the human being, when confronted with a problem or driven by a need, resorts to thought, reflection, deliberation, and the use of reason. Once we "work out" a solution, we retain it in our memory and revert to that action when we are confronted with a similar problem or situation in the future. It is clear that these attributes have been vital in the survival and dominance of our species. Imagine a scene in which some of our earlier ancestors are attempting to get some tree fruit that is beyond their reach. After several hours of jumping and not being able to reach the fruit, one of them picks up a nearby stick and waves it at the tree, accidentally knocking the fruit down. The lesson may not have been learned the first time, but if it were accidentally repeated the person would probably "discover" that a stick can be a useful tool when it comes to getting this particular fruit. The stick may very well become a part of that person's learned behavioural repertoire for dealing with the need for food. The lesson here? Humans are tool-users and we have the capacity to remember how we did something, so the next time we face a similar situation we have a learned solution at hand.

An additional capacity afforded by our large and complex brain is the ability to develop complex and abstract patterns of communication. No other species seems to have developed as complex and varied forms of communication as humans have. This is not to argue that non-human animals do not communicate, for it is clear that they do, through sounds, physical gestures, colour changes, and even odours. The well-known example of the honeybee communicating the direction and distance of food to other bees through a series of complex dancing motions illustrates the sophisticated information that animals can pass on to each other. Many animals have ways of communicating with other members of their species to provide information about matters such as the presence of danger or their availability for mating. A variety of animals can also communicate with the members of other species, as in the case of a dog baring its teeth and growling or a cat arching its back and hissing – to indicate to all present that it considers their actions a threat and that it is prepared to take action.

Most of this non-human communication is governed by instinctual processes and is thus quite different from human communication. Animal signals make up what Charles F. Hockett and Robert Ascher (1964) refer to as closed call systems. In a closed call system the reasons for an animal producing a signal, the signal itself, and the response of other animals are often fixed; that is, they are instinctual and not within the conscious control of the animal. Stated differently, the various signals that non-human animals use to communicate are often inborn, species-wide, and unlearned reactions to particular stimuli, and to the extent that other animals respond in some manner, that response is often also inborn, species-wide, and unlearned. No deliberate or conscious thought goes into producing or interpreting the signal.

It is common in the social sciences to refer to the kinds of signals we have been discussing as *gestures*. A gesture is defined as a physical movement or vocal sound that is meant to communicate. The physical gestures used in the non-human world are often instinctively based. When, for example, a beaver receives a stimulus from its surroundings that it perceives as a danger or as representing a threat, its instinctual response is to slap its tail on the water. Other beavers hearing or observing the slap receive it as a specific stimulus and respond in an instinctively determined manner by diving, fleeing, or otherwise attempting to move to positions of safety. Similarly, the white-tailed deer indicates the presence of danger with a wave of its tail. Other members of the species know that gesture as a message that danger is present, and they will attempt to flee. Non-human animals also use a variety of vocal gestures, such as a wolf's cry, the song of a bird, or a frog's croak. To the extent that these gestures are instinctual, they are produced automatically by stimuli in the environment, and other animals receiving them likewise respond in a preprogrammed, species-wide, and invariant manner.

Human beings likewise use gestures; however, the nature of the gestures we use and their significance for our survival make the use patterns among humans qualitatively different. It is clear that as a species we are unique in the extent to which we use gestures and in the kinds of gestures we use. In our communications with each other we do not just use physical movements, although "body language" can be important in human communication. More than any other species we communicate through the use of vocal gestures, and we are unique in our use of written gestures, like those you are reading now. The special and different dimension to our use of objects and vocal gestures is found in the *symbolic nature of our gestures*.

In his classic 1944 essay on the nature of human beings, Ernst Cassirer (1977) explicitly notes that humans inhabit a symbolic and not just a physical universe. Cassirer's basic point is that there are few, if any, gestures that humans use that have a "natural," unlearned, or instinctual basis to them. All the gestures we use in the process of our communications are symbolic in nature. This means that, whether they are physical movements, vocalizations, or physical objects, all our gestures have arbitrary meanings attached to them. In this sense the word "arbitrary" refers to the fact that the gestures, symbols, and signs we use to communicate have the meanings that the users assign to them and not any instinctual basis. For example, many four-letter combinations taken from the English alphabet are generally considered to be offensive. Why do people find these particular combinations offensive? It is not because we have an instinctual response to specific combinations. On the contrary, certain words are considered to be offensive, obscene, or profane because they have, by some arbitrary and historical process, been defined that way. Our symbols of human communication are arbitrary designations or expressions without some species-wide "natural" meaning attached to them. After stressing the importance of symbols in human existence, Cassirer argues that we can define humans as *animal symbolicum* because the use of symbols is the key to understanding the human capacity to think, communicate, and respond. Indeed, it is the key to understanding most human behaviour.

Consider the difference between human symbolic communication and non-human instinctual communication within the context of a particular process, mating. When a non-human animal is ready to mate, it indicates its state to others by means of an instinctual behaviour we can call a sign. Because the behaviour is instinctual, all other members of that species receiving the sign will respond accordingly, indicating that they are either ready or not ready. Can you think of a similar pattern in human affairs or human conduct? Are there patterns of behaviour, words, body language, or indeed physical objects, such as clothing, that mean the same thing across cultures and historical epochs? Those of us who happen to live in a Western culture know a variety of actions, body movements, or phrases that are used to indicate romantic interest in another individual; but to what extent are these actions and symbolic behaviour understood correctly in other cultures? Cross-cultural studies tell us that the simple act of making eye contact with another person has a broad range of different meanings in different cultures.

In a fascinating essay, "The Sounds of Silence," Edward Hall and Mildred Reed Hall (1982: 83-87) examine the culture-specific uses of various forms of body language, including the use of the eye and eye contact, the meanings of distance (how far we position ourselves from others when we are in conversation with them), and even the meanings attached to different leg positions. One of their essential conclusions is that the meanings we attach to these various modes of non-verbal communication are learned; that is, they are cultural.

Sociologists argue that there is no evidence that a behaviour or symbol with a particular meaning in one culture is going to have a similar meaning in another. A simple act like the raising of a clenched fist can mean many different things in different cultures. In our culture such a physical gesture can have a variety of meanings, ranging from joking with a friend or indicating "third down" in the Canadian Football League to physically threatening someone; or it might even be a sign of defiance and determination to continue some ongoing conflict. Similarly, a series of words such as "I feel really cool" could mean a number of different things depending on the speaker and the context within which the words are uttered. Human communication is complex, and it is clear that the meanings of the gestures used can only be understood within the social and cultural context of a system that assigns meanings to various kinds of symbols.

The most common forms of gesture used by humans are systems of vocalizations and written symbols. We know that over time, sets and systems of symbols tend to become codified and established into what we call language, and an understanding of the role of language is one further key to the study of human behaviour. The insights of the domain of linguistics, the study of language, are useful in explaining the nature of human communications. Andrew Crider and his co-authors define language as "a form of communication characterized by semanticality, generativity, and displacement" (1989: 296).

Semanticality refers to the requirement that a language have an established system of meanings to it. We recognize that very young children will vocalize, although we don't accept the sounds as language because they lack the systematized meaning that we assume is essential to language. The distinction between a series of sounds we call a language from another series of sounds that might be randomly produced and called noise is found in the fact that the sounds we call language have systematic meanings attached to them.

Generativity refers to the flexibility of human language. Speaking a human language is a creative process that brings innumerable combinations of words into different arrangements to convey different meanings. In the course of our daily communications we use many words over and over again, but as we arrange and rearrange the order of these words the meaning varies.

Displacement refers to the ability of human languages to transcend a particular time and place. Human languages allow their users to communicate about events that occurred in the past, or that are occurring in the present in distant locations, or that might occur in the future. In short, we communicate about phenomena and events beyond the limits of our immediate existence. We are not confined in our communications to the here and now.

Human beings have developed elaborate systems of vocal and written symbols, and the use of those systems is governed by widely understood rules and modes of combining sounds and words. Those systems of language allow the creative combination of sounds and words to communicate vast amounts of information. The development and use of such systems of symbolic communications have been an essential part of the process of human survival, an essential part of our human behaviour. Once we have "worked out" or discovered a solution to one of our many problems we can pass on that information, thereby enabling others to benefit from our experiences. Because we use these systems each new generation does not have to solve the same problems all over again, and humans can accumulate knowledge, understanding, skills, tools, and artifacts. We do not have to continually "reinvent the wheel."

Vocal Capacities

The human ability to develop symbolic systems of communication depends on our large and complex brain; but the emergence and use of language are related to our complex sound-producing organs. The human larynx, throat structures, tongue, and lips all contribute to our capacity to make an enormous variety of sounds. The thousands of existing languages and dialects used around to world in human communication indicate how flexible our sound-producing capacities are. The development of the symbolic codes that make up these languages is a spectacular feat that only a species with an amazing brain could accomplish. The actual vocalization of the many arbitrary sounds that make up the systems of sounds we call language is an equally demanding feat that only a creature with our particular vocal capacities could master. Our domesticated dogs, cats, cows, and horses can make a fair number of different sounds, but no matter how hard we try, or how much time we spend with them, we can't teach a cat to sound like a dog or a cow to sound like a horse. But our children quickly develop the ability to make sounds similar to all of these animals as well as, potentially, the sounds of many different human languages.

Long Dependency Period
It is ironic that the amazing creature we have been describing – mobile, with free appendages, intelligent, communicative, and vocal – should also be so relatively incompetent at birth. If we were to develop a scale of how competent and capable of looking after themselves various animals are at birth, the human species would rank near the bottom. It is a biological fact that we are incapable of caring for ourselves at birth and that we depend on the care and attention of others for a long period of time after birth. Richard Leakey has turned his attention to the question of why humans have such a long dependency period. He concludes that the problem is in part due to the fact that human babies are born too early. His explanation runs as follows:

> This may sound odd, but it has to do with the extraordinarily large brain of which we are so proud. The large brain is associated with a slowing down and a lengthening of our species' life history factors, such as sexual maturity and longevity. If we were to do the calculations for length of gestation based on our brain size, we would arrive at a figure of twenty-one months, not nine months. As a result, for almost the first year after birth human babies live like embryos, growing very fast but remaining essentially helpless. (Leakey, 1992: 159-60)

Leakey further argues that a gestation of twenty-one months would produce a baby that is physically incompatible with the size of the human birth canal, and thus the necessity of being born somewhat prematurely. He notes that one of the important post-natal changes is the continued rapid growth of the brain, which "more than triples in size between birth and maturity" (160). He suggests that our extended dependency period is also linked to the emergence of the patterns of social learning that, we shall see, characterize human beings (145).

The precise length of this dependency period varies from culture to culture. In Canada, for example, if you asked the parents of a typical first-year university student about the length of the dependency period in our society, you might receive a cry of anguish in return: "Nineteen years and counting!" Apparently, our lack of instincts makes us ill-equipped to survive, while our long period of dependency provides the required time for learning what we need to know to survive.

Flexibility of Needs and Drives
Our biological and physiological makeup gives us the ability to digest and use a wide variety of protein sources, illustrating one of our central biological characteristics, the flexibility of our needs satisfaction. The materials that satisfy our basic needs for food, clothing, or shelter are almost infinitely variable, differing radically from location to location and from historical period to historical period.

Constant Sex Drive
The idea of the human sex drive as constant does not mean – depictions in the movies and on television aside – that humans are in a continuous state of readiness for sexual activity. The point refers instead to the human capacity to reproduce at any time of the year. Unlike most other animals, humans have no particular seasons during which we "go into heat" and during which time fertilization must take place.

Longevity
Although some animals do live as long or even longer than humans, for the most part our species has a relatively long life span. And because we live for quite a long time we have abundant opportunities to use all the other various human characteristics in the pursuit of solutions to our various problems.

What do these unique characteristics have to do with how we as a species meet our needs, solve our problems, and deal with our drives? For one thing, sociologists conclude that human beings are not well equipped instinctively to deal with their needs, drives, and problems; instead, they argue, humans have developed *social modes of conduct* to satisfy their needs, solve their problems, and allow them to deal with their drives. These patterns of behaviour or modes of conduct are social, that is, they involve social interaction with others. As a discipline sociology is very much interested in understanding and analysing these modes of social conduct. In the process of undertaking this task sociologists have adopted an approach that places emphasis on the concept of culture.

Culture: The Work of Ruth Benedict and Margaret Mead

To survive and prosper as a species humans have developed "ways of doing things." This notion of "ways of doing things" will serve as a preliminary definition for a central concept in the study of human behaviour: *culture*. The field of cultural anthropology has provided essential material for anyone seeking to understand human behaviour, and in their work Margaret Mead and Ruth Benedict in particular have provided valuable examples of cross-cultural studies, that is, of several different sociocultural systems that represent different ways of doing things.

Patterns of Culture
Ruth Benedict's *Patterns of Culture*, first published in 1934, examines three different peoples who had developed three different modes of organizing their lives and solving their problems – three different ways of doing things.

The first people Benedict discusses are the Pueblo Indians of the American Southwest. She describes three groupings, the Acoma, Zuni, and Hopi, who lived in an arid region with poor soil and little wild game yet enjoyed a relatively comfortable material existence. They raised sheep and had developed a system of irrigation to water orchards and cornfields, as well as sophisticated bow and arrow technology for hunting game. They had also developed advanced architecture, which they used to construct elaborate cliff dwellings and large, well-planned urban settlements.

For the Pueblo society, as Benedict notes, rituals, ceremonies, dances, and rites associated with strong religious beliefs were central organizing dynamics in yearly social cycles. Much of the adult life of males was spent in preparation for, and actually conducting, religious activities. The religious activities of the Pueblo people were highly ceremonial, involving complex rites and rituals that had to be conducted in a precise manner with little or no room for innovation or variation. Males spent long periods of their lives learning the correct performance of these rites and rituals.

The family structures in traditional Pueblo society were organized along matriarchal lines, so that the women controlled lines of descent and owned and controlled the material assets in the household. Both the house and the corn stored in it, while they may have been produced by males, were owned by the women. Economic activity was organized communally, with much of the produce ending up in a common or communal storehouse that housed the collective property of the women. The communal and co-operative orientation of the society meant that it was rare for individuals or family members to go without having their basic material needs taken care of. Sharing and mutual care were important.

The Pueblo people were peace-loving. Indeed, the avoidance of strife and conflict was of paramount importance. The ideal individual sought to co-operate with others at all times, to avoid strong emotions, and never to stand out from the crowd. Benedict notes that the statement "No one ever hears anything from him" (91) was among the highest praise a man could receive. Although the language Benedict used was cast in the masculine, it is safe to assume the same would apply to women. The ideal individual always put the needs and interests of the collectivity first, claiming no personal authority. Individuals attempted to avoid office, agreeing to a position of authority only after their arguments about why they should not hold office had been shown to be inadequate. When they did gain an official position of some sort, individuals demonstrated as little authority and leadership qualities as possible.

For the Pueblo the universe was essentially a place of harmony. There was a time and a season for everything. As little was made of death as possible because it was widely accepted that death and life were part of a larger cycle of existence in the universe.

The typical Pueblo personality as Benedict saw it, then, was one of dedication to the community and the welfare of others. Such a person would be peace-loving, inoffensive, and subordinate to the group. These people would value sobriety and harmony and go out of their way to avoid conflict, competition, or any behaviour that would make them stand out from the larger collectivity. They would live their lives in the knowledge that the universe was indeed a place of harmony and peace. They would understand that "The seasons unroll themselves before us, and man's life also."

Ruth Benedict follows her description of life among the Pueblo with a picture of how another people in a very different part of the world organized their existence: the residents of Dobu Island, located near the shores of New Guinea.

The Dobu also lived in a difficult environment, this one an island that was volcanic and had little good soil. The area also lacked substantial sea-based resources such as fish or other sea life. The Dobu had nevertheless developed elaborate patterns of behaviour to deal with their various needs and were surviving handily when Europeans arrived in the area. These modes of organizing and conducting themselves were radically different from those of the Pueblo.

The Dobu had a reputation for being dangerous. Indeed, Benedict notes that before European colonization of the region the Dobu were cannibals. Whereas the Pueblo Indians valued peace and harmony, the Dobu "put a premium on ill will and treachery and make of them the recognized virtues of their society." By the cultural standards of twentieth-century North America the Dobu were "lawless and treacherous" (121). According to Benedict theirs was a society in which no one trusted anyone and everyone seemed to be only interested in seeking personal gain, at the expense of others if necessary.

The Dobu had no religion in the sense of an acknowledged deity or a series of codified beliefs, although they believed in and practised magic. There were no formal political structures, no acknowledged leaders or chiefs, and no legal system, at least not one formally organized and acknowledged as legitimate by most members of the society.

Personal conduct was essentially governed by the simple principle that you could do almost anything you could get away with. As Benedict notes, this was not a situation of anarchy in that there were limits and rules concerning the expressions of aggressive behaviour. These limits or rules were based on concentric circles of acceptable violence, which start with members of the matriarchal family. As members moved out from the immediate family, differing degrees of hostility and aggression were acceptable for various relatives, fellow villagers, and finally those in neighbouring villages – those located in the outermost imagined circle. The limits were provided by the expected response of others in the community to a gross violation of these boundaries. Each person, knowing that violations of the limits would not be tolerated, recognized limits on personal behaviour. Put more simply, you could not get away with it so you did not do it.

The essential staple of the Dobu diet was the yam. Given the poor soil, crops were meagre and hunger an ever-present problem. Each mature member of the society maintained an individual garden for growing yams, and a person's seed yams were deemed to be a part of their heritage. Husbands and wives each maintained a separate garden and grew their own yams, although they did pool their produce for the purpose of feeding their children. This is one of the few instances of any degree of co-operation among the Dobu.

Relationships between wife and husband were based on considerable hostility and mistrust. The Dobu were sexually active before marriage, with much of this sexual activity occurring in the home of the girl. A formal marriage ceremony took place after the mother of a female prevented a male from leaving her home after he had spent the night, perhaps after the male had become accustomed to spending a lot of time with the particular girl. There was no acknowledged phenomenon equivalent to the Western conception of romantic love, a point Benedict makes clear: "Faithfulness is not expected between husband and wife, and no Dobuan will admit that a man and a woman are even together even for the shortest interval except for sexual purposes" (127).

Dobu culture valued an extreme form of individualism. Individuals did not expect to receive favours from anyone, and they certainly gave none. According to Benedict, "All existence is cut-throat competition, and every advantage is gained at the expense of a defeated rival" (130). Benedict's final comments on the Dobu summarize their culture and personalities:

> Life in Dobu fosters extreme forms of animosity and malignancy which most societies have minimized by their institutions. Dobuan institutions, on the other hand, exalt them to the highest degree. The Dobuan lives out without repression man's worst nightmares of the ill-will of the universe, and according to his view of life virtue consists in selecting a victim upon whom he can vent the malignancy he attributes alike to human society and to the powers of nature. All existence appears to him as a cut-throat struggle in which deadly antagonists are pitted against one another in a contest for each one of the goods of life. Suspicion and cruelty are his trusted weapons in the strife and he gives no mercy, as he asks none. (159)

Benedict's third society, the Native people of the Northwest Coast of North America, represent a radical contrast to both the Dobu and the Pueblo peoples. The Indians of the Northwest, in particular the Kwakiutl, were a people of great material wealth. The locale they inhabited was bountiful, with a rich variety of resources including abundant marine life, game, timber, and other products of the forest. As a result the Kwakiutl were a people of great possessions, a commercial people, and they had sophisticated networks of trading relations including a complex system of currency that used shells and sheets of copper as the means of exchange. The commercial aspects of the society were developed to the point that they had arrangements for loans and the charging of interest payable in currency.

In traditional Kwakiutl society wealth was considered strictly private property and tended to belong to males. Two types of possessions were important: material and non-material. On the material side were fishing areas, hunting grounds, berry-picking territories, houses, currency, and other material forms of wealth. But individuals could also own non-material items, including names, rights, myths, songs, and stories. For the men in this society the ownership of possessions, both material and non-material, provided the basis of their position in the society. In Kwakiutl society men were very much concerned with their position in a social hierarchy, and they were constantly attempting to demonstrate their superiority through the accumulation of possessions. For students of twentieth-century North American society, this idea is not at all alien; however, in Kwakiutl society there was a significant difference in how members used their personal wealth to demonstrate superiority.

A central feature of Kwakiutl society was the potlatch, a complex ceremony involving the exchange of massive amounts of wealth. Although there were significant variations in the details of how the potlatch was conducted and what kind of transactions took place, one aspect was common: it was essentially an opportunity for individual men to demonstrate their superiority either by giving more wealth to a rival than the rival would be able to return, or by publicly destroying their own wealth. The potlatch was an event or ceremony that might be held in conjunction with any number of events: a birth or a death, a high-status marriage, the raising of a carved pole, a naming, or even an accident. Because they occurred frequently, the events had a significant impact on the social distribution of wealth across the society. All participants at a potlatch received some form of gift, although those nearer the bottom of the social hierarchy received less. As a result of the potlatch, no one person or family went without the necessities of life, although because of the society's abundant material wealth, the process went beyond the simple sharing that was more common in Pueblo society.

In her description of the Kwakiutl, Benedict provides rich detail of the exuberant behaviour that characterized many aspects of their culture, including religion. Whereas the Pueblo peoples were deeply religious, their religious rituals were routinized to an extreme degree, with each step being choreographed in detail. The religious activities of the Kwakiutl were characterized by attempts to reach states of ecstasy during which individuals lost control of their behaviour. Indeed, Benedict reports that at times dancers had to be tethered with ropes to prevent them from doing harm to themselves or others around them.

Benedict's Main Thesis

Ruth Benedict's book is a classic in its field and deserves to be read in its entirety because she provides a wealth of detail and an analytical style that is impossible to summarize. For students of sociology, Benedict's study of different cultures raises important questions. First of all, she offers information on an array of diverse cultures, behaviour, and personalities. How are we to make sense of this material? What does her study tell us about human conduct, society, behaviour, and, indeed, "human nature"? If by "human nature" we mean biologically based, unlearned, species-wide, and invariant behaviour, is there such a thing?

According to the evidence provided by Benedict, there are few if any species-wide, invariant, unlearned, complex behaviours by which humans solve their basic problems and meet their basic needs. One of the central points she makes is that in our attempts to understand human conduct and personalities, the concept of culture is more appropriate than the concept of instinct. She argues that it is possible to understand human beings and human behaviour as flexible, variable, and malleable to the point that we are capable of organizing our societies and developing personalities in a fashion similar to that found in Zuni or Dobu or Kwakiutl society. She says it is possible that other humans can come to *learn* to act in a manner similar to the typical resident of Dobu or Hopi society. Benedict's argument raises important questions about just how "flexible" or "malleable" we are.

Sex and Temperament in Three Primitive Societies

Margaret Mead's *Sex and Temperament in Three Primitive Societies* adopts an approach similar to that of Benedict. First published in 1935 and reprinted numerous times since, Mead's study also discusses the social organization and behaviour characteristic of three different societies, although her focus is more on a comparative analysis of the general temperament and characteristics of females and males. The cultures she discusses were located physically much closer to each other; all of them were located in New Guinea. Mead provides a wealth of interesting data on the cultures she studies, including social structures, physical organization, and typical patterns of behaviour. Most important for our purposes is what she says about the essential differences between these peoples.

The three cultures Mead discusses are the Arapesh, the Mundugumor, and the Tchambuli. Although each of these peoples inhabited quite different physical environments, it is the differences in their social organization that are striking. The Arapesh, for instance, are a people who lived in a harsh mountain environment and spent a great deal of their time attempting to wrestle the bare necessities of survival out of that difficult terrain. Although this environment is similar in many ways to that of the Dobu, the mode of social organization developed by the Arapesh was quite different. Mead characterizes the Arapesh as a peace-loving people whose conduct was marked by co-operation and sociability. In her focus on the typical conduct of the female and male members of society, Mead notes that there were few outward personality differences. Indeed, this was a people who had taken virtually every step possible to minimize the differences between the sexes, although certain activities were organized on the basis of sex. Heavy lifting was one. The mountainous environment demanded a lot of lifting and hauling, and most of the heavy work was done by women because it was common knowledge in this society that women were physically better suited for such work.

In their sexual activities, Mead saw a uniform lack of interest and ambition among both females and males. Indeed, she concludes her discussion of the Arapesh by noting how difficult it is for the Western mind to understand what the Arapesh typically believe about women and men: "That both men and women are naturally maternal, gentle, responsive and not aggressive" (1971: 157).

The Mundugumor and the Arapesh were, like the Dobu and the Pueblo, a study in contrasts. Whereas the Arapesh were a peace-loving agricultural people, the Mundugumor were hunters and formerly cannibals. Unlike the Arapesh, the Mundugumor were a rich people with abundant natural resources in their region. While the very poor Arapesh valued children and lavished a great amount of love and attention on them, the typical Mundugumor child was not valued; children were ignored and even mistreated. Infanticide, the killing of children, was not uncommon, and as Mead notes, those not hurled into the river after birth were "treated most summarily and exposed to many risks to which young children are not subjected among the most primitive peoples" (185).

Given the biological connection between sexual activity and reproduction, one of the reasons for the lack of interest and affection for the young might be the Mundugumor's attitudes toward sexual activity. The Mundugumor tendency to be individualistic and violent was carried over to their modes of conduct surrounding sexual intercourse. Both females and males were sexually active and neither simply waited passively for the other to take the initiative. The act of sexual intercourse was marked by extreme passion and even violence, after which each of the participants showed signs of the encounter in the form of scratches and bites.

There were also several forms of marriage among the Mundugumor. In spite of their propensity for sexual activity, the Mundugumor valued virginity: a virgin was highly valued as a marriage partner by both sexes, as testified to by the fact that a virgin could only marry another person who was also a virgin. But the most common form of marriage was between partners who were both known to have had sexual experiences. The final form of marriage was arranged marriages, often as a result of some larger social process such as peacemaking.

If a Western mind has difficulty understanding a society in which both sexes demonstrate little sexual ambition or a society in which both sexes are relatively aggressive, it will reel at the conduct of women and men among Mead's third group, the Tchambuli. Although property among the Tchambuli was organized along patriarchal lines, with men formally owning gardens and household property, women were the central economic actors. The primary sources of food for the lake-dwelling Tchambuli were the fishing activity of the women and their work in the gardens. The major activities of the men were related to their ceremonies and their art. As Mead notes:

> Every man is an artist and most men are skilled not in some art alone, but in many: in dancing, carving, plaiting, painting and so on. Each man is chiefly concerned with his role upon the stage of his society, with the elaboration of his costume, the beauty of the masks that he owns, the skill of his own flute playing, the finish and *élan* of his ceremonies, and upon other people's recognition and valuation of his performance. (231)

The women's position of dominance in economic matters carried over into the realm of personal and sexual matters. The women initiated courtship, mating, and marriage. Men worked hard at their ceremonies and on occasion as traders, hoping that their tasks would receive approval and praise from their wives. The wife, Mead states, controlled the real property required to survive, and her attitude toward her man was one of "kindly tolerance and appreciation" (239).

The Anthropologists' Central Lesson

The work of Mead, Benedict, and others in the field of cultural anthropology reminds us that while all humans around the world face a series of common problems that must be solved if we are to survive as individuals and as groups, we do not go about solving these problems and meeting our needs in similar ways. Indeed, we have developed remarkably diverse and different ways of solving our problems and dealing with our drives and needs. Each of the societies that Benedict and Mead studied had developed unique and successful modes of conduct for dealing with its individual and collective needs and problems. Each of these peoples had developed systems of action and interaction, modes of conduct, sets of beliefs and ideals, as well as tools, technology, and associated skills and knowledge. Each of them had established a culture that formed a basis for its individual and group survival. Each of these cultures was in turn characterized by a set of beliefs, stocks of knowledge, and established practices that allowed its members to exist in their particular environment.

But before we attempt to develop generalized statements concerning human beings on the basis of the cultural anthropologists' studies, we should note that their works have been subject to considerable criticism and debate. Margaret Mead's work in particular has been the subject of systematic criticism – although Lowell Holmes, who extensively studied the criticisms and Mead's work, concluded that there was much to recommend her work as a valid source of knowledge concerning human cultural behaviour (Holmes, 1985). To better appreciate what it is like to have an outsider describe your culture – that is, someone who might not understand the meaning and significance of many of your actions – North American readers might consult Horace Miner's "Body Rituals Among the Nacirema" (1985). Among the features of the culture Miner describes are practices revolving around the oral cavity:

> The Nacirema have an almost pathological horror of and fascination with the mouth, the condition of which is believed to have supernatural influence on all social relationships. Were it not for the rituals of the mouth, they believe their teeth would fall out, their gums bleed, their jaws shrink, their friends desert them, and their lovers reject them. They also believe that a strong relationship exists between oral and moral characteristics. For example, there is a ritual ablution on the mouth for children which is supposed to improve their moral fiber. (150)

As you contemplate these bizarre behaviours and try to locate this culture, reverse the spelling of Nacirema. By the way, did you brush your teeth or use mouthwash this morning, or ever hear of someone getting his or her mouth washed out with soap?

The Characteristics of Culture

The concept of culture is widely used in the social sciences and, like many other concepts, is subject to considerable misunderstanding because different thinkers have used the term in different ways. Although social scientists have used a variety of definitions, they agree on one point, namely, that the term does not simply apply to art, classical music, and the ballet. Indeed, social scientists tend to argue that eating a hot dog and drinking a soft drink at a football or hockey game is as much a part of Canadian culture as watching the Royal Winnipeg Ballet. In defining cultural activities social scientists follow the lead of Edward Tylor, who, in 1871, defined culture as "that complex whole which includes knowledge, belief, art, morals, law, custom, and any other capacities and habits acquired by man as a member of society" (quoted in Schusky and Culbert, 1967: 35).

While Tylor's definition still provides a basis for understanding culture as being linked to virtually all aspects of human existence, others have further elaborated on the term. In the early 1950s Alfred Kroeber and Clyde Kroeber studied various definitions of culture and developed a composite definition that has also become a standard reference in the field. They stated:

> Culture consists of patterns, explicit and implicit, of and for behaviour acquired and transmitted by symbols, constituting the distinctive achievements of human groups, including their embodiments in artifacts; the essential core of culture consists of traditional (i.e., historically derived and selected) ideas and especially their attached values. (Quoted in Theodorson and Theodorson, 1969: 95)

In their *Modern Dictionary of Sociology* the Theodorsons also provide a more compact definition: "The way of life of a social group; the group's total man-made environment, including all the material and non-material products of group life that are transmitted from one generation to the next" (95).

Teasing a definition out of these various positions, we can conclude that culture is best understood as a group's total way of life, including two aspects of human existence. First there are the shared *non-material human products* such as beliefs, myths, customs, habits, skills, or knowledge. The second aspect is the *material dimension*, the group's material artifacts and material products that have been developed over time as the group undertook the solving of its problems and the meeting of its needs. The material aspects of North American culture include everything from a Coke bottle to a street light, a hockey stick, and the latest high-technology recording of Beethoven's Fifth Symphony.

Ernest L. Schusky and T. Patrick Culbert (1967) provide a concise list of the essential features of culture. According to them, culture is shared, learned, cumulative, diverse, and complex. First, it must be *shared* by a group of people. Not every particular or idiosyncratic individual action or belief is cultural. In most Western societies the stamping of your foot when you sneeze and giggling after an inadvertent burp are not considered cultural patterns of behaviour, while using a phrase such as "excuse me" or "pardon me" is. One behaviour is widely shared by members of most Western societies while the other is not.

Culture is also *learned*. Human beings seem not to have an instinctual preprogrammed behaviour that leads them to engage in specific behaviour after they sneeze or burp. Indeed, the importance and meaning of a biological or physiological occurrence such as sneezing or burping are themselves cultural, because a loud burp after a meal is entirely appropriate, even complementary, in some cultures. Our attitudes toward such occurrences as well as our responses and behaviours are entirely learned.

As you read these words on a sheet of paper – words that first appeared as an electronic image on the screen of a word processor – consider the third characteristic of culture, its *cumulative* nature. The fact that you are in possession of a book made of paper and containing certain gems of wisdom in the English language is testimony to the accumulation of knowledge in Western society. But focus for a moment on the physical product in your hand. The knowledge and skills required to produce such an artifact are staggering, and it is essential to understand that this capacity has emerged out of the accumulation of knowledge stored and passed on from one generation to another, indeed from one century to another. Perhaps a better example might be a jumbo-jet airliner. Consider the accumulated knowledge and skills that made possible that particular physical artifact and its operation. Our culture is, in part, the legacy of thousands of years of history and development, thousands of years of humans accumulating skills, beliefs, and knowledge as well as developing technology and passing these on, largely through language. Cultural phenomena must thus be understood as the cumulative outcome of the creative efforts of generation after generation of humans.

One of the essential characteristics of culture that emerges from a consideration of the work of anthropologists such as Mead and Benedict is its *diversity*. Any cursory anthropological examination of different cultures indicates the diversity in their organizational patterns, modes of behaviour, and action. What are the common elements in the forms of social organization and behaviour described by Benedict and Mead? The answer surely is that there are few if any common elements other than the fact that each of the peoples had developed social patterns of behaviour and action to solve problems and deal with needs.

Indeed, every attempt to describe human behaviour on planet Earth and to make generalizations about common patterns arrives at one conclusion: human culture is incredibly diverse and varied. Added to this is its *complexity*. Culture encompasses every aspect of humanity's socially developed products in both the material and non-material spheres.

For sociologists, culture remains a general concept that serves to draw our attention to the fact that humans develop social solutions to their individual and collective problems. The problem with the concept is that it may be too general to aid the analysis of specific behaviours and the development of the sociological imagination. What we need to do is locate culture in its larger context, as a part of human social structures.

Terms and Concepts

Need – one of the basic requirements that must be met if we are to survive. Among our basic individual physiological needs are the requirements we have for food, liquids, sleep, clothing, and shelter. Psychologists and others have argued that humans have a variety of emotional or psychological needs that must be met if we are to develop the full range of our human physiological and psychological potentials.

Drive – an impulse to action produced by a need. The basis of a drive is an organic condition or state. In sociology we assume most drives are directed by an organism's life-sustaining tendencies.

Instinct – a complex behavioural pattern that is unlearned, genetically transmitted, invariant among members of a species, and manifested the first time a triggering mechanism is present. Some examples of instinctual behaviours are the complex mating behaviours of many animals, nest-building among birds, and hunting behaviours in animals such as weasels. A behaviour is instinctual if an animal raised in isolation from other members of its species exhibits that behaviour the first time the triggering stimulus is in place.

Reflex – a simple involuntary behaviour that is unlearned and species-wide. As opposed to an instinct, a reflex is a simple action such as blinking an eye or moving a leg when tapped below the knee.

Gesture – a physical and/or audible action used in communication. A beaver slapping its tail on the water is a physical gesture to signal that danger is present, while a human yelling "watch out" is an audible gesture. The use of and response to gestures in many non-human animals are instinctual.

Symbol – a gesture or sign that has an arbitrary, cultural, learned meaning as opposed to one that is species-wide, unlearned, or instinctual. A beaver slapping its tail on the water is a physical gesture while a human yelling "watch out" is a form of symbolic communication. There is no unlearned, species-wide, invariant response among humans to the sounds that in English mean "watch out."

Language – a system of communication that uses a variety of gestures and symbols. Language is essential to human existence and survival, because social interaction and complex processes such as socialization and cultural transmission are dependent upon its use.

Culture – the totality of the various material and non-material aspects of human existence that characterize how a specific people live and "do things." The non-material dimension includes beliefs, myths, knowledge, ideas, ideals, values, habits, and traditions, while material artifacts are those human-made and natural products that have acquired a socially defined existence and use among a group of people. Culture is complex, shared, diverse, and cumulative.

3

SOCIAL STRUCTURE AND THE LANGUAGE OF SOCIOLOGY

It is a sociological truism that in order to understand our behaviour and the behaviours of others we must locate the individual and his/her behaviours within the context of her or his society or social structure. To understand fully the relationship between individuals and their social structures, we must grasp the essential character of human social structures. The process of determining the basic characteristics of a phenomenon is commonly referred to as analysis.

The verb "analyse" refers to a process of examining something in order to find out what its basic elements or components are. If chemists analysed the substance in the cup of coffee you had this morning they could provide you with a list of compounds and elements present in the liquid. We analyse, that is, resolve things into their elements or constitutive parts, so we can better understand the phenomena around us. The result of the process is an analysis.

The process of analysing something can produce results that violate our common-sense impressions of the phenomenon. When we throw water on a fire we do not stop to think that we are really adding a combination of two gases, one that is essential for combustion and another that is highly explosive. Yet, chemical analysis tells us that is exactly what water is composed of. When literary critics analyse plays or novels by looking at their characters, formats, settings, dynamics, and composition, they may provide us with new insights into the material. Analysis is often essential to understanding, and this is certainly the case in sociology. Before we can understand the role of a society and its impact on the people within, we must know something about its basic structures, components, and processes.

One last word of warning. When we analyse something we are often performing a somewhat "unnatural" act in that we take apart and study the elements of what seems like a "natural whole" – what seems already familiar and known to us. We may think, because we have lived in a society all our lives, that we pretty much understand the world around us on the basis of our common sense and lived experience. We may therefore find it "unnatural" to look at our everyday lived reality and experiences within the context of the basic concepts of the socio-logical perspective. The wholeness of our lived social reality is very real, but it is also, when systematically examined, too complex to be auto-matically or simply understood. To assist in making sense of this complex process of social living, sociologists use a specific set of con-cepts to refer to different parts of that whole, concepts that are the basis of the discipline and its modes of thinking.

Culture and Society

The culture we are born into and in which we develop influences and moulds much of our behaviour. There is virtually no evidence in the field of cultural anthropology of complex behaviours that are species-wide, invariant, and unlearned. All human beings have needs, drives, and problems they must solve if they are to survive, but there appear to be few if any inborn complex behaviours to deal with these needs, drives, and problems. From all the evidence it seems that we are, above all else, cultural creatures. Still, in the discipline of sociology the concept of culture is usually considered part of something larger: society.

Society is a term used just as much in everyday language as in aca-demic discourse, and it can take on many different meanings depend-ing on the context. If many of you reading this book were asked what society you belong to, the answers might include the university debat-ing club, the engineering students association, or even the Society for the Prevention of Cruelty to Animals. These answers, in fact, relate to one of the first dictionary definitions: "an organized group of persons associated together for religious, benevolent, cultural, scientific, polit-ical, patriotic, or other purposes." The definitions in a standard English-language dictionary range widely, from the concept of people living as collective members of a community to the idea of "the social life of wealthy, prominent, or fashionable persons" (people, for instance, "step out in society"). The term can be used in the sense of a highly structured, large-scale, national organization ("Canadian society"); in an even more broad sense of a social system character-ized by some economic form ("modern industrial society"); or in its older, once-primary meaning, companionship or fellowship (see, for instance, Williams, 1976: 291).

Clearly, sociologists have to begin once again by defining the term as precisely as possible in order to assist our understanding of our social life. *The Modern Dictionary of Sociology* provides a starting point: "A group of people with a common and at least somewhat distinct culture who occupy a particular territorial area, have a feeling of unity, and regard themselves as a distinguishable entity" (Theodorson and Theodorson, 1969: 398). The authors note that the concept of society typically applies to groups that have a comprehensive set of social institutions capable of taking care of most of the basic needs of a population over an extended period of time.

In his useful book *Keywords*, Raymond Williams (1976) draws attention to the fact that the term "society" has been used in many different ways over the past several centuries. David Jary and Julia Jary (1991: 467) provide two definitions, both of them useful. First, they say society is "the totality of human relationships." Second, it is "any self-perpetuating human grouping occupying a relatively bounded territory, having its own more or less distinctive CULTURE and INSTITUTIONS." The common points in most definitions of society include notions of territory or geographical locale, enduring and ongoing organized social relationships, a degree of self-sufficiency, and some sharing of culture.

Keeping all of these considerations of meaning in mind, the definition of society we will use here is: *the totality of social relationships and interactions among a collectivity of people occupying a territory who, over time, survive by meeting their needs and solving their problems.*

We should note that a society is not necessarily the same thing as a nation-state, although the two are often confused. The established geographic boundaries of a nation-state may or may not be the same boundaries that define a society. It is also important to note that many societies have disappeared when their social relationships and interactions were not able to sustain the lives of the collectivity, while other societies have been absorbed, conquered, and taken over by outsiders. The phenomenon of Western colonialism has been one of the most important processes in defining and redefining the social map of the planet, often with catastrophic results for many indigenous and aboriginal peoples.

Within this framework, Canada or Canadian society, Australia or Australian society, or the United States or American society represent more than just the shared material and non-material products defined as culture. When we refer to Canadian society we imply some generally accepted territorial boundaries inhabited by a people who share a specific way of organizing and structuring their efforts to solve their various problems and deal with their various needs and drives.

Australia is likewise more than the shared products of its inhabitants. When we refer to Australian society we refer to a geographic locale as well as the specific modes of organizing religious, economic, educational, sexual, and other activities – all the factors that make up the unique characteristics distinguishing the people of that continent.

What is more, this definition of society draws our attention to another point: the human actions, interactions, and behaviours that occur as individuals attempt to solve their problems within geographical boundaries are not random and accidental; they are structured and organized. The structured nature of human behaviour is an essential attribute and is at the core of sociological analysis.

The Elements of Social Structure

This sociological definition of society raises a key point: the importance of understanding just how our behaviour, conduct, and actions are organized, patterned, and structured. While most sociologists use the term "society," it is also appropriate, and helpful, to use the term "social structure." The concept of *social structure* draws our attention to the essential characteristic of human social existence: its organized nature. Whatever characteristics human behaviour exhibits, it is, for the most part, not haphazard or random. We rarely act in a totally unpredictable and unorganized manner. Most of our lives are spent within the context of structured, patterned, and regularized social activities, interactions, and practices. Indeed, the discipline of sociology centres on the study of these social arrangements, structures, patterns, and modes of organization.

The Development of Social Structures
A rich and interesting – and often ambivalent – literature has addressed the issue of how we came, as a species, to develop our various social structures. For our purposes, however, the historical origins of our social structures are of less interest than an essential sociological point that is beyond contention and debate: as a species we have developed a great variety of social structures, social behaviours, and social organizations in our ever-continuing efforts to solve individual and species needs, drives, and problems.

Institutions
As a species, human beings meet needs, solve problems, and deal with various drives through conscious, intentional, knowledgeable social action and interaction. These deliberate actions are what we call *social*

practices. Over time these social practices become regularized, routinized, patterned, and established as "the way things are done." As they become firmly established, the social practices become a solidified part of life in the form of *institutions*.

In everyday English, "institution" tends to be associated with a specific type of organization, like a prison or a mental health-care facility. But the sociological literature contains a number of different definitions. Many of sociology's definitions stress the importance of norms, values, and rules of conduct in structuring human interaction. Although the concept of structuring or ordering human activity is important, it is necessary to relate the behaviour that is organized or structured to the satisfaction of some need or the solving of some problem. For our purposes, an *institution* is defined as: *a set of organized relationships, structured interactions, patterned behaviour, and regularized and routinized collective actions that are geared to or serve to meet some problem, need, or drive*. Significantly, if we rearrange the modifiers in this definition to read, for example, *organized* instead of *patterned*, or *routinized* instead of *organized*, or *structured* instead of *regularized*, the definition still works. The essence of the definition rests in the idea that institutions are not so much places, physical locations, or buildings as they are *social arrangements* for dealing with our needs, drives, and problems.

Institutionalization

It is possible that the various institutions that are part of modern industrial society developed by accident or by chance, that is, as a result of someone discovering that a certain action or practice "got the job done." It is also possible that some institutions were planned and deliberately developed as arrangements to help meet some individual or social need or solve some problem. The process, whether accidental or deliberate, by which social actions, behaviour, patterns of interactions, and relationships become routinized, regularized, and ultimately widely accepted and recognized as the appropriate way of dealing with a problem, need, or drive is called *institutionalization*. When we say behaviour is institutionalized we simply mean that the behaviour has come to be structured and organized into widely accepted and recognized patterns. This follows from the sociological position that an institution is not necessarily a place or a physical structure, but is rather a patterned, organized, and structured group behaviour that facilitates the solving of a problem or the meeting of a need.

Given that humans have a variety of different individual and species needs and problems that must be solved if we are to survive both as individuals and as a species, it follows that we have also developed a number of different institutionalized behaviours to deal with those needs and problems. Given that the behaviours and patterns of inter-action required to deal with the needs are very complex, it follows that institutions tend to be complex. One way of encouraging the analysis and understanding of such a complex phenomenon is the development of a classification system. One such system, which allows us to clas-sify institutions according to the need they meet or the problem they solve, is provided by Hans Gerth and C.W. Mills in their book *Char-acter and Social Structure*.

Institutions and Institutional Orders

Gerth and Mills distinguish between institutions and institutional orders. An institutional order is essentially a cluster or collection of institutions geared to meeting similar needs or solving similar prob-lems (1964: 25). For instance, the arrangements or behaviours that we engage in when we attempt to provide for our material needs form our *economic institutions*, whereas the *economic order* consists of all those institutions in a given society that are geared to the production and distribution of the material necessities of life. Within the economic order in our society there are particular economic institutions such as the large industrial corporation, the small business, the family farm, and the fishing co-operative. In sociological analysis we draw atten-tion to the fact that when we refer to these entities as institutions we are not focusing on their physical assets or their geographic locale, but rather on the fact that they represent patterns of behaviour, specific modes of social organization, and structured interactions.

It is well known, to use a familiar phrase, that humans cannot live by bread alone or, put somewhat differently, that we have needs other than those directly tied to material or physical survival. Human sur-vival depends on solving a host of other problems, such as cultural transmission, biological reproduction, and collective or social decision-making, as well as spiritual questions. In our efforts to address and deal with these problems we have developed numerous modes of conduct and behaviour that have become routinized and regularized – that is, institutionalized – into what we refer to as the educational order, the family order, the religious order, and the political order.

First, the *educational order* or the educational system refers to those structured practices, patterned interactions, and organized relation-ships that various peoples have developed to facilitate the transmission and enhancement of culture. Included under the rubric of the educa-tional order, in many Western societies at least, is a range of specific institutions such as the kindergarten, the public school system, secondary, private, and alternative schools, universities, community colleges, and technical schools. Each of these specific institutions plays its own part in our overall efforts to enhance and transmit the knowledge and skills that are a part of our culture.

Second, the mere meeting of our individual material needs is inadequate to ensure species survival, because without continuing arrangements to support biological reproduction the future of the species would be limited. In sociology we understand that set of behavioural arrangements and patterns of organized interaction that have developed around the process of biological reproduction and the care and nurturing of the very young as constituting the *family order*. Familial institutions are thus the means by which we facilitate biological reproduction and child care. The sociological literature tends to view the social arrangements we call "the family" as also being involved in the provision of various forms of emotional support for its members. According to the analytical logic of sociology, as an institution the family – whether it is nuclear, extended, or same-sex – is not so much a place or a specific set of persons, but rather a method of organizing behaviour and interaction to ensure biological reproduction, relations of mutual support, and the care and training of the young.

Third, although there are various explanations about why this is the case, the human species tends to ask profound and even ultimate questions concerning the meaning of our lives and our position in the larger scheme of things. We may never know if we do this because of how we were made by a creator or if it is the product of the considerable intellect we have evolved over the thousands of years we have been on the planet. These considerations are less important for sociologists than our very tendency to ask the ultimate questions and, even more importantly, the interactions and conduct resulting from our attempts to answer them. This realm of human social experience and behaviour is referred to as religion.

The *religious order* and religious institutions are those practices and behaviours that surround our efforts to seek the answers to ultimate questions and to celebrate and collectively ritualize the mysteries of life. In seeking to come to grips with the meaning of the events of birth, life, and death we have developed complex and intricate systems of beliefs and associated social practices that include the rites and rituals of various religions. Although sociologists are more interested in the actual social interactions and conduct of religions than in the doctrinal content of a particular set of beliefs, they do not ignore doctrine and teachings, especially if their acceptance becomes a factor leading to specific kinds of actions and practices.

Fourth, as societies become more populous and complex they require a means of developing social policy and establishing social goals. As peoples become organized into autonomous nation-states, the establishment of formal relations between and among the various social groupings becomes crucial: this becomes one of the essential aspects of the *political order*. Those social arrangements that we refer to as the political order or the political institutions encompass certain relations and behaviours: for instance, the allocation of leadership roles and the making of decisions about rules and regulations that form social legal codes.

Need/problem faced by species	Institutional order	Examples of specific institutions in Canada
Provision and distribution of material necessities	Economic order	The corporation, family farm, trade union, small business
Cultural and knowledge transmission and enhancement	Educational order	University, trade school, public school
Social decision-making, international relations	Political order	Parliament, Senate, courts, provincial and local governments, lobby groups
Spiritual needs, answers to ultimate questions	Religious order	Various and specific churches and sects
Species reproduction and early child care	Family order	Nuclear and other family forms

The political order is the entire constellation or configuration of social practices and arrangements that facilitate these objectives. The specific or internal institutions making up the political order vary from place to place and time to time. In a liberal democracy such as Canada the institutions include Parliament, the judiciary, provincial and local government structures, lobby groups, and special coalitions or social movements.

Institutions and institutional orders, then, are the basic building blocks of human society. To grasp the essential character of any human society or social structure, we must have an understanding of its basic institutional structures. Better still, we must also carry the process of analysing further, by dissecting institutions into their component parts. An analysis is not complete until we have broken down the phenomenon being studied into its smallest, most basic units.

Status

An examination of the behaviour that makes up the patterns of interaction and social organization we call institutions reveals a certain *structure* – in that there are parts within an institution that exist in orderly relationships with each other. For those parts, or positions, within an organization we use the term "status"; and the structure of an institution refers to the specific organization of the statuses that compose it.

As used here, status does not refer, as it usually does, to a ranking within a hierarchy or to a position of prestige. A *status* is, more simply, a position within an institution. Within a Western university, for instance, the statuses include president, caretaker, librarian, secretary, dean, vice-president, instructor, cafeteria worker, carpenter, student, and so on. These statuses, without being ranked in any particular order, indicate that the modern university is in fact a collection of different positions.

Similarly, the various statuses within various religious institutions could include priest or minister, member of congregation, church elder, church council member, or Sunday school teacher. Within a typical Western nuclear family we can find various statuses such as wife, mother, husband, sister, brother, daughter, son, and father. Each institution is composed of a number of different positions or statuses, and attached to each status are certain behavioural expectations that serve to direct the actions and behaviour of those in the status.

Role and Role Set

Just as there are statuses in each institution, within each status there is a role, a generally expected way of behaving, acting, and interacting. A *role* can be defined as a culturally expected or defined behaviour attached to a particular status. In a modern university, for instance, behaviour expected of a librarian or a caretaker is quite different from that expected of a president.

The extent to which these statuses and roles are strictly defined or somewhat flexible varies from one historical period to another and from institution to institution and society to society. In Western society the role of kindergarten teacher is strictly defined, so that people occupying that role may find they have considerably less flexibility and room for variations in approaching the basic task of teaching than, for instance, university professors. University professors might, for example, argue that it is appropriate to utter a word generally considered to be an obscenity if it accomplishes a particular pedagogical objective. Kindergarten teachers using the same approach would probably be called to account for their actions shortly after any of their pupils relayed the details of the day's activities to their parents.

The very term "role" implies an analogy and draws our attention to certain comparisons with formal theatrical acting. If status represents a person's part in the play, the character itself, role is the more detailed script. The theatrical analogy brings up another essential feature of the term: an individual's role is usually acted out in concert with other roles and statuses.

There is also more than one role attached to each status. In your status as student, do you act or interact in a fundamentally similar manner when you are having coffee with friends, requesting help from library staff, discussing an assignment with your instructor, and meeting the dean of your faculty? The answer for most students is no, because there is no single role attached to the status of student. Rather, there is a set of roles that sociologists call a *role set*, which means a collection or cluster of roles. The concept of role set implies that sociologists expect to see different behaviours within the same status, depending on the status and role of the other party in an interactive situation.

Role Conflict and Role Strain
Two additional concepts associated with the analysis of roles are role conflict and role strain. *Role conflict* refers to instances of conflict between two or more of the roles in a role set. For instance, instructors are usually responsible for the enforcement of standardized, uniform grading criteria for all students, so that in their role as instructors their relationships to all students must be as equal and uniform as possible. Imagine what could happen if an instructor becomes friends with a student, or if a friend enrols in the class. If the friend fails the course, role conflict can emerge as the role of instructor conflicts with the role of friend. Take another example: a supervisor in a formal work environment wants to maintain friendly interpersonal relations with others within the plant but is also responsible for enforcing new directives to speed up the work process and improve productivity. This kind of enforcement can have a negative impact on the workers under supervision, creating conflict. If the expected behaviour

of one role conflicts or is at variance with the expected behaviour of another role, role conflict results. Conflict also arises when an individual is involved with two or more roles and the behaviour of one role contradicts the behaviour of another role.

Many of you struggling to read these words are involved in *role strain*, which is commonly described as a situation in which a particular role may involve a set of expectations, and the successful accomplishment of those expectations strains the energy and resources of the status holder to the point that the person is unable to meet all the expectations. A university student may be expected to do the necessary work to get passing – or better – grades, engage in sports, participate in university clubs, plus live a "normal" social life and fulfil family responsibilities. The person on the other side of the podium could also very well be involved in role strain, because university instructors are expected to teach, contribute to university administration, undertake research, publish, and engage in public service – not to mention maintain their own personal lives. When people complain that there are just not enough hours in the day to do all they have to do, they are most likely in a situation of role strain.

Values and Norms
Our discussion of roles raises questions about the basis or origin of the cultural or social expectations that define the behaviour appropriate for various positions in an institution. Where do these behavioural expectations come from? What is the source of the knowledge that we draw on when deciding how to act in a particular role?

We know that all human societies have certain ideas, ideals, stocks of knowledge, rules, and regulations that guide the actions and interactions of individuals. Sociologists refer to these elements as values and norms. A *value* is a general and abstract principle or idea about what is good or bad, desirable or undesirable, right or wrong, or appropriate or inappropriate. Discussion of values often refers to qualities of behaviour such as honesty, faithfulness, freedom, patriotism, or equality. A particular value does not contain any specific instructions about how we need to behave in order to live a life according to that value.

What sociologists call norms do provide us with more precise instructions. Indeed, in sociology norms are commonly understood to be more specific expressions of values. If honesty is a part of a society's value system, a command or suggestion such as "Do not tell lies" represents a normative instruction. A *norm* is a specific rule, regulation, or instruction that indicates specifically how to behave and act or what is appropriate and inappropriate.

Norms indicate what is expected of us in our day-to-day behaviour; they guide our behaviour in our various roles. For example, most men born and raised in North America feel entirely comfortable shaking hands when they meet someone for the first time, especially if the person they are meeting is another man. For men, this is accepted – and practised – as a normal greeting. Many North American men feel equally uncomfortable when a stranger embraces and kisses them. For women in North America, an embrace or a kiss on the cheek is a more common formal greeting, even when meeting strangers. Why do men and women feel that these different forms of behaviour are the appropriate modes of conduct? The answer is that the behavioural forms are a part of the norms or the normative orientation of North American society.

In their analysis of norms sociologists commonly use a further analytical distinction between folkways, mores (pronounced mor-ays), and laws. They consider each of these as a type of norm varying in how specific the "instructions" are and in the implications that follow from violations of the norm. *Folkways* are norms or behavioural instructions that govern a large variety of everyday situations and interactions. Folkways deal with common everyday matters and a violation is considered rude or bad manners, but not a sign of moral depravity.

Once folkways become established and accepted they tend to govern various aspects of our everyday lives, from how to behave in a supermarket queue to what colours are considered to be appropriate to mix and match in our wardrobe. The violation of a folkway can draw attention to a person's action or personality, but generally most people do not feel that the transgression represents a serious violation of society's morals. Picking your nose in public is usually considered a violation of a folkway because it is generally deemed to be an unpleasant and inappropriate activity, but people who do this are not necessarily considered morally depraved or wanting, nor would they be subject to any formal punishment.

Mores are norms or behavioural instructions that hold great significance, and their observance is deemed to have moral implications for the well-being of individuals and society. The violation of mores is considered to be a much more significant breach of appropriate rules of conduct than the violation of folkways. If a man walks down Yonge Street in Toronto on a hot July afternoon wearing nothing above his waist, some onlookers might consider it a breach of a folkway, but in all likelihood a passing police official would take little notice. If a woman walks down the same street with no clothing above the waist she would probably be arrested. But even if the woman's actions did not contravene a law, for many people she would still be violating the mores of Canadian society: women are absolutely not supposed to bare their breasts in public.

Consider another example: someone goes to a professional football game and in the heat of the moment yells an angry obscenity at the referee. Others sitting nearby might feel a little uncomfortable, because swearing in public still carries a certain stigma and is often considered to be inappropriate behaviour. Sociologists might consider this behaviour the violation of a folkway. If the same person is in a church service, disagrees with something said, and utters the same obscenity at the same volume, or is on the street and shouts an obscenity at a police officer, nearly everyone would consider this action as a serious violation of proper codes of conduct. Sociologists would consider such actions to be the violation of mores.

The original conception of folkways and mores was developed by William Graham Sumner in his 1906 classic volume, *Folkways*. Sumner also distinguished folkways and mores from *laws*, which for him were norms or more often mores that had been formally codified and enforced. For instance, in many societies the concept of equality is represented by the norm that we should treat all people as equal regardless of their national origins, religion, and sex. These types of norms are often codified into laws prohibiting discrimination and enforced by both the police and human rights commissions.

Like norms and values, folkways and mores are subject to change. There may be groups in society that hold values and subscribe to norms that are different from those of the dominant culture. If such a group accepts some of the values and norms of the dominant culture but has other values and norms as well, they are referred to as a subculture. For instance, to the extent that Finnish Canadians accept the general value system and normative orientations of mainstream Canadian society while maintaining other values and norms unique to Finnish culture, they are said to compose a subculture. A subculture can usually exist with no major conflicts within a society.

In many societies there are groups who reject most if not all of the values and norms of the dominant culture, subscribing instead to alternate beliefs and practices. In sociology these groups are called counter-cultures. The "hippies" of the late 1960s and early 1970s who rejected mainstream North America and posited an alternative lifestyle dominated by alternative values and norms represented a counter-culture, as do present-day Hutterite and Amish communities. The essence of a counter-culture is the advocation of a value system and normative orientations that are distinctly different from the dominant culture and mainstream society.

Much of our conduct is influenced, structured, and prescribed by what we know about how we are expected to act. Indeed, as we go about our normal daily routines of work, shopping, attending classes, going to church, and other social activities, we usually don't have to think about what to do in most situations. We just seem to know what to do. The knowledge that informs our behaviour as we stand in a lineup at the supermarket or wait for our professor finally to come to the point is an important part of the values, folkways, norms, and mores that facilitate the everyday interactions that are so essential to everyday living in society.

Groups
Although we are very much institutionalized creatures, not all of our time is spent engaging in patterns of behaviour and interaction geared to meeting a basic need or solving a basic problem. There is a good chance that many of you reading this text will soon decide you've had enough and put the book down, call a friend, and go out for a coffee or some other refreshment. If we assume that in this new activity no basic need is involved – that is, the liquid intake is not really related to substantial thirst – and that what you are wanting to do is relax and talk to a friend, your conduct now falls outside the context of an institution. In this case we have to drop the concept of institution as an explanation and refer instead to the behaviour as occurring in a group.

In sociological analysis a *group* refers to people who interact in an orderly or patterned way and share a certain specific set of norms and values. According to Theodorson and Theodorson's classic definition, a group is: "A plurality of persons who have a common identity, at least some feeling of unity and certain common goals and shared norms" (1969: 176). The key to the sociological conception of a group is thus the idea of an orderly or regularized interaction among persons who share a normative system and have a sense of their identity and common purposes or goals. When you have coffee with a friend, socialize at the mall with your mates, play a game of pickup basketball on the driveway, go to a bonspiel on the weekend, or just drive around on Sunday afternoon, you are engaging in group interaction. Although these kinds of activities are an important part of our lives, they are not necessarily related to meeting a particular need in the way that institutional behaviour is. Rather, they occur because we share goals and values with others, or have a sense of common identity and feelings of unity.

Sociologists make an analytical subdivision between primary and secondary groups. A *primary group* is small in size, cohesive and intimate, and involved in face-to-face interaction that takes place over a relatively long time and in a number of different settings. Perhaps the best example of a primary group is your own collection of friends, or a clique in high school. In all likelihood this kind of "crowd" is small, perhaps five people or less. These groups tend to be cohesive and intimate, and the members feel extremely close to each other. They know intimate details about each other's lives, things hidden from parents. When you are in this kind of a group the members become your closest friends, and you take their opinions and advice seriously. You interact with them on a daily, indeed hourly, basis – these are the people you might spend all day with and then when you get home you phone them up within ten minutes to check on what's happening. When you are emotionally involved with members of a primary group, your whole being – your behaviour, your personality – becomes caught up in it.

Compared to a primary group, a *secondary group* is larger in size and less intimate and cohesive. It is more impersonal and usually geared to some specific activity or purpose: a sports team, for example, or a club that engages in a special activity, such as drama or photography. In this kind of group the various members usually don't know the intimate details of each other's lives. For instance, if you are on a softball team and you have an "off day" at bat and one of your teammates offers less than constructive criticism, you could most likely shrug off the comments with less difficulty than if your best friend had made critical comments to you. Other examples of secondary groups are church groups, people who regularly meet to play cards or chess, or casual – as opposed to close – friends at work.

The differences between primary and secondary groups can be subtle. A group of casual friends at school or work can become closer and closer as the interaction becomes more personal and intimate, so that a secondary group becomes a primary group. Likewise, a group of close friends can drift apart, becoming more casual acquaintances who only meet occasionally for routine and non-intimate interaction. This group would make a transition from a primary to a secondary group, illustrating in turn an essential characteristic of social life: it is a dynamic, ever changing process.

The sociological discussion of groups also includes two other terms: aggregates and categories. The concept of *aggregate* refers to a collection of people who essentially just happen to be together for a common but temporary purpose. When you stand with others to wait for a bus or a train, attend a course in introductory sociology, or have dinner in a restaurant you are part of an aggregate. The people who find themselves in these situations tend not to interact with each other in a manner characteristic of either primary or secondary groups.

A further distinction is made between an aggregate and a *category*.

In undertaking their analyses social scientists often divide and subdivide the populations they study according to various classification schemas. They might, for instance, use the category of university student to differentiate analytically those who attend university from those who do not. In this relationship there is no implication of group interaction or even of an accidental coming together as in an aggregate. As a category university students simply represent a division of the population based on an arbitrary attribute. Categories can be established on the basis of endless arbitrary divisions, including everything from age to level of education to place of birth.

Formal Organizations

One final component of a typical Western industrial society is the concept of formal organization. Imagine, once again, that you've had enough of reading this book and you want to make an effort to salvage the rest of your day. You decide to do something worthwhile, like engage in a community service. You go out and do some work for the United Way or an AIDS action committee or rape crisis centre. By joining and participating in these formal organizations you are interacting in yet another part of the social structure.

In sociology the term *formal organization* refers to a collectivity that has a formal structure, specific purposes and objectives with clearly delineated rules, and regulations and procedures that govern the conduct of its members or volunteers. People often do not formally join institutions or primary and secondary groups, but they do formally join certain organizations. Within such organizations there might be a formal structure of offices, with formal procedures for selecting persons to fill them as well as definite lengths of tenure.

The essential characteristics of formal organizations are the formal procedures and regulations that govern interaction within them. Some institutions, such as the multinational corporation, share some of these characteristics. But many institutions, such as the family, do not, and because many formal organizations do not relate to basic needs and problems, we make a distinction. One of the most systematic sociological treatments of formal organizations is found in Peter Blau and Richard Scott's *Formal Organizations* (1963).

In the internal structuring of interaction and behaviour within groups and formal organizations, the concepts of status and role also come back into play. Even in the most intimate primary peer groups there are statuses and roles. In a high school group, for instance, there is often one person who becomes the group "clown," another who becomes the group "brain," and perhaps someone who is the group "toughie." These statuses and the associated roles can be vital in influencing people's behaviour. Similarly, there are formal statuses with attached roles in many formal organizations.

The Tools of Sociology

The key to understanding what sociologists mean by institutions, groups, and formal organizations resides in the notion of structured or organized behaviour that is determined by the shared common knowledge of the human actors – bearing in mind always that human behaviour and action tend not to be random or unpredictable.

The language of sociology has developed slowly over the years as sociologists have analysed society. In using this terminology we must take care to avoid assuming that a sociological analysis means merely the naming and labelling of aspects of human life. For sociologists the terms provide the tools necessary for the larger operation: building an understanding of the composition and operation of society.

The act of creating and developing solutions to our needs, problems, and drives is a social act that, by definition, involves other human beings in complex, highly structured modes of action or interactions. Sociologists argue that the structures of these organized interactions can be better understood through the concepts of institution, role, status, value, norm, and group. The analysis of these modes of conduct is an essential project in the discipline of sociology.

Terms and Concepts

Social analysis – both the process of taking society, social processes, and social phenomena apart in order to better understand them and the resulting understanding and knowledge that we acquire. The verb "analyse" refers to examining something by resolving or breaking it down into its component parts. The noun "analysis" refers to the results of the process of analysing something.

Social structure – sometimes used interchangeably in sociological analysis with society. Social structure may be a preferable term because it draws attention to the fact that the human relationships, interactions, actions, and behaviours that make up society are both social and struc-tured, as well as ordered, patterned, routinized, and regularized.

Institution – a pattern of behaviour, a set of organized social rela-tionships, routinized interactions, or structured social relationships geared to solving some basic individual or group need or solving some individual or group problem. In sociological thinking an institution is not to be confused with a physical place such as a building dedicated to some specific activity such as health care. An educational institution is thus not necessarily a specific building or place but a complex set of structured and organized behaviours and patterns of interaction through which we attempt to transmit some aspect of our society's stock of knowledge.

Institutionalization – the process by which behaviour, actions, and interactions become routinized, regularized, organized, and structured into ongoing patterns. Institutionalization is the process of either deliberately or unintentionally "building" institutions by engaging in recurring and structured behaviour to meet some need or solve some problem.

Institutional order – a cluster of specific institutions that are all related to meeting a basic need or solving a problem. The economic order refers to all those economic institutions, from the family farm to the small main-street business to the chain store and the giant corporation, that are a part of how the material needs of people in our society are met.

Status – a position within an institution, group, or organization. The term does not necessarily imply a hierarchy or ranking of positions, just the existence of different positions. In a university there are typically a number of different statuses, including student, instructor, secretary, librarian, caretaker, and dean.

Role – the set of culturally defined behaviours that are appropriate and expected or inappropriate and unacceptable for a given status. In drama, when we play a role we act according to a set of instructions in the script. In our social behaviour we act according to a set of "instructions" provided by the society's script: its normative orientations, value systems, and ideological dictates.

Norm – a specific expression of a value. Norms are behavioural prescriptions or instructions that apply to behaviour in various roles and statuses. There are two different kinds of norms. A *folkway* is a norm that is generally accepted and governs a wide range of activities; but it tends not to involve serious moral considerations, and a violation is more a breach of manners and bad taste than a matter of serious concern. *Mores* are norms that are more strictly adhered to and considered a matter of public morality. The violation of mores is often a violation of a moral dictate and can be punishable in a formal manner by agents of social order such as the police. In Canadian society picking your nose is generally considered a violation of a folkway, while appearing nude in public is a violation of mores.

Value – a general and abstract principle or idea related to what is appropriate and inappropriate behaviour, what is desirable and undesirable, right and wrong, good and bad. Values are by nature general and might include vague and general instructions like "be honest" or "be polite" or "respect your elders."

Group – two or more individuals who share a set of normative orientations and value commitments, have a sense of identity and/or common goals and purposes, and interact in an ongoing and orderly way over an extended period of time. As opposed to institutional interaction, group interaction may not be directly linked to meeting some basic individual need or solving some problem.

Primary group – a small number of people in an intimate, face-to-face, long-lasting, cohesive relationship or pattern of interaction. Primary-group interaction and primary-group members are considered important by the actors involved. An example is a typical high school or adolescent clique or gang.

Secondary group – larger than a primary group and not involving as much intimate and face-to-face interaction. Typically, secondary-group interaction is shorter in duration and has less meaning and significance for the participants. A baseball or hockey team is typically a secondary group.

Formal organization – a formally organized collectivity with a specific purpose or objective. The formal organization typically includes a constitution, formal officers, and membership procedures and rules to govern conduct. Many community organizations, charities, and service clubs are formal organizations.

4

SOCIALIZATION

The sociological imagination demands more than a thorough analysis of the basic structures of human society, although clearly this is necessary. The sociological imagination demands that we understand the connections between our social structures, made up of institutions, statuses, roles, values, norms, and so on, and ourselves as individuals. The concept of socialization is the essential link between an individual and the social structure. It is one of the most important concepts in the discipline of sociology.

Although, again, there are minor differences in how sociologists define the concept, there is general agreement that socialization refers broadly to the process of social learning. *Socialization*, for our purposes, refers to the life-long social learning process that is essential to human existence and development. As a result of this process, we not only learn how we are expected to live our lives, but also acquire a culture and develop a personality.

The Biological Processes

Let's return to a discussion of your physiological being, your physical body and its various biological processes. When do you get hungry? Are there particular times of the day that you tend to get hungry and seek out and enjoy food? Usually there are. A key question is why, in most parts of North America, do we tend to feel hungry shortly after we get up in the morning, then again around twelve o'clock noon, and later around 6:00 p.m.? Do we have a genetically based biological need for nourishment at these specific times in our twenty-four-hour day? There seems to be little evidence that humans as a species are genetically programmed to eat at certain times of the day, because there are enormous variations across cultures in when people eat various meals. Anyone from North America who visits India or Chile, for example, finds that by the time dinner is served at between 9:00 and 10:30 p.m. they are past being hungry. Could it be that, as we grow up and develop in a particular society, we learn or are trained to be hungry at certain times of the day? Could it be that the process of getting hungry and desiring food, which we normally think of as natural and biological, is in some important way influenced by the overall structure and pattern of our social existence? The sociological answer to these questions is a resounding "yes," because we know that both meal times and diets are among the most diverse of cultural features.

Leaving aside the question of when hunger strikes you in the daily cycle, let's consider what you will accept as nourishment in the satisfaction of that hunger. We know that the human body needs a certain amount of protein, and we know that most locations around the world contain bountiful sources of protein. Yet most of us are relatively fussy about what we will accept. For many people born and raised in North America, the choices of meat-based protein are limited to certain parts of beef and pork-producing animals, poultry, certain fish and seafood, and mutton and lamb. For most North Americans, food coming from skunks, snakes, lizards, worms, grubs, insects, rodents, and the friendly feline and canine species is not acceptable. Indeed, many of us might have difficulty putting snake meat in our mouths, let alone swallowing it and keeping it down.

Many foods are considered delicacies in one culture but are not acceptable sources of protein in another. Does your palate allow you to enjoy very spicy flavours, like the ones we find in traditional foods in India? When we consider our ability and willingness to consume certain foods and not consume others we are confronted with the question of why. Is the explanation biological, that is, are some *Homo sapiens* born with a genetic propensity to throw up after eating snake meat while others lack this gene? Do some people have a gene that allows them to consume very spicy foods while others do not? There is no evidence that this is the case, and it seems more likely that for the most part we enjoy and consume foods we have become accustomed to through a long process of learning.

In our physiological processes such as sight, more is involved than the biological processes of light waves striking certain kinds of nerves that stimulate the transmission of electrical messages to the brain. In this case, too, a significant degree of social learning is involved. For instance, Canadians born and raised in most southern parts of the country know what snow is, and they can look out across a snow-covered field and recognize several different kinds of snow. Depending on what they see, they might describe the snow as sticky, wet, powdery, or crusted. Despite these adjectives, the English language has only one word for snow. In Inuit culture, though, there are many words for snow. There are different nouns for falling snow, snow on the ground, snow packed hard like ice, slushy snow, and other forms. Individuals born and raised in that culture commonly have the ability to perceive and recognize the various kinds of snow at great distances. A person born and raised in the southern coastal area of British Columbia, with its year-long moderate temperatures, would in all likelihood be unable to recognize, let alone identify by name, different types of snow.

Once again we must face the why questions. Are the Inuit biologically or genetically programmed with the capacity to perceive and identify different types of snow at great distances while people in the south are not? A more logical and supportable argument is that snow is a dominant factor of life in the North and physical survival there depends on knowing about snow conditions and being able to communicate on this subject with others. Given this fact, a central part of the social learning process in Inuit culture is recognizing types of snow and acquiring the appropriate language to describe them.

Another example illustrating the link between social learning and the process of perception relates to the issue of physical attractiveness or beauty. Have you ever said that another person is "good looking" or "attractive"? Have you ever noticed that you find certain "types" of people sexually attractive? If you answered yes to either of these questions, then what particular set of physical characteristics or features do you define as attractive? Furthermore, is there a species-wide, transcultural set of physical attributes that defines "attractiveness"? The answer to this is "no." What is considered attractive or sexually appealing varies radically from one historical epoch to another and from culture to culture. At a particular time in history a man might be considered attractive if he is slim, bronze in colour, and tall. In that same culture at another historical moment the ideal man could be heavier, with pale skin, and so on. Our definition of what constitutes a beautiful and sexually attractive person is not present in our genes; rather, it is a part of a society's values and norms that we are taught and learn through socialization.

In sexual conduct, to take another example, what are the typical behaviours of homo sapiens as they prepare for and engage in sexual activity? The question of what particular physical appearance stimulates the sex drive aside, once the sex drive is stimulated, how do we behave? Are there universal, species-wide, invariant, unlearned behaviours that characterize sexual conduct? On the contrary, the behaviour associated with human sexual activity is as varied and diverse as the characteristics associated with masculinity and femininity. All we need do is think about the various different styles of hair, dress, and makeup that characterize what is defined as masculine and feminine in different cultures at different times. The sexual behaviours that are typical in a given society are cultural in origin, and they are learned at the level of the individual through socialization.

Another aspect of human behaviour is related to a basic physical need, but is still fundamentally influenced by socialization: the need for shelter and clothing. The inhabitants of many regions of the planet require, if they are to survive, shelter and clothing to protect them from the elements; but if we consider the patterns of human dress we are immediately struck by the diversity of apparel that has been developed to deal with this problem. The essential point, at least in understanding the importance of socialization, relates to how we come to accept as "natural" the norms and values concerning dress. We can all think of clothes we like to wear and feel comfortable in, clothes in which we just feel "natural." Conversely, we can all think of clothes we loathe wearing and that we feel uncomfortable in, clothes we would not be caught dead wearing in public. So, what determines the clothing we find acceptable, and what determines the clothes we avoid like the plague? Is it in our genes? The answer is once again "no." The types of clothing we prefer and the clothes we feel comfortable in are related to the social learning process that we have experienced over the course of our entire lives. Our culture and the socialization that goes on within it influence how we protect ourselves from the physical environment through our dress.

The Human Personality

In stating that there is much more to our personalities and character structures than just our biological processes and how we deal with our basic biological problems, we move into an area of major controversy in the social sciences. Although many volumes have been written on the issue of human personality, authors have had apparent difficulties in defining the concept of personality. One massive introductory psychology text, Gleitman (1986), offers no definition while Andrew Crider and his associates (1989: 471) define personality in terms of the unique patterns of behaviour and mental processes characteristic of individuals and their positions in the environment. Frager and Fadiman (1984) discuss a variety of different approaches to personality without venturing a definition. Peterson (1988) adopts an approach that has merit for our purposes here, noting that while personality is by necessity a "fuzzy term," it can be understood as a "family" or collection of attributes.

Perhaps the best definition has come from psychologist David Statt (1990), who says human personality is the sum total of how we think, feel, and behave. Statt notes that while all of us share patterns of thought, emotion, and behaviour with others in our society, at the same time we also possess and exhibit unique and individual patterns of thought, emotion, and action. As a result of this, our personalities are composed of the shared and unique traits and characteristics that make us what and who we are.

The concept of *personality*, then, refers to those general, individual, characteristic, integrated attributes of an individual that define his or her uniqueness and distinctive being in the world. Our personalities are composed of extremely complex sets and patterns of traits, attributes, beliefs, and behaviours that relate to a very complex series of issues including, among other things, religion, politics, war, peace, co-operation, competition, relations to persons of the same or opposite sex, sexual behaviour, age and aging, and physical appearance and ability. Our personalities or character structures also have to do with how we experience fear, anger, aggression, or frustration. They are connected to what makes us anxious and how we deal with anxiety. On the other end of the emotional spectrum, what makes us happy, how we express joy, what gives us pleasure and satisfaction, and the sorts of things we really enjoy doing are also important elements of our personalities and characters.

The sociological position holds that key aspects of our personalities – our beliefs and attitudes, our value systems and general attitudes – are better understood by reference to our social environment and experiences than to our genetic heritage. Put simply, there is no evidence that some people are born with a genetic propensity to be Christian, Jewish, Muslim, or atheist. Similarly, there does not seem to be a gene that makes us sympathetic to left-wing or right-wing ideas or makes us exhibit any of the other great number of traits that make each of us what we are. In summary, it is clear that a good deal of our personality and character structure is fundamentally influenced by the life-long social learning process called socialization.

Types of Socialization

Within the discipline of sociology there is a general assumption that socialization has an impact on virtually all aspects of our being. The norms, values, folkways, and mores that we acquire through socialization become important in the development of our personalities and subsequent behaviour. Even some aspects of our bodily or biological functions are influenced by the social environment and the social learning process. Our language, our political beliefs, how and what we perceive, and our religious beliefs and practices are all influenced as well. Indeed, we can argue that who we are and how we act must be understood within the context of the life-long socialization process we all experience.

Within the discipline of sociology there is a tradition of distinguishing between several different types of socialization. These include primary and secondary socialization, resocialization, and anticipatory socialization.

Primary Socialization

Our survival as individuals and the long-term survival of our species depend on our ability to interact successfully with other human beings to solve our basic problems and meet various needs. This continuing interaction, which is the basis of our social existence, is predicated on the sharing of a basic stock of knowledge, part of which is a system of symbols used for communication, that is, language.

The learning of language is thus an essential aspect of *primary socialization*, which refers to social learning that involves the acquisition or transmission of the basic stock of knowledge essential to social interaction in a particular society. In addition to language, primary socialization includes the learning of behaviours such as eating habits, table manners, and toilet training. Through primary socialization we also begin to learn about the basic statuses and roles typical of the various institutions in our society, as well as the norms and values that influence behaviour.

As children observe the roles played by their caretakers they begin to learn what it means to be both female and feminine and male and masculine. For instance, by being intensively exposed to the daily routines and patterns of interaction in a middle-class nuclear family, children learn not only about expected roles but also how to deal with emotions such as frustration, anger, and pleasure. Indeed, children learn what causes frustration, anger, and pleasure. Each day, to the extent that there is a rigid division of labour and clearly understood distinctions between male and female roles and clear definitions about what is masculine and what is feminine, children, regardless of their gender, learn about what men and women are like, how they act, and even how they view themselves in relationship to the other gender. A young male child who is told, after falling and skinning his knee, not to cry but rather to act like a man and not a girl, is learning about masculinity and toughness and how this supposedly differs from the expected or "appropriate" feminine response.

If children constantly see women in the household performing domestic labour and men involved in other tasks such as doing repairs or relaxing while domestic labour is performed, they are being taught lessons about roles in the family and appropriate conduct for men and women. People born and raised in a traditional North American nuclear family in which there is a traditional sex-based division of labour tend to find later on in life that it can be difficult to radically change the patterns of domestic work. Even couples committed to changing sex and gender roles often find that it is a daily, perhaps endless, struggle to avoid falling into traditional roles.

Secondary Socialization

As human beings mature and develop they begin to engage in ever more complex and numerous social interactions. In many Western societies much of the primary socialization occurs within the scope of those patterns of interaction we commonly refer to as the family. As children develop and the range of their interactions becomes more complicated, they enter new institutional and group settings, such as the school or church, where they learn more complicated patterns of language and are introduced to society's norms, values, and behavioural expectations.

Secondary socialization is the name given to the learning of these more complex and subtle aspects of a society's language, symbols, norms, values, folkways, mores, institutional structures, roles, statuses, and group interactive processes.

Resocialization

The process of resocialization refers to deliberate and intentional attempts to modify or replace some aspect of an individual's earlier socialization with new or alternative beliefs, viewpoints, norms, or values. Many of the basic arguments put forward in an introductory sociology course, for instance, could be considered an example of resocialization because they often run counter to much of what students have previously been socialized to believe. For example, it is common for people in our society to believe there is such a thing as human nature, meaning that much human conduct occurs because of basic instincts or biologically based propensities. Many people in Canada would tend to agree with a statement such as, "Human nature being what it is, there will always be war and conflict." Behind this statement is the argument that there are basic behavioural patterns that are innate, unlearned, and invariant. Moreover, it suggests that humans tend to be preprogrammed to be aggressive, selfish, and competitive. But an introductory sociology course might attempt to resocialize students by teaching them that there is no evidence indicating humans are governed by predetermined, instinctual, and unlearned behavioural tendencies. This book is attempting to resocialize you to accept the idea that in a fundamental way you are the product of your social environment, an argument that may contravene messages you have received from a variety of other sources. Resocialization is also evident in how individuals are treated after they enter the army, where systematic efforts are made to inculcate them with new attitudes, beliefs, and modes of dress, speech, and behaviour. Similarly, if you are accepted into the Royal Canadian Mounted Police, systematic efforts will be made to change certain of your behavioural patterns. The same could be said of those who end up being incarcerated in prison, where systematic efforts to rehabilitate inmates are really nothing more than systematic efforts to resocialize them.

Anticipatory Socialization

As supposedly intelligent and knowledgeable creatures, we are often in a position to think about and plan our lives, or at least anticipate what might happen to us. When we realize we might soon be in a new situation, we sometimes try to figure out in advance what will be expected of us, what the dress codes might be, or whom we might be interacting with and what the protocol implications might be. In addition to just thinking about these issues, we might try to adopt the necessary views, actions, mannerisms, or dress, or we might even try to practise the actions we could be called on to perform.

For many students the first day at a new high school or university is a stressful situation – they do not yet know the rules. As a result, in situations like these some people may try to find out as much as they can in advance so they won't make fools of themselves or commit serious social blunders. If you join an exclusive golf and country club you will likely make sure that you understand and conform to the dress codes and other such rules, again to make your entry as smooth as possible. This process of adapting to a new situation in advance and thereby making adjustment to that situation easier is known as *anticipatory socialization*.

Socialization as Intentional and Unintentional

When we discuss social learning, or socialization, we are dealing with an extremely complex process that is sometimes the result of systematic and deliberate efforts and sometimes the more indirect and less deliberate outcome of social interactions. To understand socialization fully it is necessary to pay attention to this dual aspect.

Much primary socialization is quite intentional and deliberate, as in the systematic teaching of table manners, eating habits, and toilet training. But while parents intentionally attempt to teach their children a specific pattern of behaviour, they may also be unintentionally teaching them how to handle frustration and anger. When parents lose their tempers, for example, the children will, whether we want them to or not, learn about handling emotions.

Although it is often difficult to make a precise distinction between the intentional and unintentional, there is a clear example in the teaching and learning of language. Most of us have either observed or engaged in efforts to teach a young child some part of our language. For example, a child's caretaker holds up a metal or plastic object with a concave-shaped part at one end that is attached to a long, slender part. The caretaker says "spoon," attempting to get the child to repeat the word. We all learned some of our linguistic skills in this way. But if we consider the very large number of words that a child typically learns during the first two years of life, it is remarkable how few of those words were systematically taught and learned. A great deal, if not most, of the language we learn during our formative years is "picked up," that is, taught and learned in an unintentional manner as parents or caretakers and children go about their everyday normal routines. The distinction between deliberate, intentional socialization and the learning that occurs outside of intentional instruction will become more apparent as we consider the various agents of socialization.

There is a rich sociological literature dealing with the various deliberate and subtle dimensions of the socialization process. In her article "Killers of the Dream," Lillian Smith describes the socialization of white Christian females in the American South during the early decades of this century (Smith, 1971). Harry Gracey's (1977) essay with the provocative title "Learning the Student Role: Kindergarten as Academic Boot Camp" provides an excellent overview of the many things that are "taught" in kindergarten as well as the methods employed.

Agents or Agencies of Socialization

The concept of socialization as a life-long process of social learning leads to a further concept: the existence of agents or agencies that do the teaching that results in the learning. In sociology we use the term

agent or *agency of socialization* to refer to the institutions, groups, organizations, situations, and statuses within the social structures that, in
a variety of deliberate and non-intentional ways, mould, shape, and
influence our beings, personalities, and development.

The precise and specific array of important agents of socialization
varies from individual to individual, culture to culture, and historical
moment to historical moment. In most modern Western societies the
list of important agents of socialization includes family structures, the
education system, religion, the media, peer groups, state agencies, and
economic institutions.

Family

As suggested earlier, much of the primary socialization that allows us
to acquire the basic knowledge and skills necessary for subsequent
social interaction takes place within that set of relationships referred
to as the family – although we have to take care to avoid discussing "the
family" as if there were only one form or set of relationships that characterizes all activities under the rubric of family interaction. In most
situations children's parents have an enormous impact on their development. It is often parents who teach children the rudiments of language and communicative skills, elementary eating habits and
manners, culturally defined appropriate conduct for the elimination
of bodily wastes, as well as basic norms and values relating to many
aspects of existence. Our first introduction to the female and male roles
often occurs in the family. Members of the family, often without real-
izing it, demonstrate various ways of dealing with anger, frustration,
anxiety, and affection.

Because many of our basic norms, values, and ideas about masculinity and femininity are acquired through interaction in the family,
the family is one of the most important agents of socialization. But its
role in gender socialization raises again the issue of deliberate versus
subtle or unintentional socialization. The human infant seems to revel
in mimicking (though grownups do this as well), and this is clearly a
main method of learning. Despite what they may be trying to teach
formally about sexual equality, when parents go about the daily routine
of domestic labour (housework) they are instructing the child about
sex and gender roles, duties, and behaviour. The almost infinite variety
of subtle and unintentional ways by which socialization takes place has
been extensively researched. In a study of the transmission of sex roles
and gender behaviour, Sandra Bem and Daryl Bem note that even
when their children are as young as two days old, there are noticeable
differences in how parents treat girls and boys. Girls are touched more,
hovered over more, smiled at more, and spoken at more (1982: 56-57).

Although we may not know precisely how, such differences will tend to influence subsequent personality development.

Educational Institutions

Perhaps no institutional order is more directly involved in the socialization process in a systematic and deliberate way than the educational order. One dictionary defines education as "systematic instruction, schooling, or training in preparation for life or some particular task; scholastic instruction; bringing up."

The primary task of the educational order is to train, instruct, or school individuals in a variety of aspects of a culture, especially the elements of its formal stocks of knowledge: society's accumulated learning, skills, beliefs, traditions, and wisdom. In Western societies this includes an ability to read and write in one or more languages, an elementary knowledge of mathematics and the sciences, as well as an appreciation of the society's history and geographic and physical environment. The educational order attempts to ensure that children acquire the basic skills necessary for interaction and participation in society.

School also introduces other aspects of a society's norms and values. For example, in school an individual is taught about gender roles, both in the formal content of the curriculum and the classroom and in the less formal playground environment. In the content of textbooks and library books as well as in playground interaction, children learn about being a girl or a boy, competition, and what it means to win or lose. Through the actions and words of teachers on the playground they learn about what is appropriate, what is encouraged, what is inappropriate, and what is officially taboo.

The formal school situation might be the first time that a child has to take orders and instruction from an outsider or stranger, that is, from someone not a blood relative. In school, children learn about neatness, punctuality, discipline, respect for others, and respect for authority, as well as patriotism and the role of competition in society. In a discussion of what has become known as the "hidden curriculum," Canadian sociologist John Harp (1980) notes that a number of studies have focused on the importance of children learning competitive patterns in school, beginning at the kindergarten level. The sense of competition may not be as systematic and formally organized in the early years, but young pupils learn to compete for the attention and even affection of their teachers by demonstrating their skills in painting or printing – or even by encouraging the teachers' interest in their entries in show-and-tell contests. While what we learn at school includes the core content of the basic curriculum, our education goes well beyond this, because most of the time we spend at school is really time spent with peers. In case you are prone to thinking this sort of thing only occurs with young children, see Howard Becker and Blanche Geer's "The Fate of Idealism in Medical School" (1980).

Peer Groups

Not all socialization takes place within the structures or social arrangements we call institutions. Indeed, during certain periods in their lives, North American adolescents spend large amounts of time with their peers. The peer groups that are important vary as an individual matures and passes through the various stages of life.

During childhood, neighbourhood friends may be the most important peer group, while during adolescence a school-based crowd or clique becomes more important. The peer group is often a child's first experience in a situation that is not dominated by adults, and thus the child has more flexibility to explore interactive processes. Later in life the peer group that plays an important part in socialization may become centred around friends at work, in church or a club, or at university.

The primary group is, by definition, a group of people who really count and are important. The members of a clique in your school can have a profound impact on your conduct. Many of our habits, values and norms, and language and dress codes are acquired as a result of interaction with our peers. The fact that our ways of seeing the world and thinking about it are influenced by these interactions means that we are learning – that is, we are being socialized. These peer groups thus form an agent of socialization.

Mass Media

North Americans spend a great deal of time with mass media: watching television and videos, reading newspapers and magazines, going to movies, or listening to CDs, tapes, and the radio. In the process of watching, reading, and listening we are exposed to countless messages and signals touching on countless aspects of our social and physical being and behaviour.

For example, we acquire much of our information about events in the world, both locally and internationally, from the mass media. Many of us rely on the mass media for the latest "news," and this information becomes central to how we understand, interpret, and generally feel about the world. Our sense of optimism or pessimism, joy or despair, relief or anxiety is influenced by what we see, hear, and read. The latest news on international relations, hunger and starvation in the Third World, political tensions in Europe or the Middle East, or death squads in Central America has an impact on us and our personalities. Because our attitudes, beliefs, and values are being influenced, we are being socialized even as we simply watch, read, or listen to the news.

For anyone interested in the media, Noam Chomsky's *Necessary Illusions* (1989) is compulsory reading. Chomsky presents a chilling picture of the power of the media and those whose interests are supported by the media to mould our lives and what is commonly called public opinion through the manipulation of information. A similar argument is also developed in another book, Joyce Nelson's *The Perfect Machine* (1987), a must read for anyone who watches more than one hour of television a week.

But there is more to the media's role than just providing news. Indeed, a great many people who watch television avoid watching the news programs, preferring instead to be "entertained" by the dramas, sports, variety and game shows, and situation comedies that make up the bulk of television time. Watching television to escape from the pressures of life is also part of the ongoing social learning process. People do in fact acquire much of their knowledge about how the world works from watching entertainment television. Unfortunately, as sociologists have found, the knowledge acquired can be dubious. All you need do is ask a local police officer how many children think police work is mostly about chasing dangerous criminals at high speeds, making massive drug busts, and collaring murderers. Ask anyone who operates a private detective agency or who is a lawyer or a medical doctor if they think the television portrayal of their occupations is accurate. Nevertheless, it is clear that we do learn as we are being entertained. The learning may be of a subtle and unintentional type, but we are learning about many things, including roles and jobs, men and women, the role of violence in solving problems, minorities and how they behave, and children and aging.

Another component in the socializing content of the media is the role of advertising. Advertising has become an essential part of our lives. It is everywhere we go – not just in commercial mass media but on billboards, buses, and T-shirts. The central task of advertisers is to convince us to buy a particular product, and they accomplish this by the direct and indirect manipulation of our norms, values, beliefs, and behaviours. For example, if we become convinced that the perfectly normal human process of perspiring is disgusting and revolting and that we should do everything in our power to avoid that disastrous state of affairs, we become ready in turn to cover our bodies with various chemicals that solve the "problem." If we can be convinced that the most important thing in life is spotless laundry, we become prime candidates for a new soap product. The advertisements that we see and hear (even smell now in some magazines) are designed to "teach" us something. That is, they are designed and planned to be a part of the social processes by which we learn of life's problems and how we should solve them.

Through all of this we are being instructed about what is important and what is not, what it means to be feminine and masculine, and how men and women relate to each other. Advertisements often suggest, for example, that how we appear in a physical sense is far more important than how we feel inside or how we react to others. As typically pictured, men are in command while women are obsessed with domestic cleanliness. As a child watches these images and messages day after day, year after year, the learning takes hold in a powerful way.

Religion

Much of the socialization or social learning that occurs within religious institutions is deliberate and systematic. Churches often have programs of instruction for people of every age, from nursery and Sunday schools for the young through various youth groups, adolescent membership rites, and premarital counselling to groups that help older members cope with the death of a spouse. At all of these stages there is continuing systematic instruction and, presumably, learning regarding various particulars of the church's beliefs, practices, doctrines, and rituals.

Religious socialization is important because of the comprehensive nature of the issues, concerns, or aspects of life covered. The norms, values, beliefs, and behaviours systematically taught by formally organized religions touch on most aspects of an individual's life, including everything from gender roles and sexual conduct and how we dress to our attitudes toward the rich and poor. What we eat, how we see nature, how we deal with death, and how we respond to others with different beliefs: these are only a few aspects of our personalities that are influenced by religious beliefs and practices. Clearly, socialization plays a fundamental role in the acquisition of religious beliefs: even the most ardent biological determinist is not going to argue that some of us are born with a genetic propensity for Protestantism, Hinduism, or Buddhism. Our religious beliefs are learned, the product of our socialization.

Economic Institutions

Socialization also takes place within economic institutions. People who have had butterflies in their stomachs on the first day of a new job or who have hoped just to get through the first day or week on the job without making a complete fool of themselves have felt the impact of the workplace on their behaviour. An essential part of the first few days on any new job is learning "the ropes," that is, learning about the norms and values and language and roles that are a part of the routines of the job. If you learn about the various aspects of a job in advance, that represents a case of anticipatory socialization, while learning about them on the job is simply socialization.

A part of workplace socialization might include obvious things such as learning new and specialized languages, dress styles, codes, and expectations, as well as more subtle aspects of the work environment like obedience to authority, the importance of being punctual, and even making personal sacrifices for the employer. Among the best treatments of the work process and its enormous impact on virtually every facet of people's lives is Studs Terkel's *Working* (1974).

The concept of "good corporate" material implies a recognition, on the part of corporations, that certain individuals have the potential to be socialized and resocialized in a way that produces a budding executive. When corporations hire people who have certain basic skills and abilities and mould them to become future executive material, they are engaging in socialization. A person who joins a trade union for the first time also tends to become socialized into accepting a new set of roles, norms, values, and language.

State Agencies

Another type of socialization and resocialization occurs after an individual joins a branch of the military or a police force. In the case of military training, the concept of "boot camp" is very much about socialization and resocialization. It is common for people joining the military to undergo radical changes in both their physical appearances and their character structures. Changes to physical appearance result from the rigorous physical fitness regimes, cropped hair styles, improved posture, and new dress codes that accompany military training. Changes to personality could include a strengthened sense of patriotism, a more willing acceptance of authority and responsibility, and the decreased sense of individuality that comes with a stress on teamwork. A systematic account of the personality and character changes that result from several years of military service could well serve to highlight the changeability or plasticity of the human personality.

The Cultural Determinist Position

The arguments concerning the central role of social learning in the development and structuring of the human personality take what can be called a *cultural determinist* position. This position holds that most, if not all, of our behavioural patterns and personality characteristics and traits can be accounted for by reference to the process of social learning, or socialization.

Such an approach allows little, if any, room for arguments that attempt to explain human behaviour or personality in terms of biological or genetic factors. Yet the cultural determinist position has distinct shortcomings: much of our human behaviour is directed toward meeting basic needs and dealing with basic drives that are, to the contrary, deeply rooted in our biology. Clearly, biology cannot be ignored.

On one hand, the process of socialization does not create the drives that manifest themselves in hunger or thirst, nor does it cause our sex drive to emerge or give us the mental capacity that leads us to ask the ultimate spiritual questions of religion. On the other hand, it would seem that without socialization and the social context we would be quite unable to deal successfully with our various drives and needs. The human personality, then, must be understood as a unique product of the interaction between biologically or genetically produced physiological and psychological possibilities and socialization.

If I, as an individual, am to survive and if my species is to continue to exist, I must eat, drink, excrete bodily wastes, deal with my sex drive, clothe myself, and take care of my young. What is unique about our species is the important role that social surroundings and socialization play in the development of the modes of conduct through which these needs and drives are addressed.

Our personalities or character structures are composed of a series of norms, values, folkways, mores, ideas, beliefs, roles, behaviours, attitudes, knowledge, and understandings that influence how we conduct ourselves. They are also based on a myriad of beliefs and attitudes relating to everything from politics and sports to religion. What is the origin of these various elements of personality? How do we explain them? The sociological answer comes through connecting our biological beings with the experiences we have had in our families, in the educational system, in religious settings, among various peer groups, through media exposures, and so on. In short, we explain development and personalities by analysing the entire complex of social institutions, settings, situations, and experiences that have been a part of the socialization process, which has moulded our unique biological possibilities and potentials into what they are at this moment in time.

In their classic work, Logan Wilson and William Kolb (1949) use the term "original nature" to refer to the biological basis of human development. They are careful to note explicitly that the concept of original nature is different from the concept of human nature. *Human nature* is usually associated with arguments maintaining that there are specific inborn and unlearned behaviours and characteristics that are associated with human beings regardless of their social environment. An example of an argument based on the existence of human nature might be the proposition that all humans, everywhere and always, are violent, selfish, self-centred, and competitive. Wilson and Kolb say that proponents of such a position frequently use the phrase "You can't change human nature" to argue that such characteristics and behaviours are indeed genetically programmed and unchangeable. *Original nature* refers to the biologically based potentials, structures, and abilities that the human organism possesses at birth or that emerge as a result of normal physiological growth and maturity.

This original nature includes physiological characteristics and structures such as our reflexes, drives, and intellectual capacities. Physiological features such as skin colour, facial features, natural hair colour, and, to a certain extent, body size are biologically determined. A particular skin colour does not by itself necessarily have a bearing on personality or character structure; however, if a person's skin is dark and she/he lives in a racist society, the social processes that the individual is exposed to as a result of having that physiological characteristic could influence personality in direct ways. In such a case, do we point to the biological basis of personality or to the environmental factors?

The Cases of Feral Children

The interaction between biological givens and environmental or social conditioning becomes most obvious when a human being misses all or a substantial portion of what we call the normal socialization process.

The word "feral," indicating as it does a state of wildness or of being untamed, is not necessarily the most appropriate term to describe what are in essence unsocialized humans, but it has become widely used in sociology. A long mythology surrounds people who for one reason or another have been deprived of what sociologists call a normal socialization process. The stories date back at least to antiquity and the accounts of Remus and his twin brother Romulus (legendary founders of Rome), who were set adrift on the Tiber River by enemies, only to be washed ashore and suckled by a wolf. In more modern times, an extensive literature has developed around the subject of feral children. In his book *Wolf Children and the Problem of Human Nature*, Lucien Malson (1972) presents an extensive review of stories and accounts of feral children, finding their origins in everything from ancient mythology to the modern press, some collaborated, some not. As its main focus, Malson's book reprints the diaries of Jean Itard, which provide detailed accounts of the discovery and subsequent development of a feral child called Victor.

Victor

The diaries of Jean Itard are of interest in the study of socialization because they represent one of the few systematic records of the behaviour of a human child who apparently survived for many years without significant human contact. There is no way of knowing at what age or under what circumstances the child Victor was abandoned. He was about twelve years old when he was finally "captured," though he had been caught and held several times before January, 1800, when he was placed in a hospital and subjected to systematic medical and scholarly attention.

The boy was examined by a variety of specialists, including naturalists and the famous psychologist Pinel. Victor, also referred to as the Wild Boy of Aveyron, demonstrated no capacity for language and conceptual thinking. His preferred foods were berries, roots, and raw chestnuts, and he made a murmuring noise while he ate. He seemed to dislike sweet and spicy foods. The boy liked to watch storm clouds and enjoyed rain. At first he constantly tried to escape. He seemed to enjoy cold and damp sleeping conditions, preferring, for example, the floor to a bed. He would sniff at everything that he was presented with and at first seemed not to notice loud noises very close to him, although he did seem to hear sounds like that of nuts being cracked. In his summary of Itard's initial observations, Malson notes that Victor seemed to show none of the characteristics we commonly associate with human civilization.

Victor's behaviour and condition stimulated considerable interest and study, and the overwhelming conclusion of the specialists of the day was that he was a congenital idiot, probably biologically defective. Itard, a medical doctor with a strong interest in psychological development, disagreed, arguing that Victor was most likely a normal child who had experienced an unusual childhood and that childhood experiences explained his condition. Itard took the opportunity to prove his point by working to transform the "wild child" into a normal human being through an intensive socialization process.

We know a great deal about the work of Itard and his housekeeper Madame Guérin, because Itard wrote two detailed accounts of his work with Victor. Interestingly, although Madame Guérin did a great deal of the actual work and provided essential care for Victor, she has tended to receive little credit and attention in the literature. Itard's reports, written to and for the government of the day, form the basis of what are referred to as his diaries.

In the reports Itard described their slow, laborious, and at first seemingly hopeless work with Victor. At the outset just preventing Victor from running away was their main concern; however, gradually they were able to begin to teach Victor to follow simple directions, to distinguish between an object and the word that described the object, and to use letters, words, and even sounds. Victor gradually exhibited not only conceptual and intellectual growth but also emotional growth. There is solid evidence that he came to be attached to and love his care-takers. Although he never mastered speech, he was eventually able to understand words and communicate his simple and basic needs in writing.

Victor was eventually entrusted to the care of Madam Guérin, and he lived with her until his death at the age of forty. There is little sys-tematic data on Victor's subsequent development, but we know from Itard's earlier reports that he was able to help with routine household duties and chores such as chopping wood and gardening.

Victor's case eventually formed the basis of the François Truffaut film, *The Wild Child* (1969). But, as interesting as his case is, we might feel the need for more up-to-date data. Indeed, there have been peri-odic reports in the popular press about abandoned or feral children, and there have been two well-documented North American cases in this century.

Anna and Isabelle
In an article in the *American Journal of Sociology* in January, 1940, the well-known U.S. sociologist Kingsley Davis reported on the case of a child who had spent most of her life imprisoned in a single room in the house of her mother's father. This girl, called Anna, was the second illegitimate child born to her mother, and Anna's grandfather was so enraged by what he saw as the indiscretion of her mother that he refused to even look at the child. As a result Anna was kept in seclu-sion in a second-floor room and given only enough attention to keep her alive.

Evidence gathered concerning Anna's history indicates that at the time of her birth in a private nurse's home she appeared normal and was even described as beautiful. But, Davis reported, when she was removed from the room in her grandfather's house and brought to a new home about five years later, she was suffering from serious malnutrition and was completely apathetic. She lay in a "limp, supine position, immobile, expressionless, indifferent to everything" (Davis, 1949: 555). She seemed to show little response to various stimuli, so at first the onlookers believed she was deaf and even blind. Anna did not know how to walk or talk; indeed, in a subsequent report Davis noted that she did not do anything that indicated intelligence (1949: 174).

Davis described the treatment Anna received in the various homes she was placed in and, finally, the private home for mentally handicapped children in which Anna made her greatest strides. She was not given any systematic or particularly rigorous regime of training, but, as Davis noted, two years after her discovery Anna "could walk, understand simple commands, feed herself, achieve some neatness, remember people, etc." (1949: 175). About three years later she had learned to talk, although she mainly used phrases. In addition, she worked with beads and pictures. She was concerned about keeping clean – she washed her hands habitually – and was able to run. Her general disposition was described as pleasant (176).

Anna's physical health never did recover from the effects of her malnutrition and isolation, and she died in 1942 at the age of ten. In his 1949 article Davis compared Anna's case with that of another girl who had also spent the first years of her life under unusual circumstances. The second girl, given the name Isabelle, was discovered shortly after Anna and had also been kept in seclusion because of her illegitimacy. Isabelle had been looked after by her mother, a deaf mute, and had received considerably more care than Anna. Nevertheless, she spent the first six years of her life secluded in a small room, and when she was removed and placed in an institution she showed few of the characteristics we associate with a child her age. She was in poor physical condition. She suffered from severe bowing of her legs, was unable to talk, and, at first, appeared to be deaf. She was subjected to a series of personality and intelligence tests and the results, predictably, showed little sign of intellect or ability.

Isabelle's treatment program was considerably more systematic and rigorous than the one given Anna. Those caring for her concentrated their efforts on teaching her elementary language skills, and while their efforts produced no results at first the persistence of the team paid off. Once Isabelle began to learn language her progress took a dramatic leap forward. She moved quickly through a series of learning steps until her measured IQ had tripled in a year and a half. Davis reported that she struck him as "being a very bright, cheerful, energetic little girl" (1949: 179). She was still behind others of her age in school, but had made such rapid strides that her future seemed no more uncertain than any other child's.

Genie

Perhaps the most familiar case of a contemporary feral child is the case of Genie. Genie was taken into custody in November, 1970, after surviving thirteen years of nearly total isolation in a small room at the back of her parents' home in a Los Angeles suburb. We know that Genie's father became a very disturbed man who insisted on not having any children. After finding his mother's body on the street, the victim of a hit-and-run accident, Genie's father seems to have completely abandoned the normal world and he spent his last years as a recluse with his family as his virtual prisoners. He was convinced that Genie was mentally challenged and would die before she was twelve. In order to protect Genie from the world, her father kept her isolated in a small dark room. Genie was harnessed to an infant's potty seat much of the time, and when not in that position was placed in a sleeping bag modified to serve as a straitjacket and confined to an infant's crib with a wire mesh attached to the sides and top. Genie's mother appears to have been a victim of her father's wrath as well in that she seems to have regularly suffered physical abuse from the time of their wedding. As her eyesight deteriorated, she was unable to stand up to the father in order to protect Genie (Rymer, 1992)

When Genie was thirteen her mother finally summoned her courage and decided that it was time to change Genie's circumstances since she was obviously going to live beyond the age of twelve. Genie was brought to the attention of the police, after which her parents were arrested and charged while Genie was admitted to hospital. On the day he was to appear in court, Genie's father committed suicide and her mother was eventually acquitted of the charges against her on the grounds that she, too, was a victim of abuse and as such had not been able to intervene.

Russ Rymer describes Genie's condition at the time she was taken into custody:

. . . she weighed only fifty-nine pounds and was only fifty-four inches tall. She was in much worse physical shape than at first suspected: she was incontinent, could not chew solid food and could hardly swallow, could not focus her eyes beyond twelve feet, and according to some accounts, could not cry. She salivated constantly, spat indiscriminately. She had a ring of hard callus around her buttocks, and she had nearly two complete sets of teeth. Her hair was thin. She could not hop, skip, climb, or do anything requiring full extension of her limbs. She showed no perception of heat or cold. (1992: 43)

In addition, he notes she could speak only a few words. During the period that followed Genie became one of the most studied humans in history, and thus we know more about her than about any other feral child. Rymer notes that Genie's means of expressing emotions were also unusual. When frustrated, for example: "She would scowl, tear paper, or scratch objects with her fingernails. When she was very angry she would scratch her face, blow her nose violently into her clothes and urinate. But she would not make a sound, and she would not turn her anger outward toward another person" (54).

In the first years after being taken into custody Genie became an important source of information concerning human development, although Rymer provides a detailed account of what must be termed a measure of mistreatment by various scientists and experts who were eager to study and learn from Genie. Among the important findings that emerged were new data about the relationship between language acquisition and the physiological development of the brain. Rymer summarizes the startling implications of these findings in the following manner:

> If Genie was any indication, we are physically formed by the influence of language. An essential part of our personal physical development is conferred on us by others and it comes in at the ear. The organization of our brain is as genetically ordained and as automatic as breathing, but like breathing, it is initiated by the slap of a midwife, and the midwife is grammar. (68)

Rymer further explains that language is "the mechanism of the human brain that actually triggers the brain's growth." He goes on: "What are human beings? Beings whose brain development is responsive to and dependent on the receipt at the proper time of even a small sample of language" (69). Maya Pines draws a similar conclusion in a study of Genie, quoting an expert who studied Genie to the effect that without language normal physiological brain development does not occur (1981: 32).

In the final analysis, the case of Genie seems to represent a double tragedy because, as Rymer argues, in the haste of researchers to learn from her experiences she became what has been termed the most tested child in history, but her emotional needs seem not to have been at the top of many agendas and as a result an opportunity to undo more of the damage Genie suffered may have been lost. At last report Genie was living in a home for mentally challenged adults.

The Lessons

Although the precise backgrounds of Victor, Anna, Isabelle, and Genie are different, their cases provide certain insights into human conduct.

Perhaps the first point to consider is the actual behaviour of these children who had been denied a "normal" socialization process. Are there any common patterns of behaviour or conduct present in humans who are substantially unsocialized? If we are looking for specific characteristics or traits, the answer is no. These four children did not exhibit uniform behaviour that could be defined as aggressive, violent, gregarious, co-operative, loving, competitive, or anything else. They did exhibit the human capacity of locomotive activity, which Thomas Williams (1972) calls gross random movement, meaning that people have the innate physiological capacity, based on our muscle, bone, and tendon structures, for a great many random and different motor movements. Isabelle, Victor, and Genie each demonstrated this ability early on, and Anna later displayed the ability. Other than this the children had little in common.

The conclusion we can draw from these studies is that when reared in isolation, or at least under conditions of relative social isolation, human beings do not tend to develop identifiable and distinguishable characteristics. Instead we seem to possess, as Ruth Benedict argued, enormously wide and varied potentials and possibilities. Furthermore, to develop fully our human potentials and possibilities, we require a social environment and social contact with others.

Terms and Concepts

Socialization – the life-long process of social learning that human beings undergo. As one of the most important concepts in sociology, it is variously defined as everything from the process of cultural transmission to the acquisition of a personality. Socialization influences virtually every aspect of our beings and personalities from key physiological processes to our character structure. Social learning occurs in practically every social setting, and nearly all of our social experiences contribute to what and who we are.

Agents of socialization – The institutions, groups, organizations, sources, social situations, and locations within which we are socialized. Agents of socialization include statuses in institutions as well as social and cultural settings in which we learn certain ways of acting and behaving. For example, as you prepare to get a driver's licence you encounter a number of different agents of socialization including driver-training teachers, parents, other drivers, and traffic situations. If you learned to drive in a small community and subsequently move to a big city, the traffic situations you encounter on the expressway then literally become a site of social learning and thus an agent of socialization.

Primary socialization – the basic social learning that typically occurs during the first few years of a life. Primary socialization is the acquisition of basic knowledge of a society's values, norms, folkways, and mores and thus includes learning things like language, eating practices, everyday rules of conduct, and etiquette.

Secondary socialization – the process of acquiring the more complex and subtle knowledge that we need in order to interact and behave appropriately in the many complex roles we engage in as we mature and become involved in more and more institutions and group behaviour. Primary socialization may not teach us how to act in school, a lecture hall, a union meeting, or a board room; however, as a result of secondary socialization we acquire this knowledge later in life.

Resocialization – The social learning process that involves deliberate and sometimes systematic efforts to change an aspect of what was previously learned. In an introductory sociology course, efforts may be made to resocialize you in order to have you understand and accept the sociological perspective. If you join the military or the RCMP you will also certainly be resocialized.

Anticipatory socialization – learning values, norms, behaviours, and modes and rules of conduct in anticipation or in advance of some situation when you might need them. Before entering a new social or institutional setting we frequently learn what might be expected of us – how to dress, how to talk – in order to make our entrance into that new setting easier and to avoid embarrassing mistakes.

Feral children – children who have for some reason missed a significant portion of the "normal" socialization. Sometimes referred to as "wolf children," feral children typically have survived in a degree of social isolation that usually results in death. Among the well-documented cases are Victor, Anna, Isabelle, and most recently Genie.

5

THEORIES OF SOCIALIZATION

Most social scientists acknowledge that the concept of socialization is fundamental to understanding how our personalities are formed and our behaviour is structured. But once we've learned the basic tenets – the types of socialization, the possible agents and agencies – further questions arise. Exactly how does socialization take place? How does the process make its distinctive impact on our personalities and social behaviour?

These new questions bring on new theories. Social scientists have spent long hours trying to explain the more intricate workings of social-ization and, as always, the answers to "what makes socialization work" are contentious. Here we will explore several key theories of learning and personality development in order to determine their value in coming to our own understanding of the socialization process. We begin with one of the earliest arguments.

Conditioning Theory

Classical Conditioning
Classical conditioning was one of the first theories developed to explain how animals, including humans, learn.

We commonly, and correctly, associate the term classical condi-tioning with the work of the Russian physiologist Ivan Pavlov – though Pavlov was originally interested not in learning theory but in the study of the digestive processes of dogs. As a part of his research Pavlov pre-sented dogs with food and measured their salivation response. As he was carefully making his observations he noticed that after a while the dogs would salivate when they saw the food dish, that is, before they

actually got to take the food into their mouths. Based on these observations Pavlov concluded that the dogs had learned to associate their
dishes with food, and that the dish itself had become a stimulus to
produce salivation.

The dogs did not have to be trained to salivate when they were presented with food, because the salivation was a natural response. In
other words, the food was a natural or unconditioned stimulus, and
salivation was the natural, unconditioned response. What happened
was that the dish, as a stimulus to salivation, became a substitute for
the food. The dish became a conditioned or learned stimulus, and salivation at the sight of a dish was a learned or conditioned response. A
conditioned stimulus is one that has become associated with an original stimulus; and thus it is a learned and not a natural stimulus.
Although it is considered natural for a hungry dog to salivate when food
is presented, there is nothing in the natural repertoire of a dog's behaviour that causes it to salivate at the sight of a dish. The conditioned
response is the one elicited by the conditioned stimulus. To prove his
point, Pavlov subsequently conditioned dogs to salivate at the sound
of a bell, something that originally would not be associated in any way
with food.

While there is debate about the extent to which classical
conditioning explains human conduct, it is clear that we do learn some
things this way. Imagine a child's first encounter with a hot stove.
The child, reaching out and touching the stove, feels the pain at the
same time that a parent shouts, "Hot – don't touch!" After repeating
this unfortunate lesson a few times the child comes to associate the
words "Hot – don't touch!" with pain. So when the child is about to
touch a hot barbecue in the back yard and someone shouts "hot" the
conditioned response is avoidance. The child has come to associate
the word "hot" with pain and will avoid objects if others say they are
hot.

Imagine another situation involving parents, their children, and a
snake. The parents have a pathological and irrational fear of snakes,
and each time they encounter even a harmless garter snake they shout
out and jump away. After a few such encounters the children come to
associate a snake with an unpleasant experience, and the snake
becomes a conditioned stimulus that brings on a conditioned response
of fear or flight.

The American psychologist John Watson developed the most forceful arguments relating to the usage of conditioned learning for human
development. In an oft-quoted statement, Watson declared that there
were almost no limits to the capacity of conditioned learning to mould
the human personality:

Give me a dozen healthy infants, well-formed, and my own specified world to bring them up in, and I'll guarantee to take any one
at random and train him to become any type of specialist I might
select – doctor, lawyer, artist, merchant-chief, and, yes, even
beggar, and thief, regardless of his talents, penchants, tendencies,
abilities, vocations, and race of his ancestors. (Quoted in Robertson, 1981: 107)

Watson, fortunately for the sake of his potential human subjects, never
carried out the project. The general approach was subsequently criticized, largely because of its simplicity. Others working in the area of
human learning suggested that the classical conditioning approach was
not adequate to account for the complex patterns of learning that
humans experience.

Operant Conditioning

The most famous proponent of a second school of conditioning theory,
operant conditioning, is B.F. Skinner.

Skinner approached human behaviour as if all actions were
responses to stimuli. He did not believe we could understand, or that
we should try to understand, what went on between a stimulus and a
response, because science had to concern itself only with observable
phenomena. Skinner's focus therefore is on operant behaviour rather
than, like classical conditioning, on respondent behaviour. Operant
behaviour can be produced by a stimulus; however, the stimulus may
not necessarily precede the behaviour, as it does in classical conditioning. When a chicken pecks on a button and receives food as a
reward it eventually learns to peck the button in order to receive food.
Skinner is well known for advocating the use of rewards in teaching
and for the Skinner box (Schultz, 1975: 245-50).

According to the theory of classical conditioning, an organism learns
to associate an "unnatural" or secondary stimulus with an original
stimulus, and as a result the second stimulus or conditioned stimulus
becomes enough to elicit a response. Operant conditioning refers to
situations in which an organism actually learns to behave in certain
ways as a result of the response it receives when it acts or behaves in
that way. For example, if an initial action is followed by a positive
reward the organism taking that action will learn that it is the appropriate way to act in order to receive the reward. However, a negative
reward (punishment) will deter the organism from taking the action
that produces it. If an initial action is followed by a punishment the
organism will learn to avoid that action. For example, if a hungry
chicken accidentally pecks a green button in its cage and food is

released, the chicken, with a sufficient number of successful repetitions of the action, will come to learn that pecking the green button is the way to acquire food. In a similar fashion, an organism encountering a negative experience or some form of punishment will learn to associate the action with its unpleasant consequences and avoid the behaviour. The proverbial slap on the wrist can be understood as a form of operant conditioning.

These approaches are usually linked under the general heading of behaviouralism (Salkind and Ambron, 1987: 199). A major criticism of the approach from sociologists is that it presents an overly simple view of human personality and human development because the human learning process is said to follow a pattern similar, if not identical, to that in non-human animals. Many social scientists and philosophers have argued that humans and the patterns of learning they exhibit are indeed qualitatively different from non-humans and non-human patterns.

Jean Piaget

Jean Piaget (1896-1980), a renowned Swiss psychologist, challenged many of the arguments of conventional conditioning theory, arguing that the formation of the human personality is more complex than indicated by the behaviouralist position. Piaget is also important because he offered a perspective on personality formation based on a recognition of the roles of both biology and society.

For Piaget the biological component is self-evident, because humans are biological creatures who undergo processes of growth, development, and maturation. Much of our personal, intellectual, and moral development is predicated on a certain sequence of physical growth and maturation. The processes of becoming a mature, intelligent adult are a complex interaction of biology or heredity and experience or environment.

The role of physical biological maturation is apparent in Piaget's ideas about the human stages of development. Each stage involves both physiological or biological maturation and development of the individual as well as the emergence of unique and distinctive cognitive skills and methods of learning. Indeed, Piaget is best known for his arguments about cognitive structures, a notion that refers to the tendency of all human children to exhibit common or standard rules for problem-solving and reasoning at each stage of development. The discovery of sequential patterns of development that move a child from the use of one set of rules to another led Piaget to theorize that these changing patterns of cognition were tied to or related to the correlated physical and psychological development or maturation of the individual.

Based on observations of his own children and experiments with others, Piaget concluded that there were four distinct stages or periods of development:

1. *Sensorimotor.* A stage covering birth to about two years of age.
2. *Preoperational.* Lasting from about two years old to age seven.
3. *Concrete operational.* Years seven to about eleven.
4. *Formal operational.* Lasting from about age eleven to full maturity in adulthood.

Piaget associated unique or distinctive modes of cognition, reasoning, knowing, social and psychological development, and learning with each of these stages.

Sensorimotor Stage

In a collaborative work with Barbel Inhelder (Piaget and Inhelder, 1969), Piaget further subdivides the sensorimotor stage into six substages; here we need only note the general flow of their discussion. During the first stage, human infants gradually come to understand that they are unique and distinctive beings with an existence apart from others. Children tend to experience the world directly, that is, they physically manipulate objects they encounter by attempting to touch or hold them. In doing this they are essentially exploring the world and learning about their senses and motor capacities, as well as using their senses and motor capacities to learn about the world. Cognitive activity is at a low level, due in part to linguistic capacities.

Although early on in this stage children are not capable of comprehending things outside their immediate sight, they eventually develop a sense of the permanence of an object; they come to realize that an object continues to exist even if they do not actually see it at a given moment. For example, a typical ten-month-old child playing with a toy will immediately lose interest in that toy if the object is covered up. The child will simply transfer attention to something else. When the same experiment is done with older children, they will try to find the objects they had been playing with.

Imitation is a key part of the learning process during the sensorimotor stage. By the end of the period children are beginning to master the use of language, an important prerequisite for the process of symbolic thought that characterizes the child's cognitive capabilities in later stages. Piaget argues that the use of symbolic thought becomes apparent when a child uses one object as a substitute for another. The ultimate expression of the capacity for symbolic thought is the child's use of language.

Preoperational Stage

At about two years of age children mature to the point that they pass into the second stage of cognitive development, which lasts until they are about seven. The preoperational stage is marked by a dramatic increase in linguistic capacities; however, the children are literal in the use of language and the focus of all understanding still tends to be their own being. They are self-centred. At this age they are unable to understand fully the world from the perspective of others and unable to describe things from a hypothetical or abstract perspective that is different from the one they are physically located in. If you ask children in this stage a question about how something might look from a different perspective or angle, they tend to ignore your question because they simply cannot envision or comprehend the possibility of an alternative point of view.

At this stage children's understanding of language and physical perspectives is limited. They will use language in a way that seems to be unaware of the perspective of the listener. They will also use language in a quite literal fashion, accepting little or no ambiguity in terms. Their literal and limited cognitive capacity is illustrated by what Piaget calls conservation. For example, if you take two glasses of water that are the same size, each containing an equal amount of water, and show them to children in this stage, they will probably agree that the glasses contain the same amount of liquid. If you pour some of the liquid from one glass into a thinner and taller glass, the water level becomes higher in that glass. The children will tend to argue that the taller, thinner glass with the higher water level contains more liquid. Similarly, if children are shown two rows of similar objects such as blocks or dominos that are equally spaced and equal in length, they will probably tell you that each row contains the same number of items. If you spread out the items in one row so that it appears longer, these children will tend to say that the new row contains a greater number of the objects. These responses indicate that the children have not come to understand the principle of conservation, namely that changes in the physical arrangements of objects do not change their quantity. The logical capacity of reversibility develops later, and children then come to realize that every action has a logical opposite.

Concrete Operational Stage

Around the age of seven children pass into the last of Piaget's key child-hood stages of cognitive development. During the concrete opera-tional stage their cognitive capacities begin to illustrate the types of logic that we commonly associate with adult thinking. They begin to understand the logical principle of conservation, that all judgements cannot be merely based on how things appear.

While there are still limits on the cognitive abilities of children, espe-cially in the area of abstract reasoning, they make great intellectual strides during this stage. Among the important cognitive capacities they develop is the ability to understand complex social relations. A child develops the ability to understand that the same person can be a mother, a sister, a daughter, an aunt, even a friend depending on the position of the reference person. The world, the child comes to realize, is not nearly as simple and literal as it once seemed.

The children's increased cognitive capacities demonstrate a much more significant use of logic and a degree of abstract reasoning, but they are still somewhat limited and dependent on practical and con-crete intelligence. This means that they can operate most effectively when there are actually objects in the immediate environment to be manipulated. Children move into the realm of fully abstract reason-ing during the final stage of development.

Formal Operational Stage

According to Piaget, at about eleven years of age children pass into the last stage of development, which lasts through adulthood. The formal operational stage is the culmination of the development of cognitive capacities. It is the stage during which our full capacity for abstract and logical reasoning emerges.

Our final cognitive ability is the capacity to reason abstractly and to use hypothetical concepts and thinking. When confronted with a problem we are able to think through a wide range of possible solu-tions in advance. Because of our capacity for abstract thought and abstract reasoning, we do not have to experience things directly to be able to think about them and solve problems related to them. During this stage of our development we acquire the capacity to work with analogies and abstract ideas as well as to accept arguments that might appear to be contrary to the apparent facts. The full human capacity for using abstract thought, symbols, and logic becomes apparent. We can think in terms of hypothetical possibilities and communicate our ideas to others who readily accept them, even in the absence of imme-diate, concrete, experiential data.

Moral Development

In his studies of the moral development of children, Piaget found that children pass through two stages of development. He called the first period, which lasted from about years four through seven, the stage of *moral realism*. Children in this stage of development tend to take the presence and legitimacy of rules and regulations for granted. They tend not to question the origins of rules but accept them at face value and treat them as sacred and not to be questioned. In this stage children exhibit what Piaget calls unilateral respect for the adult or other person in charge of administering the rules.

In one case that Piaget describes as an example of typical behaviour of moral realism, children were told stories about two boys. When called for dinner the first boy went immediately, but on the way into the dining room he accidentally bumped into a tea cart, breaking fifteen cups. The second boy accidentally broke one cup while he was climbing on a cupboard to get some jam he had been told not to eat. When asked which boy deserved to be punished more severely, the children answered that the boy who broke fifteen cups deserved more punishment because his actions had caused more damage. They apparently made no distinction between the intent of or reason for the actions and the outcome.

As they mature in a cognitive sense children gradually begin to develop a more sophisticated and complicated approach to moral issues. As this happens they move toward the stage of moral development called *moral autonomy*. Children exhibiting moral autonomy do not simply accept "black and white" interpretations of rules and moral issues. They question the legitimacy of rules and regulations, asking why actions were undertaken before passing judgements on their outcomes. In a game situation the moral autonomist might agree, providing all others involved have agreed, to change the rules of a game. Such an attitude, which exhibits a stronger sense of social being, develops as children mature in their physical and cognitive capacities.

What we find in Piaget, then, is an approach demanding that we pay attention to both intellectual and physical development and maturation in our efforts to understand the human personality. The individual human is a unique combination of a physiological developmental and maturation process that takes place within an equally unique social and learning situation. The theory argues that we all share something in common, in that we have all passed through a series of stages in both our physical and cognitive maturation. Our differences are understandable in terms of the uniqueness of the biological basis of our being and our experiences.

The Symbolic Interactionist Approach

The work of Piaget postulates a more complex learning process than the one found in the behaviouralist stream. The work of Charles Horton Cooley and George Herbert Mead, two contemporaries who influenced each other's work, presents an even more complex view of the human learning process. Mead and Cooley stressed the importance of human symbolic communication and interaction.

George Herbert Mead

It is difficult to characterize George Herbert Mead (1863-1931) within the usual boundaries of academic disciplines, because he was a philosopher, social psychologist, and sociologist. His studies cover a wide range of topics, but what is important to us here is his work as it relates to the process of socialization and social learning.

Mead's approach has been called biosocial, because it encompasses an analysis of both the biological and the social aspects of development (Morris, 1962: XV). Although there are similarities with the work of Piaget, Mead's analysis of the intersection of the biological and the social is somewhat more complicated.

In his posthumously published work, *Mind, Self and Society* (1934), Mead argues that there is an inherent connection between the development of the human mind, the human self (or personality), and society. Mead's use of the term "mind" implies an important distinction between the physical organ called the brain and the social product he calls the mind. The brain, as a physical organ, is responsible for the many distinctive capacities that characterize human beings. The mind, more akin to the personality, encompasses complex stocks of knowledge somehow stored in the brain organ. Mead explicitly notes that the complexity and size of the human brain underpin human social existence by aiding our ability to undertake two important activities: the development of a temporal dimension; and communication (1962: 117-18, 145).

For Mead, *temporal dimension* refers to the human ability to arrange behaviour and action in a temporal order or sequence based on an understanding of the future consequences of what is being done at a given moment. The human animal possesses the ability for reflexive intelligence. That is, we do not merely and simply respond to stimuli in an automatic and immediate manner. Rather, after receiving a stimulus we reflect on it, think about it, and interpret its meaning. Then we reflect on the possible actions we could take, the responses we could make, and we consider the possible consequences. Finally, in the context of these interpretative and reflexive processes, we act (1962: 117-18). This temporal dimension has a physiological basis in our brain organs and a social basis in our minds.

In addition, Mead notes that one of the peculiar characteristics of human social activity is our extensive use of communication. Indeed, we are able to learn all that we are required to know to survive only because of our extraordinary ability to communicate – thanks largely to the role of our large and complex brain.

Communication is by no means unique to humans, although in animal life many visual and audible gestures that imply messages have proved to be instinctual responses. When a beaver senses danger and slaps the water with its tail, it is making an immediate, instinctual gesture, not one that has been thoroughly, even if quickly, considered from a number of angles. Non-human animals also use gestures in even more complicated communications, as in Mead's well-known example of the behaviour of dogs before a fight. When confronted with a hostile being, dogs instinctively respond with a gesture we call a growl. Mead calls this behaviour a "conversation of gestures" and sees it as quite different from a human conversation, because the gestures tend to be simply stimuli followed by an instinctual response (1962: 63). In a non-human conversation of gestures, a stimulus produces an inborn and unlearned response, which can itself become a gesture, which produces another response in the animal making the first gesture, and so on. The key point is that gestures are instinctual responses to stimuli, and that gestures themselves become stimuli to further instinctual reaction.

Human communication is different because the gestures used are both significant and symbolic (Mead, 1962: 45). A gesture is significant, Mead argues, when it has an assigned or abstract meaning behind it, that is, when it is the result of thought or deeper reflection and intentionally communicates a meaning. Unlike dogs and their instinctual growl, when humans receive stimuli that they perceive as hostile they tend to respond only after considering the nature of the threat, possible courses of action, and the consequences of both. When humans respond, they tend to try to use gestures that both convey their understanding of the situation and indicate the subsequent actions they might take.

For instance, if you frighten me and I respond with a faint smile and say, "Don't do that," I am passing along a good deal of information about how I interpret and understand your actions, how I intend to respond, how I expect you in turn to respond, and, finally, how I will probably respond to your response. If I respond by snarling, "Back off, turkey," accompanied by a look of displeasure on my face, I pass on quite different information. My response, whatever it is, is not instinctually predetermined. Rather, it is dependent on how I understand your initial action, my relationship to you, the circumstances, and other factors.

The human response to a perceived threat is different from the animal response precisely because it includes the interpretation of the initial gesture and the use of significant gestures to respond. *Significant gestures* are thoughtful and deliberate actions intended to communicate a meaning from one human actor to another (Mead, 1962: 46). *Meaning* implies the use of symbols and gestures that are constructed and used by one actor with a clear "eye" to the role of the other actor. The communicator has thought about and reflected on the meaning of the message, determined how to respond, and anticipated the response of the other actor. In communicating in this way with others we are imagining ourselves in the position of the other and attempting to judge how that other will react to our communication. This is indeed a complex process that requires humans to use complex systems of communication.

People and Communication

What are you doing at this precise instant in your life? The answer undoubtedly is reading a book written in the English language. While you may not be paying attention to every word, you are nevertheless reading a series of words in the English language. The words you are reading are nothing more than a particular set of written symbols that humans have developed for the purposes of communication. The specific shape and order of the symbols that make up the English alphabet have no basis in nature or human instinct. They are an arbitrary, even accidental, series of shapes that have become codified into a system of abstract symbols. The use of the English language involves the manipulation of these symbols in various combinations called words. Over the centuries those who came before us have developed systems of arbitrary sounds and arbitrary meanings that have become attached to these symbols.

Human communication is based on the use of these abstract symbols. The human being is a language-using animal. Without language, how could we acquire the vast amount of knowledge that we require to be functioning members of society? Without language and the communication that it makes possible, the process of socialization could not take place, and we would be unable to accumulate and pass on our culture. For Mead, it is impossible to contemplate the human animal without the use of some form of language, whether written or spoken. Language is a key to the development and survival of the species.

For Mead the mind and the symbol are inseparable and essential aspects of being human. An essential difference between the human animal and other animals is the intersection of the human mind between stimulus and response (Mead, 1962: 117). Much non-human behaviour is a matter of the reception of a stimulus followed by automatic response. In the case of human behaviour, we have the human mind with its vast stores of knowledge intervening between stimulus and response. The mind gives humans the capacity to interpret a stimulus and ascertain its meaning, then to consider various responses and the consequences of each possible response, and finally to determine a pattern of behaviour. The development of the capacity to do this, that is, the development of the mind, is an integral part of the emergence of the human personality, or of what Mead calls the self.

G.H. Mead's "Self"
Without providing a succinct and tidy definition of the "self," Mead's use of the term tends to suggest a meaning related to personality or character. His key point is that we should understand the self as an inherently social product. We are not born with a self, but rather the self develops (Mead, 1962: 135). The development of this self is in essence the process of personality formation.

Mead maintains that the self is essentially a product of the human capacity for reflexive thought. It is because we are capable of reflection and thought that we are also capable of consciously knowing that we are a self. Mead also maintains that the development of this capacity for thought and thus the development of the self are dependent on the acquisition of language (Natanson, 1973: 12). He argues that the self emerges through a series of distinct stages.

Mead's Stages of Personality Development
Reece McGee refers to Mead's first stage of development of the self as the self-consciousness stage (1975: 72). Mead discusses the necessity of a preparatory stage of development during which the human child acquires the capacity to use language in the process of reflection and thought. McGee notes that the self-consciousness or preparatory stage occupies, roughly, the first two years of a child's life.

The key stage of self-formation begins, according to Mead, at about year two when the child enters the play stage of development. During the play stage the child begins to play at taking on the role of others. A child might play at being a teacher, a parent, or even a baby. Such behaviour obviously cannot occur unless the child has sufficient knowledge of language and the structures of the social situation to know that these various roles exist. Through playing at roles or pretending and imagining that they are other people, children begin to understand that there are statuses other than their particular positions. Getting outside one's own normal status is an important part of the process of coming to understand how to interact with others. Through play and imaginary interactions children further their knowledge and understanding of the social structure, its roles, norms, values, and statuses. At this stage in their development they may not yet have a firm concept of their self.

The play stage is followed by what Mead calls the game stage (Mead, 1962: 150-52). The interaction becomes more complex: children are in situations of interaction involving others, not just imagining those situations. Mead uses the example of a game of baseball to illustrate (154). To interact successfully in a game of baseball you have to know and understand the variety of different roles involved. The pitcher must know what is expected of that role and have a degree of knowledge about how each of the other players will act in a variety of different situations. For instance, the first time children are on the field playing a baseball game, they all have a tendency to chase the ball no matter where it is hit. Similarly, novice soccer players tend to be constantly crowded together and scurrying around the ball regardless of the position they are supposed to be playing. The coach's first job is often to teach the children that there are various positions, each with a specific role or expected behaviour attached to it. That is, the players have to "stay in their positions." Once the children learn these positions and roles the games proceed more effectively, with far better end results.

According to Mead, in our everyday and ordinary interactions in the game of life, we need to go through a similar learning process before we can interact properly (play). The learning necessary for acquiring the skills and knowledge required for interaction takes up our childhood and occurs during the play and game stages of personality formation. This learning involves the acquisition of a set of symbols that facilitates communication, that is, language, which then makes it possible to learn the specifics of a society's roles, statuses, norms, values, folkways, and mores.

Through the use of language and symbolic communication a person learns about the nature of the society's role structure, value system, and normative expectations. As this learning occurs, people become capable of interacting in complex, organized social activities requiring co-operation. What emerges in the individual's mind is an understanding of the general rules and regulations and modes of conduct that members of the society use and find acceptable and that facilitate the society's continuing interaction. In their minds people gain a conception or an understanding of what Mead calls the "generalized other" (1962: 154-55). Once we have an understanding of the general expectations and rules that govern an interactive situation, we are in a position to become players in that situation. At this point in our development we definitely begin to develop a personality; or, to use Mead's terms, the self begins to emerge.

Mead's Concept of the Self

Mead argues that the human self has two essential components: the "I" and the "me." The "I" component of the self is the biological basis of existence, the biological creature, the sensual bodily structures, our physiological, organic being.

According to Mead, because we are more than mere biologically driven or programmed beings our self or personality has another dimension or aspect: the "me." This dimension is the learned and acquired social component, made up of all we learn as we develop language, norms, values, folkways, and mores. In other words, the "me" is the sum total of the learning that we have experienced up to a particular point in our lives. It is the stock of knowledge acquired through our social existence and has great importance in the overall makeup of our personalities. This "me" is constructed and determined by the nature of the "generalized other" that individuals acquire through social interaction in specific though varied social contexts.

Mead's concept of the self implies that personality development is a life-long process that continues as long as our biological beings continue to develop and as long as we continue to engage in social interactions. Although we are not always aware of it on a day-to-day basis, our biological beings are in fact continually changing, and all of the various associated processes have an impact on our personalities. Similarly, as we go through life we are continually involved in new experiences that often involve new behavioural expectations, norms, and values, which in turn alter the "me" part of the self and thus the whole personality.

We need only think about all the changed social expectations that people experience after graduation from high school or when they get married. In those cases, the expectations of society change dramatically. The graduates are suddenly no longer "high school kids" but "young adults" under increased pressure to look after all aspects of their own lives, to go on to higher endeavours. Newlyweds similarly have to live up to a whole new set of behavioural expectations. To the extent that these new expectations come to have an impact on personal attitudes and conduct – to use Mead's phrase, on the self – that self remains in a continual process of development and transformation.

Charles Horton Cooley

Charles Horton Cooley (1864-1929) was a contemporary of G.H. Mead's, and many of their ideas were similar. For instance, like Mead, Cooley understood that the individual and society cannot be separated. Cooley also shared Mead's views on the fundamental importance of communication in human existence and development. Cooley understood that the human mind is not the same thing as a physical brain organ because the mind is a social product that develops in a social context.

Among Cooley's concepts that help explain how our personalities emerge and continue to develop is "the looking-glass self." According to him, the looking-glass self is an important part of the process by which our self-image develops and is maintained. Furthermore, it very much influences our day-to-day interactions and behaviours. As Cooley says, there are three parts or components to the "self-idea" or looking-glass self: "A self-idea of this sort seems to have three principal elements: the imagination of our appearance to the other person; the imagination of his judgment of that appearance; and some sort of self-feeling, such as pride or mortification" (1956: 184).

According to Cooley, when we interact with others we form images in our mind of how we think we appear to them – most often without even being aware of it. This "appearance" may not be merely physical. For example, a teacher can form an image of how she appears to others, not just as a physical being, but in her social role of teacher. After experiencing how others interact with her, our hypothetical teacher first forms an image of how the students in her class "see" her. She then forms or develops another image, this one of how she thinks the other or others she is interacting with judge her. For example, in her mind they see her as a good teacher, a poor teacher, a fun person, a bore, or whatever. The final part of the looking-glass self is a self-image. Depending on the nature of her image of how others see her, and her further image of how they judge her, our teacher will feel good or bad, enthusiastic or depressed, and so on, both about herself and about her role as teacher. This self-image will have an important impact on her attitudes, behaviour, and general pattern of interactions.

Cooley indicates that the images and feelings we have about ourselves are the product of the social interactions we engage in as we go about playing various social roles. Our self-image is a product of a myriad of social interactions, the responses of others to us, our judgements of what others are thinking about us, and resulting self-feelings.

Cooley's ideas in this area have stimulated considerable research in the area of interactions and behaviour. For example, Mark Snyder

(1982) reports on research on self-fulfilling stereotypes that illustrates how our treatment of others elicits behaviour consistent with what our treatment tells them we expect of them. Snyder reports that some people chosen as research subjects were shown photographs of strangers they were about to talk to on the phone and asked what they thought the strangers would be like. Later, when the researchers watched the subjects talking to the strangers they saw that the subjects treated the strangers differently, depending on what they thought in advance the people would be like. The ones picked in advance as looking sociable, pleasant, and friendly were treated differently than the ones described in advance as unfriendly, distant, and so on. What is especially interesting is that the people being talked to answered in kind: that is, they responded in a manner consistent with what was expected of them. The expectations of certain behaviour or characteristics actually set in motion an interactive process that elicited that particular kind of behaviour (Snyder, 1982: 47-50).

Cooley also points out that not everyone we interact with has equal significance in terms of their impact on our self-image. There are some "significant others," such as those in our primary groups, who are very important and whose opinions of us as communicated in our looking-glass self are very important. Others, perhaps those in secondary groups, are less significant, and their opinions have less impact on our behaviour.

The work of Mead and Cooley locates the basis of human development in our communicative abilities and our capacity for reflexive intelligence, both of which require a social environment in order to develop. Although Mead clearly recognized that we are first and foremost biological creatures, the work of Mead and Cooley, which is often referred to as the symbolic interactionist approach because of their emphasis on symbol usage and interaction, can be criticized for downplaying the biological dimension of human personality. The social scientist who is interested in an approach that systematically incorporates the role of biological processes and forces in personality development should become familiar with the work of Sigmund Freud.

Sigmund Freud

The process of human personality development has been approached from enormously divergent perspectives, and one of the best examples of this is the Austrian psychiatrist, Sigmund Freud (1856-1939). The breadth and depth of his writings defy summary, simple or otherwise, but in his efforts to understand the development and structures of the human personality Freud contributed key theories and concepts to the growth of the social sciences.

In his work Freud argued that the human body is an energy system subject to the basic laws of nature that govern the universe. Like all life forms, the human being evolved after cosmic forces acted on inorganic matter. At a point in the distant past, Earth held only inorganic matter and the planet existed in a condition of stability. Cosmic forces that we may never fully understand acted on this inorganic matter, transforming it and giving rise to the conditions necessary for the development of organic matter. The end result was the beginning of life. Since the time that organic matter emerged a continuous evolutionary process has been at work, which ultimately resulted in the emergence of the human species. The human animal is, Freud argued, an evolved dynamic energy system essentially "powered" by the biological and physiological processes that sustain all life on the planet (Hall and Lindzey, 1970: 39).

Freud maintained that the human species, like other life forms, is influenced by *instincts* – although he did not use the term in the same way that biologists do. An instinct is, for Freud, a psychological representation of a source of tension. Duane Schultz notes that "Freud's term in German, *Trieb*, is best translated as driving force or urge" (1975: 315). The tensions that are the basis of instincts have their origins in the biological and physiological processes of the body. In brief, our physiological existence produces various needs and drives, which yield excitations, which in turn are the real root of instincts (Freud [1933], 1965: 85-86). Instinctual energy is deemed to be the driving force of the human personality whose structures we now want to explore.

Id, Ego, and Super-ego

It is possible, for analytical purposes at least, to think about the human personality as being composed of three interconnected and interrelated parts: the id, the ego, and the super-ego (Freud [1933], 1965: lecture XXXI). The most basic part of the personality structure is the id, which is present at birth and is in closest touch with the physical or bodily processes. The id constantly strives to keep the human physiological and psychological systems in a situation of stable and low levels of energy or tension. This is a task of enormous difficulty, because the normal physiological functioning of the human body constantly yields fluctuating levels of energy and thus tension. This simply means that, under normal circumstances, we tend continually to get hungry, thirsty, and sexually stimulated. When tension of one kind or another increases, the id immediately attempts to address the problem through what Freud called the pleasure principle. The id, trying to solve the problems we are faced with, is concerned with immediate gratification of the drive or need because it desires an immediate reduction of the tension. It is constrained in this, however, because it is only capable of operating at the level of wishes and impulses. The id uses what Freud called the primary process, which involves the creation of images that would satisfy the need. It only dreams or imagines satisfaction, because it does not understand the difference between reality and the imagination. The fact of the matter is, however, that wishful thinking does not reduce the tension. If we are actually starving, no matter how hard we imagine food the hunger persists; and, ultimately, without real food we will die. The id cannot solve our problems or reduce our tensions.

Human survival, however, has been facilitated by the emergence of another part of the personality system called the ego, which relates to our need, if we are to survive as individuals and as a species, for contact with the objective world. The ego is the part of the personality that transcends the id and makes it possible for us to secure real satisfactions and real means of reducing tensions in the real world. Whereas the id operates under the auspices of the pleasure principle and the primary process, the ego is directed toward the reality principle and the secondary process.

The reality principle leads the organism to seek out and locate objects in the physical world that will satisfy the various tensions experienced at a given moment. The ego knows that imagining food or drink does not really deal with hunger or thirst, so, using the secondary processes, it develops a plan to secure actual satisfaction for the need or drive. The ego is not constrained by rules and regulations in its efforts to secure satisfaction, and thus the individual operating under the direction of an id and ego shows little constraint or social responsibility and is not bothered by moral or ethical concerns. In its continuing efforts to deal realistically with the fluctuating tension and energy levels that the body produces, the ego pretty much does whatever it thinks it can get away with. Reducing tension and achieving survival are its paramount concerns.

A world occupied by humans governed by their ids and egos would be unlike the social worlds we have come to accept. In his important book *Civilization and Its Discontents* (1930), Freud argued that humans come to realize that if they are to develop their higher facilities and engage in occupations and pursuits within a stable society, they must renounce the immediate gratification of all their needs and drives. Although it means less than complete and full reduction of all tensions, humans must learn to sublimate and displace some of their tensions in exchange for the larger benefits offered by living in society. The structure of the personality that facilitates the movement from an unstructured and uncivilized state of complete gratification to a civilized but constrained and not fully satisfied condition is the super-ego.

The super-ego is the part of the personality that understands that the ego must be constrained. It offers moral and social reasons for inhibiting the immediate gratification of all our needs and drives. Keep in mind that if all humans were to seek immediate and unconstrained gratification of needs and drives as they arise, life would be a jungle and Thomas Hobbes's famous description of life as being "solitary, poore, nasty, brutish and short" would ring true (Hobbes [1651], 1968: 186). As an intelligent species, however, we come to accept that such a situation is not in our individual or collective best interests. We come to realize that the full development of our individual and species potentials and capabilities requires some degree of social and moral regulation of conduct. As a result we develop collective restraints, moral codes, and rules of conduct that make it possible to substitute social peace and security for immediate gratification. These rules and regulations, which make society possible, become a part of our personality structure in the form of the super-ego, the internal agency of control that ensures our compliance. All of this is similar to the way a military garrison governs a conquered city (Freud [1930], 1982: 61). The super-ego is our conscience, the reason we have an internal feeling of guilt when we violate what we know are the established rules, even if no one else is aware of what we have done (61-64).

It is through the super-ego that the social and moral dimensions of our personalities are introduced. The regulations and constraints that the super-ego imposes do not originally come from within the individual but from society, in most cases passed on by parents. The values, norms, and ideals that the super-ego uses to constrain the actions of the ego are the values, norms, and ideals of the society in which the individual lives. Through socialization the individual comes to know what is appropriate and inappropriate, what actions will result in reward and what will be punished. Eventually each individual accepts these values, and as a result personal actions come to be guided by the internal operation of the conscience. Society's values and norms become the individual's, imposed on the ego through the operation of the conscience (Hall, 1979: 31-35).

The id, ego, and super-ego are among the central analytical concepts employed by Freud in his efforts to understand the human personality. In their study of human personality theory, Robert Frager and James Fadiman describe these as the three subsystems of the psyche. Each makes its own contribution to the distribution of energy and thereby facilitates an existence that balances pleasure and tension (Frager and Fadiman, 1984: 14).

In his later work Freud argued that there are two essential kinds of instincts, one directed to the enhancement of life and the other toward aggression and destruction (Freud [1933], 1965: 92–95). The behaviour that arises out of the presence of the life instincts, Eros, serves to facilitate the survival of the individual and species. Eros directs our activities in the search to satisfy our need for nutrition, fluids, and reproduction. The death instincts are related to the original preorganic state of all living matter. They are rooted in the desire of all living matter to reduce tensions as much as possible, with the ultimate state of tension reduction being the return to non-organic existence after death (Freud [1920], 1955: 36; Gay, 1988: 401).

Human instincts are also flexible. That is, while instincts have an aim – to remove the cause of an excitation or tension – there are usually many different objects that can accomplish that aim (Freud [1930], 1982: 16). In the human animal energy originally directed by a specific kind of tension can in fact be redirected or sublimated. For instance, in the case of sexual tension other kinds of activity can replace sexual activity and accomplish a measure of tension reduction. Sexual energy can in effect be redirected into sports, art, music, or even studying sociology. As a result of sublimation and displacement, human instinctual energies are redirected into the multiplicity of activities that characterize our species, and the pursuit of these varied activities results in the development and flourishing of our civilizations (Hall and Lindzey, 1970: 37–38; Freud [1930], 1982). The means by which we come to develop modes of conduct based on processes such as sublimation and displacement are in essence the process of personality formation.

Instincts, the forces that drive the human personality, also change and develop as the organism matures and develops. What forms of energies and excitations the organism is confronted with and must deal with will change as it matures and develops. Maturation and development also give rise to learning and the development of the types of behaviour we mentioned above. Defence mechanisms are essentially adjustments that we make when we encounter situations and conditions that prevent us from discharging tensions. Freud refers to anything that prevents the organism from discharging tension as a frustration. Among the key methods of dealing with frustrations are identification, displacement, sublimation, and the development of defence mechanisms (see Hall, 1979, for an excellent overview of these complex processes).

Freud suggested that one of the most important forms of energy that the human organism and personality have to learn to deal with is sexual energy. As Hall points out, however, his definition of sexual energy was quite broad:

Freud's conception of the sexual instinct is much broader than the usual one. It includes not only expenditure of energy for pleasurable activities involving genital stimulation and manipulation, but it also embraces the manipulation of other bodily zones for pleasure as well. (1979: 102)

The major areas of the body through which sexual energies are manifest and subsequently dissipated vary as we develop. The main centres of tension reduction, or erogenous zones, are the mouth, the anus, and the genitalia. As we mature and develop attention shifts from one zone to another, marking different stages in the development of our personality.

Stages of Development

Freud believed that as humans develop they pass through a number of distinct stages, each of them characterized by different sources of tension that require handling. Just how these tensions come to be handled during the various phases can affect subsequent personality characteristics.

The first stage of development is the oral stage. During the first year of our lives, because most of our interest is devoted to acquiring basic nourishment, the oral cavity is the centre of our tension-reducing activity. The common attempts of small infants to put anything and everything into their mouths are characteristic of this period. Later in life personality traits such as excessive sarcasm, gossiping, and constantly nibbling or eating are manifestations of certain problems that a child encounters in reducing tensions during this period.

As children begin the second year of life, a new stage of development unfolds involving a dramatic change in the location of the tension-reducing activity. As they begin the process of toilet training, the major location of tension and tension-reducing activity shifts from the oral cavity to the anal cavity. The necessary biological process of waste removal becomes an important source of tension reduction. The elimination of wastes is made all the more pleasurable for the child after the process comes under conscious control. Once again the manner by which this tension-reducing process is handled by the parents or others taking care of the child has an impact on subsequent personality development. In the case, for example, of strict toilet training, the outcome can be an obstinate, retentive, and stingy character; but the element of parental praise can produce a more creative and productive individual (Hall and Lindzey, 1970: 51).

The third stage of development is the phallic stage. At about age three the major focus of tension reduction shifts to the child's genitalia.

The ways in which sexually based energies and tensions are manifested and addressed differ in males and females, which Freud explains by citing the physiological differences between males and females. It is during this stage that children develop and resolve in some manner their Oedipus complex. The Oedipus complex, named after a character in the classical Greek tragedy *Oedipus Rex* who unknowingly kills his father and marries his mother, involves the emergence, among children, of sexual feelings for their parents. The precise manner in which these sexual feelings and attractions reveal themselves and are dealt with differs for males and females. (For an overview of these ideas, see Freud [1933], 1965, lectures XXXII and XXXIII.)

In the male child the emergence of sexual tensions and energies results in a strengthening of his affection and love for his mother. Those feelings for the mother also change, with the love developing a potential sexual aspect. The male child is aware of a possible conflict over the love and affection of the mother, given the presence of another male in the form of the father. The boy develops a fear of his larger, more powerful rival, which manifests itself as a castration anxiety. The child is afraid that his rival will punish him for his secret love for the mother by removing the offending organ, the penis, through castration (Freud, 1965: 114-15). To avoid such a painful loss the boy decides that he must avoid antagonizing the father, and he represses his sexual feeling for the mother and seeks to identify himself with the father. By identifying with the father the male child is preparing himself for the eventual role of father, when at some point in the future he, too, will have a relationship with a mature woman like his mother.

Freud notes that in the case of the female child the process is quite different, owing to her different biology. In *The Longest War: Sex Differences in Perspective*, Carol Tavris and Carole Wade summarize Freud's arguments regarding the essentials of the process in females:

> Girls too go through an Oedipal stage, Freud supposed, but with far different results. Whereas the boy worries that he might be castrated, the girl, after seeing a penis for the first time, worries that she already *has been* castrated. As Freud described it, "When she makes a comparison with a playfellow of the other sex, she perceives that she has 'come off badly' and she feels this is a wrong done to her and a ground for inferiority". . . . She is, to say the least, angry that she lacks the marvelous male organ and has an inferior clitoris. She blames her mother for this deprivation, rejects her, and seeks to displace her in the father's eyes. She becomes daddy's darling. (1984: 180-81)

The female child is ultimately forced to seek compensation for her lack of a penis through the act of mothering a child, ideally a male child who would indirectly make up for her shortcoming. The female child is thus cast for her role as a mother later in life.

After the boys' and girls' resolution of the Oedipus complex, a period of latency begins during which relatively little happens in terms of new sources of tension and energy. At the onset of puberty the adolescent passes into the genital stage, which offers the opportunity for development of a personality; and the characteristics and features that emerge are a result of the various stages the child has passed through. Significantly, most of us remain unaware that we have passed through the stages or that our personalities are composed of various components resulting from those stages. Many of the important psychic processes that influence our personality and its development occur at an unconscious level, and we may never be aware of them.

In recent times, scholars influenced by feminist thought have sharply criticized various aspects of Freud's analysis. Some notable examples are Michèle Barrett (1980), Sandra Harding (1986), Carol Tavris and Carole Wade (1984), and R.A. Sydie (1987). In *Natural Women, Cultured Men*, Sydie argues that because the major theories in sociology were formulated by men, the discipline is "blinkered" and has neglected, ignored, and excluded the social realities faced by women and the general position of women in society (1987: 10). In specifically discussing Freud, she points out that feminist theory has found two central flaws in Freud's analysis: first, it assumes that patriarchal societies are natural and inevitable; second, the psychoanalytical treatment that developed out of Freud's work reinforced the unequal positions of men and women in Western societies (Sydie, 1987: ch. 5). Clearly, there are substantial grounds for questioning many of Freud's universal claims and the scientific legitimacy of his overall approach, although his ideas do remain influential and sociologists need to be familiar with them.

Toward a Sociological Synthesis

Most if not all sociologists agree that no single approach to socialization offers an adequate account of the complex process of human personality formation and development. As a result, sociologists have incorporated or modified various insights drawn from these thinkers into a perspective that both recognizes the biological basis of human existence and stresses the role of the environment in moulding the basic structures of the human character.

To summarize, the human animal is a biological creature with physiologically rooted needs and drives. Humans face a number of basic problems that must be solved if the species and its individual members are to survive. If we define instincts as species-wide, unlearned, biologically transmitted, and invariant complex behaviours, the human animal does not seem to be particularly well endowed instinctively. Humans do not seem to have much instinctual behaviour to assist us in dealing with hunger, fear, finding shelter, sexual drives, and so on, yet we still do find ways of dealing with our needs, problems, and drives. Indeed, if we did fail to deal with those aspects of life, we would cease to exist as living organisms and as a species. All of this raises questions about how we have managed not only to survive but also to prosper.

Humans beings have used our species-specific capacities – everything from the upright posture to our constant sex drive and relative longevity – to develop systematic social behaviours to solve the many problems the species faces. Acting in concert with each other, humans have developed patterns of social interaction that represent cultural solutions and cultural behaviours.

Unlike instinctual behaviour, human cultural behaviour is diverse and learned, and it has produced a variety of material and non-material products, from the millions of human artifacts that surround us daily (material) to our languages, beliefs, customs, ideas, and ideals (non-material). These non-material and material products are the essential components of what social scientists call human culture.

An essential characteristic of human culture is its orderly, organized, patterned, and structured character. Human conduct is not random and accidental. Indeed, the most stressful moments in our lives tend to occur in situations in which we don't know what to expect from others, or when there is a lack of structure and as a result we don't understand the behaviour of others.

For sociologists, culture is a concept that must be located within the context of an even larger set of social arrangements or structures. Culture is intertwined with these social structures: institutions, statuses, roles, norms, values, formal organizations, and groups.

Human infants are born into a social structure. They enter the world as sensual biological creatures with basic needs and drives that must be satisfied; but they are incapable of satisfying their needs or dealing with the problems they face without the assistance of other members of their species. To survive, human infants require a long period of systematic physical, emotional, and social support. The development and maturation take place within the context of social structures.

The shaping, moulding, and learning that the infant, the young child, the adolescent, the young adult, and the middle-aged and older person are exposed to is the process of socialization. Through a series of social experiences we come to acquire our characters and personalities – from what we eat to our values and attitudes toward others around us to our political beliefs and practices and the ways we act when we are angry, frustrated, or afraid. Through the social learning process our possibilities and potentials are developed – or not developed.

This tremendous amount of learning – of socialization – seems to be predicated on our capacity to communicate. The use of abstract written, vocal, and signed symbols for the systematic and deliberate transmission of knowledge and information is an essential characteristic of the human species, which means that the learning of language is considered an essential aspect of human development.

In stressing the importance of the social learning process in moulding the personality, sociologists must be aware of the danger of adopting an *oversocialized* conception of human development. In a famous article, D.H. Wrong (1961) warns against adopting an oversimplified or purely culturally determined view of human beings. It is not possible simply to look at a set of agents of socialization and predict that those influences will produce a person with certain characteristics. Because each of us is the unique product of biological or genetic and sociological or environmental influences, our development must be understood as having been influenced by both factors. In a set of published lectures, R.C. Lewontin, a leading geneticist, has argued that a further complicating factor is what he calls "developmental noise" or random-chance factors in development (Lewontin, 1991: 26-27). Lewontin argues that the precise manner by which an individual organism develops is subject to chance and random variations that are not immediately linked to its genes or environmental circumstances. He notes, for example, that the way in which cells divide and produce the various organs of the central nervous system can be very much influenced by developmental noise. Thus, while we emphasize the environmental and social factors in sociology, we must still recognize that human development is the outcome of a complex process of environmentally mediated biological factors that are influenced by developmental noise.

Although the human individual is a creature with biological needs and drives and biologically based physical and psychological capacities and potentials, we require a social environment for our survival. We must learn how to solve our needs and deal with our problems, and as we learn to do so certain of our various complex potentials and capabilities come to be developed while others remain undeveloped. We may never know the precise nature of all of our potentials and capacities, and it is possible that we possess many capacities and potentials that for a variety of reasons never come to be realized. An inquiry into which of our individual capacities get developed and thus form a part of our "self" must involve the use of our sociological imagination. To understand our strengths and weaknesses, we must look at our individual life stories or biographies, always within the context of the various existing social structures.

Socialization as Unique and Shared
Linking biography and history reveals other aspects of human development. A central question that often emerges when we consider human personality and development relates to our differences and similarities. Sociologists are often asked, "If your argument is that the social environment fundamentally influences our personalities and character structure, why are each of us so unique, so individual?" Another related question is: "My sister and I must have had a similar socialization process because we had the same parents, shared a house for eighteen years, went to the same school, attended the same church, and even played with the same kids when we were young. Why are we so different?"

These are important questions, and they relate to two essential points about socialization: first, socialization is both shared and unique; second, it is always a complex phenomenon.

The argument that each of us undergoes an individual and unique socialization process is a simple recognition of the reality of our lives. No two human beings have ever shared an identical environment. For instance, consider the fact that no other person has the exact social learning experiences that you have had. Even if you had an identical twin, there is no way that brother or sister could have shared every single one of your social learning experiences. It would be both a logical and physical impossibility. Even if two individuals have the same parents, share the same house, attend the same school and church, take vacations together, and read the same books, they do not share identical environments, because no matter how many of their experiences are similar, they will still have many totally different experiences. They may have had different friends, different teachers at school, watched different movies and television shows.

Indeed, a sociologist would argue that while siblings have the same biological parents, the personalities and character structures of the parents who raised and socialized them will have changed, matured, and developed during the period between the births of the children. Socialization is a two-way process, and while parents are socializing a child there is a reciprocal process at work that changes the parents themselves. In the normal course of living, people change and develop in countless ways, both in their physical beings and in their personalities. This is in keeping with George Herbert Mead's notion of the "self" as being composed of a biologically based "I" and a socially produced "me." As we develop and mature biologically, the "I" goes through considerable change. Similarly, as society along with its values, norms, and folkways changes, so, too, does the social "me." Are you identical today in every way to what you were like a year ago, or two years ago? I suspect not – and I hope not, because the constant process of development and change is one of the reasons human beings are so interesting.

The building of the human personality is also an extremely complex phenomenon. Once our personalities or character structures begin to develop they become a factor in their own subsequent development. For example, because you are human you possess an amazing brain, with unbelievable capacities. Your brain allows you to think, reason, reflect, communicate, and learn. As you engage in these actions socialization occurs, and your personality and character emerge and develop. Your developing personality has an impact on how you respond to different experiences in your life, which in turn influences how and why you learn certain things and how and why you react to certain situations. As your personality develops and forms it becomes a part of the complex social interactions you participate in, social interactions that are an essential part of the ongoing socialization process. The result is a life-long process of development, learning, and interaction.

When we speak of the socialization process as shared we refer to all of the common learning experiences shared by members of a society. There are a great many things that people born and raised in North America have in common as a result of socialization. Many of the society's dominant values, norms, folkways, and mores have become part of our personalities simply because we grew up and live in this society. There are, for example, certain acts, words, or behaviours that most of us find acceptable or unacceptable in certain circumstances, and our definitions of what is acceptable or not under certain circumstances are learned. Socialization explains both our individual differences and our similarities.

As for the unabating complexity of socialization, how could a lifelong social learning process be anything but complex? The more we come to understand socialization, the more we realize that it is a process we may never fully understand. My own personality has been influenced by every institution in my society, as well as by scores of groups, organizations, and individuals. If I am to understand this process I must also understand how the institutions themselves operate, how they are related to each other and the entire social structure. If I am to understand fully how my personality has been influenced by various norms and values I must also understand the nature of these phenomena. Where do they come from? What is their role in society? If I am to understand myself as the product of a unique socialization process, I must understand the nature of the larger social structures within which this socialization occurred. The full development of the sociological imagination requires an understanding of how those social structures work.

Terms and Concepts

Classical conditioning – learning that involves the association or substitution of a new behaviour or response with a stimulus. Present a hungry dog with food and it will salivate. Classical conditioning occurs if you ring a bell each time you present the food; eventually the ringing of the bell will be enough to produce salivation: the dog has been conditioned to salivate at the sound of the bell.

Freud's concepts of id, ego, and super-ego – in Freudian theory, the three major dimensions of the human personality. The id represents our basic instinctual biological being and its behavioural tendencies, which mostly involve fantasies about reducing tensions. The ego is the dimension of our being that impels us to direct action in order to reduce various tensions without, however, moral or ethical guidelines. The super-ego represents the internalization of the social and moral controls that we have developed to facilitate an ongoing civilized social existence.

G.H. Mead's "self" – akin to the concept of personality; the total bundle of characteristics, attributes, and features that define a person as unique. Composed of an "I" that is the sensual biological dimension and a "me" that is the socially learned behaviours, values, norms, and attitudes. The biologically based "I" and the socially constructed "me" are not in isolation but rather are dynamically integrated in the "self." The "I," "me," and "self" all tend to be dynamic and changing, yet there is a degree of consistency.

G.H. Mead's play and game stages – according to Mead, the two most important stages of development for the human self or personality. The play stage involves playing at various social roles, becoming aware of the complexities of social interaction, while in the game stage we actually occupy different roles and learn the appropriate behaviours for those and other roles.

Generalized other – our knowledge and understanding of the attitudes, values, norms, expectations, and expected actions of others in different roles and the community at large in our social milieu. Our actions and interactions are affected by our understanding of the generalized other.

The looking-glass self – a concept developed by C.H. Cooley to illustrate how our self-image and the behaviours that emerge as a result of that image are socially constructed through interaction with others. The looking-glass self is essentially a process that involves: (1) forming images of how we think others perceive us; (2) making assessments as to how we think others judge us on the basis of these images; and (3) developing a self-image and/or self-feelings that influence our behaviours and actions in that situation.

Operant conditioning – learning that involves the association of a consequence, a reward or punishment, with some behaviour. If a specific behaviour produces a positive reward while another behaviour produces a negative reward, an organism will learn to behave in a manner that produces the positive reward and avoid the one that produces the negative reward.

Piaget's stages of development – the four stages that children pass through, in chronological order: (1) sensorimotor, birth to about two years; (2) preoperational, from two years to seven; (3) concrete operational, from seven to eleven; and (4) formal operational, from eleven to maturity. Each stage reflects the dynamic relationship of physiological maturation and social environment as the child develops from a sensual being to a mature human being capable of abstract and hypothetical thinking.

Significant gesture – Mead's term for a gesture or symbol used deliberately and consciously in social communication.

Temporal dimension – the human capacity to understand the temporal ordering of events, which allows us to take into account the consequences of our actions prior to acting and to adjust our actions on the basis of our understanding of their perceived future consequences.

PART II

Theorizing Society

Chapter 1 presented a challenge for the student of sociology by advocating the development of our sociological imaginations. The sociological imagination is an intellectual capacity or frame of mind that allows people to better understand their lives, their behaviour, the behaviours of others, and the social world they live in. The first task involves arriving at an understanding of the impact that society has on our personality, character, behaviour, and lives in general. As Mills points out, however, this is not enough because the full development of the sociological imagination requires that we understand how our society is structured and organized, how women and men interact and behave, how and why it changes or remains stable, how wealth and power are distributed, and so on. In Part II the reader will be introduced to some of the ideas, arguments, and propositions developed over the past century and a half about how society works. The field you are entering is commonly known as sociological theory.

This section has three chapters. The first, Chapter 6, introduces what we might call the founding figures and the streams or schools of theory that developed out of their work. In Chapter 7 we consider how the ideas of the founders have been revised and reworked in the middle and late twentieth century to produce several streams of contemporary sociological theory. In Chapter 8 we will cast serious doubt on the heuristic capacities of the three major streams or schools of sociological theory that were dominant prior to the late 1960s. The reason we are questioning the adequacy of the arguments and theoretical positions that have dominated sociology has to do with their failure to include systematic efforts to theorize and explain an essential dimension of the human condition – sex and gender relations. In Chapter 8, therefore, the reader is asked to come to grips with the most important development in sociological theory this century, namely, the emergence of feminist theory.

6

SCIENCE, THEORY, AND THE ORIGINS OF SOCIOLOGY

Sociology is a social science that, as a first step, requires its practitioners to describe the world and the events that make up daily existence. For most of us that probably doesn't seem a difficult task. Indeed, much of our daily conversation is composed of providing others with descriptions of things we have observed or experienced.

For instance, take the book you are reading and close it. Then raise the book a metre or so off your table or desk and release it from your hand. Next, describe precisely what happened. In most cases your description would provide an image of the book falling and give an idea of the sound the book made when it hit the surface of the desk, table, or floor – possibly a good hard thump. According to one dictionary, to describe something is to "set forth in words; recite characteristics of; qualify as" or to "mark out, draw." Description involves the systematic symbolic presentation of our perceptions of the characteristics of some phenomenon.

But sociology goes beyond this first step. It is fairly straightforward to describe what happens when you lift up a book and then let it go; but scientists must not only describe events, they must also seek to answer questions such as "Why did the book fall to the table or floor?" When we ask this sort of question the focus of our intellectual energies shifts from describing to explaining. While describing an event or phenomenon is an important part of understanding what happened, descriptions alone do not allow us to probe or answer the "why" questions. Most practitioners in virtually all disciplines and branches of scientific knowledge production seek to do more than merely describe the world: they also seek to explain it.

In the case of the dropped textbook you might offer a number of different answers to the "why" question. You could argue that objects fall toward the ground because there are dragons in the centre of the earth that suck all objects toward them. You could postulate that the weight of the air pushes objects down toward the earth. Or you could contend that the pressure of light waves, most of which originate from above, pushes objects down. Finally, you could argue that all bodies in the universe exercise a force of mutual attraction toward each other, a force related to the mass of the body and the square of the distance between them. If you adopt this last explanation you would know that the force is called gravity, and you could note that because the mass of the Earth is greater than the mass of the book, this makes the book move toward the Earth as opposed to the Earth moving up to meet the book.

This admittedly simple example draws attention to a couple of essential points. First, explaining something – that is, dealing with "why" questions – means more than merely describing things. Second, answering the "why" questions can involve more than a single response. Both of these points in turn raise a series of further issues.

The argument that explanation is more than and different from description strikes at the core of what is commonly understood as the "project" or the objective of science. For scientists, the task of answering the "why" questions, of providing an explanatory capacity, falls to *theory*, which, in its simplest form, is nothing more than an attempt to offer an explanation of something. Most of us, for instance, have heard about the theory of gravity and know, even if vaguely, about the sets of assumptions and propositions commonly associated with that explanatory framework. In the case of the falling textbook, most of us would probably accept the explanation provided by that theory – a fact that raises a further important question: why would we find this particular theoretical explanation acceptable rather than, say, the idea that there are dragons in the centre of the earth sucking objects toward themselves?

The question of which explanation should be selected for a given event or phenomenon is a major issue in the scientific production of knowledge. The scientific approach calls for the systematic use of empirical data to help determine how useful a theory is in explaining a problem. Part of how we judge theories is through their capacity not only to explain events in the world but also to stand up to empirical verification. The notion of empiricism refers to the commonly accepted assumption in science that there is a real and objective external world that serves as the basis for testing whether a theory is correct or not. A theory should be capable of generating hypotheses – predictions or provisional theories about what will happen under specified circumstances – that can be tested by some method of gathering data from the objective world. There are, however, endless debates around the issue of just how you test a theory and the extent to which accepting a theory predetermines the evidence you gather.

Since the beginnings of sociology, theory has been central to all sociological work. The social thinkers who influenced the emergence and development of sociology produced extremely complex sets of arguments and ideas about how human society works and how we should go about understanding it. What follows here will provide only a brief outline of how key theorists viewed the workings of human society and how they suggested we go about attempting to understand that society.

The Historical Background

To understand the emergence of sociology, it might help to look at the insights of one of its subfields, the sociology of knowledge. The central concern of that subfield is the relationship between the social conditions and structures that exist at a given time and place and the process of the production of knowledge. The sociology of knowledge attempts to place the producer of knowledge and the process of knowledge production within its historical, cultural, political, economic, and religious contexts.

The French thinker Auguste Comte (1798-1857) first used the term "social physics" to describe the new science he was attempting to establish, later switching to the word "sociology." In developing his arguments about why a new approach to the understanding of human affairs was needed, Comte was reacting to the conceptions of humanity and society prevalent in his day. In his opinion the existing conceptions of humanity and society were faulty, and the relationship between them needed reconsideration. This meant a complete revamping of how people explained the workings of the social world – a revamping of the sources and methods of social knowledge.

The Rise of Capitalism

In Comte's era, the modes of thought associated with the term "science" were just gaining dominance. As well, the emergence of science as the most commonly accepted way of explaining the world was part of a much wider series of changes in Western societies. Most importantly, during the seventeenth and eighteenth centuries Western Europe was being transformed from a feudal to a capitalist society.

The transition from feudalism to capitalism was a radical revolution in the true sense of the word, because it changed all aspects of society. The emergence of capitalist or market society involved radical and dramatic changes to the political, economic, family, religious, military, and educational orders. In addition, an intellectual revolution changed accepted ideas about the sources of knowledge, about how we come to understand the world we live in.

In feudal society the church had played a powerful role, and one of its major influences was in knowledge production. The pervasiveness of religious beliefs meant that most people accepted the authority of the church as the definitive source for most, if not all, knowledge. They saw God as the prime mover or cause of events in the world, and they understood events in nature as being related to God, God's blessing, God's will, or God's wrath. The fact that not all events could be explained was accounted for by the viewpoint that humans could not possibly know or understand all things, and that this, too, reflected God's will.

As time passed and new ideas and modes of thought from North Africa, the eastern Mediterranean, India, and other parts of Asia began to filter into Western Europe, changes began to occur in the understanding of the relationship between the authority of the church and the production of knowledge. Among the new ideas were the introduction of Arabic numbers and a revival of interest in the ideas and philosophy of classical antiquity. The emergence of Islam with its interest in a synthesis of ideas drawn from Greek, Roman, and Indian society provided an important challenge to the notion of Christianity as a universal belief system. The Christian response in the form of the Crusades served in the long run only to undermine the power of the church, because the returning adventurers brought back different forms of thought, including knowledge of classical geometry, new philosophies, and logic. As these diverse streams of thought took hold and merged with local improvements in technology within the context of expanding economic activity, major changes began.

The Copernican Revolution

In his classic study of the intellectual developments of the period, *The Making of the Modern Mind*, J.H. Randall states: "Two great revolutions in thought had occurred, and the course of intellectual history since that time is primarily the record of the gradual penetration into the beliefs of men of the significant consequences of those revolutions" (1940: 226).

The first of the intellectual transitions was the Copernican revolution, which dramatically altered the popular conception of our physical location in the universe. Before the sixteenth century there was broad acceptance, among Western thinkers at least, of the basic tenets of the Ptolemaic astronomical system. Claudius Ptolemaeus, known as Ptolemy, was a second-century A.D. Alexandrian astronomer and mathematician who developed an astronomical system based on the premise that the Earth was the centre of the universe and the sun and certain planets revolved around it. The theory received broad support from the church and theological thinkers because it meshed with their understanding of creation. It made sense, many of them held, that God would put the earth and humanity, the centrepiece of His creation, at the centre of the universe.

The Ptolemaic system dominated thinking in astronomy and theology for centuries, but by the early sixteenth century it had begun to encounter problems. As new optical technologies were developed and Europeans began to move about the planet making stellar observations from different perspectives, the accepted system, with its explanations of planetary movements and locations, began to be questioned. At first the discrepancies between the Ptolemaic theory and the new empirical data were addressed by making additions to and placing qualifiers on the system. As a result of these additions and qualifiers the explanatory system used by astronomers eventually became cumbersome and complicated. When Ptolemy's system was used to interpret the data the astronomers were producing, the universe seemed to be a place of chaos. Scientists working in the field were forced to consider one of two possible explanations: either there was no logic and order in God's universe or the basic premises of Ptolemy's system were incorrect.

Nicolaus Copernicus (1473-1543), a Polish astronomer who studied in Italy, was convinced that God's universe was a place of order. Like other thinkers attracted to the new sciences, he believed that creation was governed by logic and that it was mathematical and harmonious. He proposed a radical solution to the problem of the order of the universe, putting the sun into the centre, with the Earth and other planets rotating around the sun. By advocating a heliocentric concept, Copernicus found himself under pressure from the authorities of the day. Church officials were concerned that his theory downplayed the centrality of the Earth and humanity in the structure of the universe. The Vatican declared his ideas to be "false and altogether opposed to holy scripture" (Barnes, 1965: 677).

In challenging the authority of the church, Copernicus was advocating an alternative way of knowing and producing knowledge. By the time his work was further developed by Johann Kepler and Galileo, using data produced by the constantly improving telescopes, the correctness of the heliocentric view was firmly established. The Copernican revolution established the importance of empirical data, or information gathered by some manner of observation, in producing knowledge. Empirical proof would increasingly become the means of determining the truth or falsity of a statement.

The Cartesian Revolution

Copernicus firmly believed that the universe was a place of mathematical order and regularity. It was the second major intellectual revolution – the Cartesian revolution – that established logical thought and correct reasoning as an integral part of knowledge production. By the time the French thinker René Descartes (1596-1650) emerged, the absolute authority of the church as the source of all knowledge was in decline. More and more intellectuals were looking to empirical data as a source of knowledge. Descartes added to the legitimacy of the scientific approach through the arguments made in his *Discourse on Method*, published in 1637. He argued that the first step in knowledge production is to wipe out all existing ideas, including those based on authority, in order to begin with an unbiased mind. The thinker would then start over again with simple and proved statements and, using the rules and procedures of current and formal logical thought, develop more and more complex truths. Knowledge and truth could thus be produced only by the rigorous application of patterns of deductive and rational thought. No statement not arrived at by the use of logical and rational thought would be accepted as knowledge.

The Emergence of Science

Although some intellectuals maintained that knowledge was totally dependent on empirical or sense data (empiricists) and others argued that knowledge came first and foremost from logic and rational thought (rationalists), a union of each of these "new" ways of knowing was in formation throughout the sixteen and seventeenth centuries.

Among the first to argue that true knowledge required the use of both correct reason and empirical data was the English essayist Francis Bacon (1561-1626), a contemporary of Descartes. But the first fully systematic exposition of the method of producing knowledge we have come to call science is commonly attributed to Isaac Newton (1642-1727). Newton's method of "analysis and synthesis" called on investigators to use both inductive and deductive logic, both observation and reason. Newton maintained that observation is the point of departure because empirical support must be provided before a statement can be accepted. Once a statement is proved to be true, it can be used as the basis for subsequent rational and logical thought, so that conclusions not provided by the immediate empirical or observational data can be arrived at through rigorous logical thought. The method of science thus involved the production of general statements by inductive thought working from data provided by the senses. Knowledge that claimed to be scientific required some form of further or subsequent confirmation or proof; and this was to come through the production of deductive hypotheses that could in turn be verified by still more empirical sense data. Observation, in the broadest sense of the word, and experience, along with reason and logic, were all deemed essential parts of the process of knowledge production. A new way of knowing was born, which was soon to prove itself in the discoveries and findings that paved the way for the transformations of the industrial revolution.

The linkage between the capacity of the way of knowing called science and the development of new technology was striking. The standard lists of prerequisites for industrial development always include the presence of machines and technology (Clough and Cole, 1967: 393). While some of the discoveries and findings that came out of the work of people in physics, chemistry, astronomy, and biology might be considered "pure science" (knowledge produced for its own sake without any direct application), much of the new knowledge was applied, that is, used almost immediately in industry and production. The outcome was an explosion of technology that formed the basis of the mechanization of industry, agriculture, and commerce. The knowledge produced by science, which was often cast in terms of the discovery of universal and natural laws, became the basis of a new economic and social order. A central idea in this new order was progress, and scientific knowledge became linked with this powerful notion.

Given the apparent successes of the scientific method in what we commonly refer to as the natural sciences, it is not surprising that some thinkers argued that this same method of knowing or producing knowledge should be used to provide systematic and assured knowledge in the social world. As the feudal order was declining and being replaced by the emerging market or capitalist system, radical social, political, and economic revolutions were also sweeping the world. Although it was obvious to many thinkers that the old order was on the way out, the nature and characteristics of the new order were not yet apparent. Among the key social, economic, and political questions that emerged was the question of social order.

As the power of the church declined, social thinkers concerned themselves with determining if the new scientific way of knowing could provide knowledge that would serve as the basis of social order, stability, and solidarity, as religion had in the past. During the feudal era, religion and the power of the church had provided a strong common set of beliefs and thus an important source of social solidarity. If people in the new capitalist order were to interact as unregulated, isolated individuals in market transactions, with each pursuing his/her own interests, and if each was to be allowed to believe whatever he or she wanted, how could a stable and ongoing community or society be possible? If everyone just acted out of self-interest without an overriding concern for the community, would the situation result in unbridled chaos? Other questions also emerged.

As the political structures of feudal society collapsed and the new nation-states emerged, theorists began to ask fundamental questions about the nature of political power. What precise form should the state take? What is the appropriate role for the monarch and the feudal aristocracy in governing society? In the past those elements had claimed absolute authority and power, but now new classes and groups were contending for power. What role should the governed, especially those involved in business and commerce, play in the operation of the state and government? As the church declined, questions emerged concerning the basic role of religion in a person's life. Similar fundamental questions were asked about the role of education, the structure of family life, even the relationships between the sexes. Nothing seemed sure or secure in the way it had before.

Liberalism and a Scientific Politics

Among the first thinkers to address these kinds of questions in the modern era was Thomas Hobbes (1588-1679). Hobbes believed that just like the rest of the universe, human society was subject to certain natural laws. He was further convinced that the new method of knowing called science was indeed the most appropriate route to the kind of "assured" knowledge that would allow humans to construct a society in accordance with the laws of nature. The methods of science were deemed to be capable of uncovering the laws of nature that governed human affairs, and once we had discovered these laws all we need do was ensure that our social, economic, and political structures did not contravene the laws.

Much has been written about the actual method that Hobbes used and the extent to which it followed what we would now call science (Macpherson, 1973: 230-50, 1968: 25-28; Nelson, 1982: 138). But the precise method Hobbes used to arrive at his conclusions is of less interest for us here than his conclusions. On the basis of his observations and an intellectual process that Brian Nelson refers to as "thought experiment" (1982: 139), Hobbes concluded that human beings are by nature selfish, egotistical, individualistic, and possessive. On the basis of this conception of human nature Hobbes went on to develop arguments about what form of social and political organization humans should endeavour to create. He concluded that the "natural" form of human society was one built on competitive, individualistic market relations overseen by a powerful state governed by an absolute monarch.

For Hobbes and other thinkers who came after him, including political philosopher John Locke (1632-1704) and economists Adam Smith (1732-1790) and David Ricardo (1772-1823), the scientific method was the only acceptable method for producing knowledge. For these intellectuals, the scientific method marked an intellectual revolution. The knowledge that many of them produced related directly to the issues of social, economic, and political reconstruction. In their own ways the later thinkers suggested that, given their findings, the most appropriate form of social organization was a market economy combined with a more liberal state. Each of them produced knowledge that served social, economic, and political interests engaged in a critique of the old feudal order – interests working for the establishment of a new market-based liberal democratic society. The first fruits of the scientific revolution served as the basis for a critical analysis of the existing order. What was called scientific knowledge became a part of continuing political struggles.

The thinkers of the seventeenth and eighteenth centuries also tended to accept and use the idea of a fixed and universal human nature. Although the specifics of their conceptions of human nature varied, most of them maintained that there were fundamental, innate human behavioural tendencies that had to be acknowledged as the basis for the structuring of society. That is, most of the thinkers we commonly include in what is called the classic liberal tradition tended to believe that human beings were by nature competitive, acquisitive, possessive, and individualistic. They supported the social relations connected to a market or capitalist economy because they believed those social relations would allow the blossoming of the natural behavioural tendencies of human beings. Their particular emphases on the scientific method and the fixed and universal nature of humanity provided a distinct background for the development of Auguste Comte's ideas. Comte objected to a good deal of the logic and assumptions of this line of thought, and he set out to provide an alternative view of humans and society.

Auguste Comte and the Emergence of a Discipline

The substantive work of Auguste Comte is little used or referred to in modern sociology, but his contribution to the development of the discipline was enormous – apart from his early use of the term "sociology."

Many of the early social, economic, and political thinkers, in applying the methods of science to their fields of study, ended up being sharply critical of existing society. As a result of this tendency, science had taken on a "critical edge," a tendency that greatly concerned Comte. He lived in France during the aftermath of the French Revolution, a period of enormous change, confusion, and turmoil. Not surprisingly, he became deeply concerned about the roles of confusion and chaos. From Comte's point of view, many of the radical changes and much of the social turmoil seemed to grow out of the findings of thinkers who claimed to be scientists, and who had become tied to an excessively critical project. Comte was not prepared to abandon science, he just wanted it to play a more positive role in social reconstruction. He also began to question some of the basic premises of the classical liberal thinkers, especially those relating to human nature.

Yet another concern was that most of the thinkers of the previous two centuries had been mistaken in what they identified as the object of their inquiries. The classical liberal thinkers had studied "man" in order to discover his basic "nature." They then went on to consider the sort of society that would be most appropriate given "human nature." Comte took exception to this approach, arguing that it was incorrect to postulate the existence of a fixed, universal, and unchanging human nature. Comte was working in an era during which European colonialists, missionaries, and military officials were providing a wealth of new knowledge about cultural diversities. In addition, the period was characterized by a growing body of historical data. When he put this new historical information together with the new knowledge about different cultures, Comte concluded that human beings were not and never had been static and unchanging creatures. Indeed, as he asserted in *The Positive Philosophy* (1838), what he saw in human history was a record of constant change, development, and improvement of both the physical condition and the intellectual faculties and abilities of humans. Comte believed that far from being the same the world over and across historical periods, human beings were quite different in different places and at different moments in history.

Comte was also concerned with the approach of the classical liberals at another level. The prevailing view of society understood it as an extension of the individual. This view led to a certain approach to social phenomena: it was considered appropriate and possible to first study individual people without reference to their society, and then to extrapolate the characteristics of society from the supposed natural characteristics of those individuals. Comte objected to this view on the grounds that society was not merely a collection of individuals. According to him, the "social" was a realm of existence of its own, governed by laws unique to it, and therefore society and the social must themselves be the object of investigation. Comte explicitly argued that individual human beings, as parts of a larger social whole, must be understood within the context of that larger whole. He further argued that the social whole of which the individual is a part can itself be understood by means of an example drawn from biology – thus introducing an important analogy into sociological discourse: the organic analogy.

A living organism is clearly more than merely the sum of its parts. If we only examine, for example, the individual organs, tissues, and fluids that make up a human body, we cannot completely comprehend the complexity of the human organism as a totality. This is because once the various individual parts are arranged in a different way, what we see is a new entity altogether, and not a human body. Indeed, under certain conditions the totality of the parts takes on a life of its own, becoming a living organism and not just a collection of organs. Using this analogy, Comte argued that we must understand human society as more than just a collection of individuals. Human social phenomena are real, they have a reality and an existence of their own, and they represent an object of investigation for the new discipline of sociology.

Comte is important to the development of sociology, then, because he broke the mould of existing patterns of thought by systematically arguing against the prevailing idea of a fixed, static, inborn human personality, or the behavioural traits commonly called human nature. He said instead that humans are diverse and, as a species, capable of changing and improving their condition, character, temperament, behaviour, and ability. He argued that throughout history humanity had developed and passed through a series of stages, each stage different in how society was organized, how knowledge was produced, and what people were typically like. He maintained that society and the social are real, different, and distinct from the individuals within them. Further, he suggested that the social is a crucial factor in shaping and moulding the individual. Lastly, he argued that society and the social realm were the objects of investigation of an emerging new discipline called sociology. The objective of sociology was to be the discovery or uncovering of the natural laws that govern the social. The knowledge produced by the application of science to social improvement would provide a positive basis for even further human progress and development.

Comte's primary contribution was the development of a distinct discipline with a distinctive approach to the study of society and the social. What is most important about Comte, then, is the fact that he ignited the interest of subsequent thinkers who all, in their own ways, attempted to provide the kind of scientific basis of knowledge of society and the social that Comte had envisioned. Some of these thinkers explored ways of studying society that were at odds with Comte's approach, but nevertheless they still claimed to be producing scientific knowledge.

Marx and the Study of Human Society

The German theorist Karl Marx (1818-1883) is one of three major thinkers, along with Emile Durkheim and Max Weber, who had a significant influence on the development of modern sociology. Each of these thinkers produced complex ideas that, once again, defy simple presentation. This problem is even more acute in the case of Marx because his name has become purposefully connected to various political agendas and regimes all over the world – an unfortunate situation, perhaps, because many of those regimes and societies bear little relationship to Marx's original ideas. In effect, the producers of a set of ideas lose control over the uses that others make of their work. The ideas and teachings of Christ, for example, have historically been used by Christians as a justification for waging war and murdering innocent humans, which seems distinctly contrary to the purpose of the original message.

If there is a single phrase that best characterizes Marx's analytical style, it is "the materialist approach." In this sense the term does not mean an obsession with the accumulation or possession of material artifacts and goods. As used in social theory, *materialist* refers to a distinctive approach to understanding human beings and human society.

Marx's materialist approach is based on a series of fundamental assumptions about what it is that makes humans unique and different from all other animals. He suggested that humans can be distinguished from other animals in a number of ways; but the central distinguishing characteristic is the fact that humans *produce* the material necessities of life. To survive, humans need to provide certain elementary material necessities such as food, clothing, and shelter, and what is unique about the human species is how these basic material needs are met (Marx and Engels [1845], 1973: 42, 48). Non-human animals simply take what they find in nature or use what nature provides in the immediate environment, whereas humans actively and deliberately go about producing what they need to survive, intervening with nature to provide for the satisfaction of material needs.

Humans, through the application of our intelligence and physical capacities, alter and change nature to satisfy our needs through actions such as the domestication of animals, the creation of new plant strains, the raising of crops, the diverting of water channels, and even the creation of new artificial products that we eat, use for travel, or clothe ourselves in. All of our basic necessities, such as food, clothing, and shelter, are the outcome or the product of humans labouring to create satisfaction for our material needs.

Productive Forces and Relations of Production

The human activity of producing the material goods, products, and services that we require for survival involves the use of technology, tools, knowledge, and skills, which Marx called *productive forces*. Marx also argued that in addition to being characterized by the use of productive forces, human productive activity is also inherently social; that is, it involves other humans (Marx and Engels [1845], 1973: 43, 50). His materialist method proceeds from these assumptions to provide a way of understanding human society. He argued that if we want to understand human beings and human society we must investigate and understand how the production of society's material necessities is organized. We must examine the productive forces that are in existence at a particular moment in time as well as how material production is socially organized. He referred to this last point as the social relations of production.

The nature of the productive processes is determined by both the level of development of the productive forces and the nature of the *social relations of production*, that is, the patterns of ownership use and control of the productive forces. The nature of the economic institutions is of fundamental or prime importance in influencing the nature and character of the other social institutions. The character and shape of the various institutional orders – the family, polity, education, religion – are fundamentally influenced by the nature of the productive arrangements.

A substantial debate has emerged about just how much emphasis Marx put on this influence. Some theorists have argued, for example, that Marx advocated an economic-determinist position, meaning that the economy or economic institutions determined all other aspects of a society. Although Marx may not have advocated such a strong position, the essence of the materialist position is that economic institutions are the most important factor in a society's general shape and character. The various other institutional orders in turn have reciprocal influences on each other and the economy; but these reciprocal influences are not of the same magnitude as the influence of material production over the whole (Marx [1857], 1973: 83-100).

Marx's Method Applied

The critical dimension of Marx's work is not necessarily found in his materialist approach, but rather in the outcome of his application of this approach to an analysis of capitalist society. Marx spent a major portion of his life engaged in a systematic and critical examination of the nature of material production and distribution within capitalist society. The major product of this work was his three-volume book called *Capital*.

Among Marx's essential conclusions concerning the social relations of production in capitalist society was the argument that capitalist society is by necessity a class society. The class structure of capitalist society is, Marx argued, based on the specific social relations of production that characterize the society. The class relations in a capitalist society are based on people's different structural relations to the forces of production, that is, their position in the economic institutions. This means that there are some people who own, operate, and control the factories, mills, mines, land, and other facilities that produce material wealth, while there are other people who do not. Those in structural positions of ownership receive income by virtue of that ownership, while those who do not own productive resources are forced to sell their capacity to work, that is their labour power, in order to survive.

According to Marx, the class structure of capitalist society is also characterized by relations of economic domination and subordination: some people own and control the major production resources in the economy while others do not have a share in the ownership of or any control over economic resources. For Marx, an analysis of class was essential for understanding the general structures of capitalist society.

Relations of Domination and Power

Marx linked the existence of classes, based on different economic positions, with the existence of ideological domination. Here *ideology* refers to sets of ideas or beliefs that justify or legitimate the social structures and arrangements of capitalist society. It was in connection with a consideration of how certain sets of values, norms, ideas, or beliefs come to be accepted that Marx made his famous statement that "The ideas of the ruling class are in every epoch the ruling ideas" (Marx and Engels [1845], 1973: 64). By arguing that there are relations of ideological domination and manipulation, Marx was attempting to illustrate the pervasiveness of relations of domination within capitalist societies. The ruling class attempts to influence all aspects of the social structure, including the very way people think.

Marx also linked economic power and economic domination to political domination. Although he made several different arguments about the precise way in which economic and political power are linked, the key point for us here is his argument that the presence of overwhelming economic power in the hands of one class makes authentic democracy impossible. This is because the class with economic power is always able to influence the government and the state to ensure that the political order acts in its long-term interests.

What we find, then, in the work of Marx is an approach that is materialist in its general orientation. Marx suggested that if we want to understand human beings within a capitalist society or the overall structures of a capitalist society, we must begin our examination with a consideration of how material production is organized. Such an approach leads to more questions. What level of technological development has taken place? Who owns, controls, and directs the use of productive forces? The answers provide essential clues for understanding the entire social structure. In other words, an analysis of the economic or material basis of a society becomes a point of departure for understanding the rest of society, a master key that helps open a series of other doors in our exploration of social complexities.

In his basic assumptions regarding the nature of reality itself, Marx's thought was very much influenced by the German philosopher Frederick Hegel (1770-1831), who produced one of the most complex and comprehensive philosophical systems ever formulated. There was one key assumption of Hegel's that Marx held firmly to. For Hegel, and thus for Marx, an essential characteristic or attribute of the universe was constant change. Everything in the universe is in a constant process of change, development, and transformation, of unfolding, a process guided by the internal logic and structures of the phenomena themselves. Marx assumed that the social scientist must take this basic fact into account when examining and explaining a given phenomenon.

Emile Durkheim

The ideas and work of the French sociologist Emile Durkheim (1858-1917) were very much an extension of the project initiated by Comte. More specifically, Durkheim was attempting to establish the scientific legitimacy of the new discipline of sociology, and he wanted to use that new discipline to assist in the establishment and maintenance of social order. The persistent issue of social order and stability had continued to be of importance in Europe and France during his era. Durkheim was concerned that not only did society seem to be devastated by conflict, but that this situation was also being described as normal by Marx and his followers, who argued that the capitalist system was inherently prone to conflict and crisis. In a fundamental way he set out to develop both an alternative to the Marxian, materialist approach to the study of society and an alternative approach to the study of capitalist or, to use his phrase, industrial society.

The Division of Labour

One of Durkheim's most important books, *The Division of Labour in Society*, illustrates these two related objectives. Durkheim discusses and presents an approach to understanding human society, and in so doing he attempts to illustrate the nature of sociological analysis. The book examines the transition from pre-industrial to industrial society, although his specific focus is the role of moral codes and belief systems in social structures and changes. Durkheim seeks to demonstrate that the basis of social order is to be found in society's moral codes, by which he means belief systems, value systems, and normative orientations. As a society evolves, changes, and develops the basis of social order, its moral codes can change, and there can be periods of conflict as the new moral codes or belief systems develop. Over time there will be a tendency for order to return as the new belief systems become accepted and internalized within the population.

An Emerging Functionalist Approach

In his effort to understand how society works, Durkheim adopted and developed the organic analogy, making the role of functional analysis much more explicit. *Functional analysis* is a mode of thought that seeks to explain the parts of a system in terms of the overall needs of the system and the particular need that each of the parts or components deals with or solves.

The survival of an organic system such as the human body requires that a number of basic problems or needs be successfully solved or satisfied. In the human body there are specialized structures, such as the various organs, that meet these various needs. One way, for example, of explaining a human heart is to refer to its function as a pump that ensures the circulation of blood throughout the organic system. Similarly, the lungs and stomach could be explained by referring to the functions they perform for the entire body. Understood in this manner, the human body is a system with a series of basic needs that must be met if it is to survive. Each of the organs that make up the body performs a specialized function, allowing the entire system to continue to survive.

When this mode of analysis, called *functionalism*, is applied to human society, it holds that we should seek to understand the various aspects or components of a social system in terms of the functions they perform for the social whole. For instance, in his study of the division of labour, Durkheim announced that he would look at the division of labour by exploring the function it performs (Durkheim, 1933: 49).

One problem that social systems face, which an organic system does not, is social order. Social order was an acute problem for many of the classical sociological thinkers because they were operating in an era in which the transformation from the old feudal order to the new capitalist system had only recently occurred. The feudal system had been characterized by the existence of a widely accepted set of moral beliefs providing the basis of social stability. In the feudal system tradition was much more important and individuals tended to view themselves as one part of a larger God-given whole. In the emerging modern market system, individuals were no longer connected to each other by traditional bonds and ties, and some thinkers were concerned about how social order and stability would be assured. Durkheim eventually concluded that within the new society a situation similar to the one that prevailed in feudal society would eventually develop. That is, a new set of moral codes or beliefs would indeed emerge, and although the content of this new moral code would be different, its function would be the same: the new moral code would provide a social cement to hold the society together.

Durkheim thus provided an alternative view of society and an alternative approach for society compared to the one posited by Marx. A materialist would argue that economic order is at the core of society. The economic order, Marx argued, is the most important factor in shaping and influencing the structures of a society. For Durkheim the value system is the most important factor. The character and structure of a society will be, in a fundamental manner, determined by the nature of its moral codes, belief systems, and normative orientations.

One of Durkheim's essential tasks was to establish the legitimacy and value of the sociological approach. It was important, he maintained, to view social phenomena and processes as social and not individual. To illustrate this point he engaged in an extensive study of what many thought was the ultimate individualist act, suicide, intending to show how sociology could cast light on even this human extreme.

Suicide

The book *Suicide* ([1897], 1995) is perhaps Durkheim's best-known work. As a result of his investigation of the phenomenon, Durkheim concluded that suicide was not simply an individual act understandable in psychological terms. A person is, Durkheim suggested, connected to society through a series of bonds that regulate conduct and aspirations and provide purposes and ideals. If these bonds are weakened and the individual is not sufficiently integrated into society, that person could be prone to one of three types of suicide. First, when a person does not have firm bonds or connections to society, the act of suicide is caused by egoism. Second, under other circumstances a person may be too strongly integrated into society and have no autonomous self or thought for her or his self. Under such circumstances the person could commit altruistic suicide, which involves giving one's life for the collectivity, as in the case of a soldier who willingly throws himself on a bomb to save his comrades. Third, Durkheim identified a type of suicide that tends to occur when society as a whole has a weakened moral code. He characterized a society lacking a strong system of beliefs and values to hold it together as being in a condition of anomie. Under such circumstances people do not feel firm anchoring bonds with the social structure, and as a result anomic suicide can occur.

According to Durkheim, then, there are sociological explanations for many of the events and processes that we assume are individual acts and processes. As a discipline sociology focuses on the study of the social forces and processes that have an impact on individuals and influence their behaviour.

The Study of the Social
Whether he was studying the moral codes that change as the division of labour develops, the role of religion, or social factors related to the levels of suicide, Durkheim insisted that those social forces and processes, which he called social facts, were real and subject to scientific study. In a book that amounts to an instruction manual for sociologists, *The Rules of Sociological Method,* he wrote: "The first and most fundamental rule *is: Consider social facts as things"* ([1895], 1964: 14; emphasis in original). A *social fact* is something that has an impact on an individual's "ways of acting, thinking, and feeling" and is "external to the individual and endowed with a power of coercion, by reason of which they control him" (3). Elsewhere in the same book he stated: "A social fact is to be recognized by the power of external coercion which it exercises or is capable of exercising over individuals" (10). If we find, for example, that someone's religious values cause her or him to act in certain ways, we would have to recognize religion as a social fact and subject it to sociological investigation, an activity that Durkheim in fact spent much of his life doing.

Durkheim made a systematic attempt to develop an approach that would provide an alternative to both Marxism and the various other theories that characterized the social sciences of his day, including those offered in psychology. While Marx and Durkheim provided quite different approaches to understanding society, each introduced a kind of set of instructions about how we can at least begin to undertake social analysis.

Max Weber's New Blueprint for Analysis

Max Weber (1864-1920) was a contemporary of Durkheim, but as a German he was influenced by a very different intellectual environment. Weber set out to establish an approach to sociology that was different from both Marx's materialist approach and Durkheim's functionalism. As a result he provided a definition of sociology that was not so all-encompassing.

All of the early sociological thinkers possessed broad backgrounds and were not the narrow specialists that modern thinkers tend to be. However, even by the standards of classical thinkers Weber's background was astounding. He studied, among other things, law, general history, politics, economic history, economics, political history, and religion before he began to formulate his unique approach in the developing discipline of sociology.

Weber's View of Sociology

Weber did not develop his systematic approach to sociology until late in his career and life. In his large and unfinished major treatise on sociology, published in German in 1922 and in English under the title *Economy and Society* (1968), Weber provided a definition of sociology that pointed the discipline in a direction quite different from that taken by the followers of Durkheim and Marx. Weber defined sociology as "a science concerning itself with the interpretive understanding of social action and thereby with a causal explanation of its course and consequences" (1968: 4). For Weber, the project or objective of sociology was to provide a basis for interpreting and understanding individual human social actions. The job of the sociologist was to provide a framework for answering important questions such as: Why did she or he do that? Why did they do that? Why do people act the way they do?

Fundamental to Weber's definition of sociology is the assumption that the subject matter of sociology, indeed of all the social sciences, is quite different from that of the natural sciences. The social or human sciences deal with human action and behaviour, and thus they are concerned with motivation. Human actions and behaviour, unlike the actions and "behaviour" of inanimate phenomena such as atoms or electrons, are motivated and must be understood in terms of these motives. The driving forces for human action and behaviour are not, Weber suggested, only external coercive forces in the social structure. There are important internal subjective motives and factors that must be taken into account when we study, interpret, and explain the individual human actor. Religion, for example, is not so much an "external social fact" as an internal and personal driving or motivating factor. As such it is one of the factors that must be examined when we attempt to develop an interpretative understanding of a particular social action.

Doing Sociology

If we accept Weber's definition of the goals of sociology, the next logical question is, how do we move in this direction? What sorts of issues must sociologists be concerned with as they attempt to offer an explanatory and interpretative understanding of individual social actions? In a collection of essays, *The Methodology of the Social Sciences*, Weber warned social scientists of the difficulties they faced in attempting to understand their particular subject matter. He argued that the world social scientists were attempting to understand was infinitely complex and presented "an infinite multiplicity of successively and coexisting emerging and disappearing events, both 'within' and 'outside' ourselves" (1949: 72).

Weber warned that the people attempting to understand this infinitely complex world possessed only finite minds and were therefore capable of grasping only a finite portion of the infinitely complex reality that would confront them. In other words, social scientists would never be able to understand completely and fully the social world they were attempting to explain. He did not, however, suggest that they abandon the project. Instead, through the illustrative analysis presented in *Economy and Society*, he argued that it was necessary at least to begin the work. Just because we can never isolate causal explanations for all human actions and behaviours does not mean that we should not try. What we must do as social scientists, rather, is face up to our inherent limitations and then "have a go at it" and begin the process of attempting to offer explanations for as many actions and behaviours as we can.

The approach that Weber suggested does not necessarily begin with the elaboration of a basic theoretical approach for the study of human society. Different societies work in different ways, so that rather than attempting to develop grand and abstract theories of human society, as sociologists we should examine the structures and workings of the society that is home to the individuals we are attempting to understand. Weber spent much of his time examining the structure and workings of capitalist or market society, because that was the society he lived and worked in. This led him to investigate and study a large number of different factors that he felt had to be taken into account in order to explain and interpret individual social action in a market society.

As the table of contents of *Economy and Society* indicates, Weber covered an enormous range of topics and issues: from economic action to status groups and classes, from social norms to the sociology of law, from religion to politics, feudalism, and the ancient city. It is an intimidating array of subject matter, perhaps, but one way of looking at it is to see it as an instruction manual or blueprint for sociological analysis. The book illustrates the infinite number of possible factors that sociologists have to pay attention to as they attempt to develop interpretative understandings of human social actions. Some of our actions might be understandable in terms of our class positions, others in terms of our religious beliefs, others within the context of the legal system of our society, and still others by considering the current structures of authority. Although we can never explain all the social actions we confront or observe, we must still make a valiant effort to explain as many of them as we can.

Weber directed us to attempt an interpretative understanding of human social actions by analysing the factors that motivate an individual actor. He listed a series of different possible factors that could explain our social action, and he provided insights into how we can actually proceed in the investigation. For example, assume for a moment that you are a religious person and that I am attempting to explain one of your social actions in terms of your religious beliefs. There are several things I must do. First, I must study and understand your religious beliefs. Second, I must offer a coherent summary of those beliefs. Finally, I must use this detailed analysis of your religion as part of my interpretative understanding of your actual behaviour.

There are no easy routes or shortcuts I can take in the first step: I must go out and study the particular set of religious beliefs you subscribe to. The second step, summarizing those beliefs, can be difficult, and for it Weber suggested a particular approach. Instead of attempting to present all of the details and specifics of the particular beliefs, Weber argued that we use what he termed *ideal types*, defined in the *Modern Dictionary of Sociology* as "a conceptualization or mental construction of a configuration of characteristic elements of a class of phenomena used in social analysis" (Theodorson and Theodorson, 1969: 193). I thus create an ideal-type representation of your religion and use this set of ideas as a basis for my explanation. I am able to make sense of your behaviour by comparing it to the ideal type. I can compare your behaviour with others in a similar position by referring to the ideal type, which provides a benchmark against which I can analyse and understand your behaviour. In what is perhaps the most widely read of his books, *The Protestant Ethic and the Spirit of Capitalism* (1930), Weber makes extensive use of ideal types in his discussion of both capitalist entrepreneurs and Calvinist religious beliefs (1958: 71, 98).

Following Weber and the other early thinkers, the task of the sociologist is to explain human social action in terms of its motives and causes. We are faced with a situation in which we will never know all the motives and causes of all behaviour, yet we can make a start. Our work will be facilitated by the use of ideal-type mental constructs or representatives of the factors we are examining. Such ideal-type constructs allow us to explain particular instances of social action and, perhaps more importantly, they give us a basis for making generalizations about the motivating factors under examination. Such generalizations, by providing systematic knowledge, will be of use to other sociologists and will contribute to the larger body of knowledge of the field of sociology.

Terms and Concepts

Theory – a set of concepts, propositions, and arguments that attempts to offer an explanation of the dynamics, operation, characteristics, and features of some phenomenon or event. Theories are more than descriptions, because they seek to explain why and how "things happen." Theory is an essential part of science, because scientific work seeks to explain, not just describe, the world.

Inductive thought – a mode of thought or reasoning that moves from the specific or particular to the general. General principles are inferred from particular instances. For instance, you might study specific manifestations of some phenomenon and then make generalizations about all cases of this phenomenon.

Deductive thought – a mode of thought or reasoning that moves from the general to the specific or particular. You begin with general or even universal statements and deduce specific or particular conclusions. On the basis of some body of established knowledge or principles, you make deductions about some particular instance or case of that phenomenon.

Materialist approach – in sociology, an approach most often associated with Marx. Based on the assumption that humans are unique creatures because they produce satisfaction for their material needs, the materialist approach assumes that the level of technological development and the social organization of material production (economic activity) form the basis or core of society and influence all other aspects of society. A materialist would argue that sociological analysis must always begin with an examination of the basic economic institutions in a society and move from there to study the other institutions and structures.

Relations of production – within Marxian theory, the social arrangements and patterns of social interaction that have been developed to facilitate material production. Included are the patterns of ownership, use, and control of a society's productive resources and capacities. In an industrial society this refers to the people who own, control, and have the power to direct the use of the mines, mills, factories, and other productive resources. Throughout history humans have developed many different types of social relations of production as they have attempted to survive and prosper; and this factor, in part, helps explain the difference between hunting and gathering societies and advanced industrial societies.

Productive forces – within Marxian theory, sometimes referred to as the forces of production. Refers to the technology, tools, skills, and knowledge that a society possesses, which are applied to material production. Throughout history humans have survived and prospered using an incredibly diverse range of productive forces, which again, in part, helps explain the difference between hunting and gathering societies and advanced industrial societies.

Power – the capacity of human actors to influence social structures, processes, and the conditions of their lives. But it is one of the most contested concepts in sociology. In its Marxian sense, power refers to the capacity of those who control the vital processes of material production to control and direct the overall structures, direction, and operation of society. Weber adopted a more individual approach, relating power to the capacity of individuals and groups to carry out their will even in the face of opposition.

Ideology – a system or set of ideas, beliefs, or values that serves to explain and justify social, economic, cultural, and political phenomena, structures, and processes from the perspective of a particular class or group. For example, a dominant ideology will explain and justify the socio-economic and political system from the perspective of the ruling class.

Social facts – as used by Durkheim, those phenomena that have an impact on the actions and behaviour of individuals and are social and external to the individual. For example, because religion can have an important influence on society and individuals it can and must be studied as a social fact, in the same way that a physicist might study the influence and impact of gravity on physical bodies.

Labour power – in Marxian theory, the capacity or ability of human beings to engage in work and productive activity. In a capitalist society a worker sells this capacity to capitalists.

Functionalism – in sociology, a general approach that assumes society can be understood as a system with needs that must be met if the overall system is to survive. Institutions operate or function to meet one or more of these basic system needs. The function of an institution is the system need it meets or the problem it solves for the overall system. Normally systems exist in a stable and orderly condition.

Weber's definition of sociology – that the objective of sociology is the explanation of individual social actions and behaviours. As a social science, sociology deals with behaviours and actions that are both meaningful to the actor (usually we know why we are doing things) and caused by motivations (there are reasons for our actions). Sociology should seek to provide interpretations of social actions by offering an interpretation of the meaning the actions had for an actor and interpreting their motivation. Interpretations of meaning and motive are key parts of a causal explanation.

Ideal type – as used by Weber, an abstract or pure representation of some phenomenon people are interested in studying or understanding. Although we may never find a real or empirical example that is similar to an ideal type, the intellectual construction of ideal types will assist in understanding the concrete real-world phenomenon under study. The "ideal" in no way implies a moral judgement, because we can create an "ideal-type" personality profile of a serial killer as readily as that of a saint.

7

CONTEMPORARY
SOCIOLOGICAL THEORY

Since the beginning of the discipline, sociologists have had an abiding concern with developing theoretical frameworks to help explain the various phenomena and issues that come under their scrutiny. But although many of the insights and arguments developed by the founding figures in sociology were astute, indeed brilliant, few sociologists of the twentieth century have been willing to acknowledge that the "classical thinkers" dealt adequately with all the key issues: indeed, an important stream of contemporary thought argues that the earlier theories are fundamentally flawed. As a result, the field of sociological theory has retained a dynamic core, with numerous new and quite complex theories emerging in the seemingly endless quest to provide a more adequate and contemporary approach to the issues of society.

The modern approaches to sociological theory involve a large number of thinkers, but the studies can be usefully broken down into a few major streams or schools of thought, most of them, not surprisingly, connecting back to the classical approach: structural functionalism (influenced by Comte, Durkheim, and others); neo-Marxism; and symbolic interactionism (influenced by G.H. Mead and Weber). But beyond these approaches – which at one time at least might have been considered various branches of the sociological mainstream – are other new challenges, particularly from the vital field of feminist thought and from the work on structuration theory as developed by Anthony Giddens. In the end, all of these various streams raise other questions. Is theory really necessary? Are there limits to abstract theory? And how, after critically evaluating the various approaches, can we use them to further the sociological imagination?

The Structural Functionalist Perspective

From the Great Depression of the 1930s until well into the turbulent decade of the 1960s, Western sociology was dominated by structural functionalism. As a stream of sociological theory, structural functionalism, which is also often referred to just as functionalism, was influenced by the ideas of Comte, Durkheim, and – to some degree – Weber, as well as by anthropologists such as Bronislaw Malinowski and A.R. Radcliffe-Brown and the economist-sociologist Vilfredo Pareto. In the United States contemporary functionalism was systematically developed by Talcott Parsons, altered somewhat by Robert Merton, and refined by, among many others, Kingsley Davis, Wilbert E. Moore, Neil Smelser, and Daniel Rossides.

The Organic Analogy Revisited

Harking back to the work of Comte and Durkheim, structural functionalists often use the organic analogy as their mode of explanation. That is, they have tended to analyse society in the same way others might view an organic system such as the human body. This overall approach is based, once again, on the recognition that if it is to survive, an organic system such as the human body has certain basic needs that must be met and problems that must be solved. For example, a minimal level of nutrients must be provided for all its organs; wastes of a variety of sorts must be removed; oxygen must be provided for the organs; sexual tensions must be released; and so on. Some structural functionalist thinkers use the phrase "system prerequisites" to refer to these basic needs and problems.

Similarly, social systems have *system prerequisites*: a number of basic and common problems that must be addressed and solved. Talcott Parsons and Robert Bales developed the first list of what these basic system prerequisites are for the human social system. They suggested that for a society to survive over time it must provide or make arrangements for biological reproduction, the provision of material needs, the establishment and dissemination of a value system, and the general co-ordination of all this activity (Aberle *et al.*, 1967: 317-31; Parsons, 1951: 26-36; Rossides, 1968: 67-68; Skidmore, 1979: 137).

In the case of a complex organic system such as the human body, complex specialized organs have evolved or developed to deal with the various specific needs or problems. The heart, stomach, kidneys, central nervous system, and other specialized organs all have a specific task or function to perform within the system as a whole. The heart pumps blood throughout the body; the stomach and the digestive tract work to enrich the blood with nutrients; the lungs add oxygen to the blood and remove wastes; and so on. Each of the organs in the system performs a function, solves a problem, or meets a need for the whole organic system. In other words, an organic system is made up of specialized structures (organs) that perform specialized functions for the whole system.

When we apply this general framework to society, we can argue that society or the social system faces certain basic problems that it must solve if it is to survive. The social system, like an organic system, is a complex phenomenon made up of component parts. While in the organic system the most important component parts are organs, in the social system the most important component parts are institutions. Like organs, institutions are complex structures that perform various functions for the entire social system. For example, one of the problems faced by a social system is biological reproduction and sexual regulation. The structure that takes care of this general system need is the family. Similarly, the economic institutions function for the entire social system by solving the problems associated with the production and distribution of the basic goods and services required for survival. The problems associated with establishing and maintaining a value system are dealt with by the educational and religious institutions, while the problems of social decision-making are handled by the political order, also called the polity.

The mode of analysis employed in the structural functionalist approach is quite commonly used in both scientific and non-scientific discourse. Pretend for a moment that a life form from another planet approaches you holding an animal heart in its hand (or whatever appendage it uses for what we would call a hand). The creature and you are somehow able to communicate, and it asks you what this object is. You answer that it is a heart, which prompts the question, "What is a heart?" How do you reply? One approach would be to explain the heart as a mass of muscle tissue; but when the creature asks for more details you find yourself explaining the heart in terms of its function as a pump that keeps blood circulating throughout the body. You might elaborate, noting that by pumping blood the heart is ensuring that nutrients and oxygen reach the various other organs and tissues and that wastes are removed. As soon as your explanation takes this turn you have begun to practise classical functionalism. You are explaining a single part of a system in terms of the function it performs for the whole.

Social Order

One of the central concerns of the structural functionalist approach, especially as it developed in the United States under the influence of

Talcott Parsons, is social order. In this case, moving beyond the simple organic analogy to understand society, we must ask how the entire complex of social institutions is organized, co-ordinated, and maintained as a working system. For example, how do people in the various institutions know what behaviours and actions are expected of them and their institutions? How is the whole social structure held together and maintained? That is, how is the multitude of complex interactions and institutions that make up an advanced industrial society co-ordinated and organized? In attempting to answer these questions structural functionalists have tended to borrow from Durkheim, adopting his arguments about the role of value systems or moral codes in binding social systems together. In his study of functionalism Mark Abrahamson notes the importance of value systems in the functionalist view of society: "The entire social system, or at least its stability, is seen as resting heavily upon shared values, even though society is also seen as having a structure and organization" (1978: 41).

A shared set or system of values, norms, beliefs, and morals is seen as the basis of social order. Because the majority of members of a society share a moral code or belief system, they will know and understand what behaviours are appropriate and inappropriate under what circumstances, what the proper functions of institutions are, and generally "how things work." As a result of its members sharing values and beliefs, social systems will tend, under normal circumstances, to exist in a state of consensus and equilibrium. Indeed, functionalists argue that social order is the norm, and as long as there is a common value system holding or binding all the elements of the system together, social order will be maintained. For this reason the structural functionalist perspective is often referred to as the *consensus* or *order perspective*.

In addition to providing the basis of social order, shared moral codes or value systems also tend to be important factors in giving social systems their general shape and character. In Parsons's work this discussion is posed in the context of a highly abstract discussion of a series of dichotomous value orientations (Parsons, 1951: 180-200). Here we can keep the language simpler. Daniel Rossides states that there are two factors regularizing human actions into the structures that sociologists call institutions: the type of technology as given in a society's cultural artifacts; and the society's sets of values and ideas. Rossides sees values and ideas as playing an important role in the overall structuring of the society (Rossides, 1968: 183). In *Social Structures and Systems* (1969) William Dobriner more forcefully developed an argument about the central role of norms in structuring society and social relationships. He explicitly argued that norms both define the very character of social relationships and provide a central cohesive force binding relationships together in a unified system (1969: 72-76).

Understanding Social Change

As a result of its key focus on institutions and other social practices and phenomena in terms of how they contribute to maintaining the social system, many social theorists have argued that structural functionalism is biased toward the existing social system and against the element of social change.

Various theorists have examined these criticisms. Two of them, John Wilson (1983: 75-76) and Percy Cohen (1973: 58-59), noted that advocates of functionalist analysis have in fact taken a variety of different positions that address the issue of social change, and that therefore this criticism may not be as valid as the critics have claimed. Parsons explicitly addressed the issue of social change in one of his later books, *Societies: Evolutionary and Comparative Perspectives* (1966). In *Social Change*, a book also published in the 1960s, prominent functionalist Wilbert E. Moore noted that at a certain point functionalists had to make amendments to their approach to allow it to deal more adequately with the issue of social change (1963: 8). As suggested by the title of his book, Moore argued that functionalism is indeed interested in and capable of dealing with social change.

Another author, William Skidmore (1979), noted that structural functionalism is certainly capable of dealing with evolutionary change, that is, gradual change in how a society or social system adapts to its environment and looks after the material needs of its members (179-80). As Skidmore suggested, this conception of change implies a slowness in the process. Ruth Wallace and Alison Wolf (1986) also noted that, as presented in the classical formulation of Parsons, structural functionalism views social change as a slow process that occurs when social systems adapt to gradual changes among the component parts of the system. In the organic analogy, as the human body ages its various organs may not function in the same way as they did previously. In the case of the heart, for instance, the entire system is forced to make adjustments to the slightly changed capacity of that organ so that fresh blood can still be delivered effectively. In the case of social systems, changes to any of the institutional orders can result in adjustments and changes to other orders, although these changes tend to be slow, gradual, or evolutionary.

Robert Merton's work made significant advances in the capacity of structural functionalism to deal with change. Merton argued that it was not correct to assume that every aspect of a social system made a positive contribution to maintaining the overall system. He noted that it was possible for a component or a part of a system to be dysfunctional (1968: 105). *Dysfunction* refers to a situation in which a component or part of a social system operates in a manner that has the effect of actually lessening the system's capacity to survive.

Using the organic analogy, we can argue that a body will continue to exist in a healthy, stable condition providing all its various organs are functioning in a normal manner. If an organ does not, for any number of possible reasons such as age, infection, or disease, perform its functions normally it could be referred to as dysfunctional. The dysfunction of a particular organ could lead to a crisis situation that if not corrected would threaten the very existence of the system. Most of the dysfunctions associated with the organs in an organic system are corrected by the internal mechanisms of the body's immune system and other biological corrective mechanisms.

In the workings of a social system, consider the case of the presence of sexist ideas in a society's norms and values. Such ideas often mean that many important jobs become labelled as being outside the interest, domain, and possibilities of women. The result is that women in the society are socialized not to aspire to those jobs, and the positions are filled mostly by men. Half of the society's potential pool of talent is thus not available for jobs that could be vital to social development and prosperity. This is surely not a desirable situation, and it should be taken as an indication that a part of the society, in this case a part of its system of norms and values, is operating in a dysfunctional manner.

When a particular institution does not perform its allotted function, the stability and equilibrium of the social system can be threatened because of the failure to meet and solve a part of the system's basic needs or problems. Under such circumstances social systems tend to make adjustments, perhaps allocating the task or function that is not satisfactorily being addressed to another institution or facilitating the development of a new institution to carry out the function. If, for example, one of the central functions of the family is the provision of child care for young children, and if both parents in a traditional nuclear family become employed in the labour force, then a new institution, such as day care, could emerge to fill the void. Under these circumstances some form of social change occurs as the transformation of family structures brings about corresponding adjustments in other parts of the social structure. The change was brought about through an adjustment to the larger system to deal with a dysfunctional part. The larger, more important point, as a functionalist might argue, is that the social system's tendency to move towards equilibrium and stability facilitates the ability of the overall system to deal with dysfunction.

Similarly, it could be argued that because structural functionalism tends to emphasize stability, equilibrium, and consensus, the theory is able to deal with social change, particularly if the change is slow and evolutionary.

Changing Social Values

In addition to social change that occurs as a result of the evolutionary adaptation of a society to its surroundings and the dysfunction of components of a social system, some social change occurs as a result of shifts in a society's value orientations and normative systems. Structural functionalists tend not to focus on the history and origin of a society's values and norms, because their concern is more with the ongoing functions of social phenomena. Because value systems and normative orientations are at the centre of society, shifts and changes in the core values are bound to have an impact on the entire social structure.

Understanding Social Conflict

For structural functionalism, the question of social conflict is even more difficult than the question of social change. The assumption that social systems normally exist in a condition of stability and are characterized by equilibrium and consensus tends to focus the attention of a structural functionalist away from the issue of social conflict. In addition, the approach does not have a well-developed conception of power, and as a result its ability to address the issue of conflict is diminished (Skidmore, 1979: 180).

For Parsons the issue of social order was not only important, but also one of the most fundamental issues facing society. Social order tended not to be a problem after a society had established a more or less stable value system and set of normative orientations. Once those values and norms were successfully passed on to individuals and ingrained in their personalities through the process of socialization, the problem of social order tended to be solved (Hamilton, 1983: 104). There would always be conflicts of a more or less minor nature – that is, conflicts that were not system-threatening – but these could usually be handled within the system.

Arnold Rose presented a classic statement about the basis of social conflicts, in noting that values are usually at their centre. Rose argued that conflicts arise because individuals and groups engage in a clash of values or attempt to stop the actions of others holding different values (1956: 492). This approach would apply to industrial conflict, religious conflict, and even conflict between different racial groups. Most stable social systems have established mechanisms and procedures for dealing

with such conflicts. These mechanisms and procedures, when successfully used, not only address the problem of a specific conflict but also
add to the stability of the whole system.

In *The Functions of Social Conflict* (1956), Louis Coser systematically
developed the theme of conflict as contributing to the general stability of a social system. Coser argued that conflict is likely to occur in
any large and complex society, but if it is limited and does not threaten
the basic values and norms of the social system, it can serve to
strengthen and stabilize the system. Indeed, a social system must tolerate a degree of conflict and provide the institutionalized means of
dealing with it. If there are "safety-valve" institutions that individuals
and groups can use to address concerns and problems that might lead
to conflict, the system will be able to make the adjustments necessary
to prevent the conflict from threatening the overall system. In addition, the institutional expression of legitimate grievances gives individuals and groups a chance to "let off some steam" and thus avoid a
potentially threatening buildup of discontent. Finally, the expression
and emergence of limits to conflict can serve to revitalize the existing
value and normative system by leading to a re-examination of existing
elements and possibly introducing fresh and innovative ideas. A functionalist might argue that conflict can even have a positive function for
the social system.

Social Inequality and Power

The structural functionalist perspective explains social inequalities in
terms of either a society's value system or its division of labour. For
some functionalists, such as Parsons, social inequalities result from
individuals possessing or not possessing certain traits or characteristics deemed desirable within the context of the value system. For
example, if the society's value system stresses the importance of material possessions, people with material possessions tend to have a higher
social position or standing.

Another explanation for social inequality from within the functionalist stream was developed by Kingsley Davis, Wilbert Moore, and
others. This approach suggests that a degree of social inequality is necessary if a complex society is to allocate its various jobs and tasks to
the individuals available in society.

In their approach to the polity or the political order, functionalists
are interested in analysing the functions that the political order performs
for society. For North American political structures, functionalists tend
to accept the approach known as pluralism. According to this approach
political power in Western liberal democracies is typically not concentrated but spread out among a plurality of centres of power. Among the

unique features and strengths of liberal democratic systems are the opportunities available to all citizens to influence government and have an impact on the political process. According to the theory, even though there are individual inequalities in Western liberal democracies, they are still basically open and egalitarian societies.

We will be discussing the structural functionalist approaches to social inequality and the polity in Chapters 9 and 10 respectively.

Structural Functionalism and Social Theory

The set of general ideas and arguments presented here under the rubric of structural functionalism represents a sort of "generic version" of the perspective. It indicates only some of the general assumptions and positions that characterize the broad theoretical stream or perspective called structural functionalism. A particular theorist would never, strictly, make all these arguments; but they do represent a summary of the key background assumptions, arguments, and propositions that inform the structural functionalist approach.

When grappling with somewhat abstract theoretical ideas and arguments, we need to keep in mind the key role that theory plays in social analysis. Theory provides the basis for explaining how something works; it provides answers to the "why" questions that emerge as we try to get through each day. In attempting to provide the basis for explanations and answers to these questions, theories also provide the basis for ways of organizing and making sense – in our minds at least – of the phenomena we experience. The social and physical worlds present themselves to us as an incredibly complex series of events and experiences, and we are required to organize all of it in some manner if we are to survive those worlds, let alone understand them. Theories provide a means of organizing the world in a way that renders it comprehensible, and the various perspectives that have emerged in the field of sociology have been developed in the attempt to make sense out of how society is organized and how it works.

Neo-Marxist Social Theory

The Materialist Perspective

Karl Marx's materialist approach to the understanding of human beings and human society was based on a series of ontological assumptions concerning the human species. Humans are unique, Marx argued, primarily because our physiological and psychological makeup allows us *to produce* satisfactions for our material needs and wants. As we have undertaken the act of material production, we have created a variety of productive forces: various tools, technologies, skills, and bodies of knowledge. Human material production is also a social act involving others, which leads to the concept of social relations of production. It is an elementary postulate of the materialist method that if we are to understand a particular society we must understand the nature and organization of its forces of production as well as of the social relations of production.

There is much academic debate among neo-Marxists about just how the social relations of production and the productive forces impact on each other and on society, but it is clear that Marx himself understood that they both make up the economic basis of society (Marx [1859], 1977: 20). Although neo-Marxists tend to accept that the various non-economic institutions do have a reciprocal influence on the economic base, for the most part they assume that the economic basis or core is the essential or primary factor in influencing and structuring the various other components or parts of the social structure. More specifically, institutional orders such as the political order and state structures as well as the educational order and its components are influenced by the nature of the economic order. In addition, the family and even the religious order will, in some fundamental manner, have their shape, character, and structure influenced by the economic institutions.

For a neo-Marxist, the nature of a society's economic structures and institutions provides essential clues that will help unlock the dynamics, structures, and character of other components of the larger social structure. The relationship between the various institutional orders and institutions is not a simple one, but in the final analysis the key to understanding the entire social structure is to understand the economic core.

Social Change

In using this basic method, neo-Marxists make an additional further assumption, namely that human societies tend to be dynamic and constantly changing. To explain the importance of social change, neo-Marxist theorists might ask you to think about what has happened in human history over the last several millennia. Having done this, they might ask if you are impressed by the extent to which human societies have remained stable and constant over the last several thousand years. Or are you struck more by how change and development, often of a dramatic and radical nature, seem to have been the normal pattern of things? Neo-Marxists would suggest that human society is a dynamic phenomenon in which change and development are a constant. They argue that the constant changes in productive forces and social relations of production have led to constant changes in the various other institutional orders.

Materialist Analysis as Social Criticism

In engaging in the act of production, the human species is in essence creating itself. Production is an act of self-creation and an expression of our unique species' powers and abilities. It is an expression of our humanity. For the materialist, material production is the most important human activity.

In *The German Ideology* Marx and Engels discussed the importance of the act of production to human existence. They maintained that how we are situated in the process of production fundamentally determines the kind of people we are and become. A part of their argument holds that, since the act of production is central and essential to being a human, humans must control not only the process of production but also both the products of their production and the relationships they enter into as they produce. If people do not have this control they experience what Marx termed *alienation*. When material production is conducted under conditions characterized by alienation, its entire role in human development and existence changes. Rather than being an expression of our humanity and creativity, productive work under alienating circumstances becomes a process that distorts, destroys, and dehumanizes.

The issue of alienation remains a central concern for most neo-Marxist thinkers (Ollman, 1976). In addition, the concept provides the basis for offering critical analysis of larger structures of capitalist society. It suggests that in any truly humane society the entire range of activities surrounding material production must be under democratic control, that is, under the control of the people who actually produce the physical wealth. Only under such circumstances will production be an activity that allows for the full development of all human potentials and possibilities.

In their analyses of the economic basis of capitalist society, neo-Marxists maintain that some mode of class analysis is essential. Although there are substantial, indeed, radical differences in how various neo-Marxists approach the study of class, there is agreement that class is a central concept that must be employed in the investigation of capitalist society. Neo-Marxists tend to assume that in a capitalist society there will be a dominant class and at least one (and very likely more) subordinate class. The dominant class is defined in terms of its structural position within the economic order; its position allows it to gain control of the bulk of the society's economic surplus. By virtue of its position as owner of the society's productive resources, the dominant class exploits other classes, most notably the working class, benefiting from their economic activities.

Ideology

Another central concept in the neo-Marxist approach – and one that is also still very much an issue of continuing debate, as well as being subject to widely differing usage – is ideology.

One usage of the term "ideology" follows quite directly from Marx's views. Marx suggested that ruling classes have a tendency to develop, or at least promote, views of the world that suit their interests and serve to justify their position. In stating that the ruling ideas of an epoch were the ideas of the ruling class, he was really arguing that ruling classes maintain their power through a number of different means, including ideas. A ruling class interested in maintaining its position within a particular set of social structures will attempt to ensure its position and prevent the emergence of opposition and conflict by articulating and promoting views of the world that justify the status quo. It should not be implied that the ruling class always does this in a conscious and deliberate manner, nor should we assume that the views expressed by the ruling class are always a deliberate and intentional attempt to manipulate the subordinate classes (although this cannot be ruled out). The neo-Marxists argue that the value systems, normative orientations, moral codes, and belief systems of a society such as ours are, in fact, in a direct and substantial manner connected to the larger process of class rule and domination. Winning the hearts and minds of the subordinate classes is an important part of maintaining control.

Neo-Marxists often use the term "dominant ideology" to refer to those sets of beliefs, values, and norms that support and justify the overall system and the position of the ruling classes in that system. The precise nature and content of dominant ideologies will, of course, vary over history. In a capitalist society the values and norms might typically place emphasis on individualism, individual initiative and responsibility, freedom of enterprise, the desirability of competition, the necessity of being aggressive in order to succeed, and respect for leadership. In addition, ideas that downplay the importance, or even existence, of class would be seen as supportive of the overall system. A neo-Marxist might argue that to the extent that all classes in the society accept these values and norms, the overall system is strengthened – and so, too, is the position of the ruling class, which benefits most from the operation of the system. The themes of ideological manipulation and domination play an important role in the thinking of some neo-Marxists. Others calling themselves neo-Marxists would disagree, arguing that placing too much emphasis on the notion of ideological manipulation is a mistake because it directs our attention away from an important characteristic of capitalist society, the tendency for the system to produce conflict.

If we assume that there are different classes in capitalist society, with different positions in the society's economic structures, it is possible to envision the emergence of conflicting systems of ideas or ideologies. While the ruling class produces and promotes sets of beliefs, values, and norms that express its interests and concerns, and while it attempts through a variety of means to impose these elements on all classes, the subordinate classes will also generate their own ideologies and ideas about how the world works. For example, subordinate classes might begin to realize that the value system, norms, and beliefs they were taught in school or that are presented in the media really don't explain the world as they experience it. Workers who are told again and again that if they work hard they will get ahead might be finding out that after twenty years of hard work they will still be barely able to keep up with the escalating cost of living. Meanwhile, corporate profit margins increase and the major shareholders of large corporations become wealthy beyond belief. Under such circumstances, if workers become familiar with socialist ideas and critiques of the structures of inequality that characterize a capitalist society, they may find that such ideas and critiques make sense; and a counter-ideology postulating a radically different set of values, norms, beliefs, and ideas representing the interests and concerns of a subordinate class could gain credence. In such a situation there would then be a clash of ideologies; or, put differently, the conflict that is always a part of a class society would take on an ideological dimension.

When a structural functionalist discusses value systems and normative orientations and when a neo-Marxist discusses ideology, they are, essentially, referring to the same thing. But each perspective views the role of values, norms, ideas, or ideologies in a fundamentally different manner. For structural functionalists, a society's primary values are the social cement that binds society together in the interests of all. For neo-Marxists, a society's primary values represent the views and interests of the dominant class, and – to the extent that they hold society together – they serve the interests of the dominant class. The values, norms, ideologies, and so on are a part of a larger strategy of domination and manipulation. But if there are conflicting counter-ideologies, those elements are part of a larger process of class-based conflict, which is typical of class societies.

The Polity or State System
The neo-Marxists' tendency to view capitalist society as a system fundamentally characterized by relations of domination and subordination

extends to their overall views about the nature of the state in capitalist society. Although there are major differences in how they see this happening, their common assumption is that the polity and the state structure in capitalist society tend to serve, over the long run at least, the interests of the dominant class. The state may serve the interests of the dominant class by direct actions, such as when state agents act to end a workers' strike, or the state may serve the interests of the dominant class in more indirect ways, by promoting general social and economic stability and legitimizing the system. A neo-Marxist might argue, for example, that the provision of social services to people out of work is a way of both legitimizing the humane nature of the system – of seeing that no one goes without – while keeping at least a minimal purchasing power in the hands of the population, a situation that ultimately benefits the producers and sellers of consumer commodities. The state may also take actions that create a favourable climate for profitable investment, thus ensuring a measure of economic growth and social stability, which is in general most beneficial to the dominant class. The key question that arises from such a position is: how and why does the state tend to serve the interests of the dominant class? Recent developments in Marxian theorizing on the state are discussed further in Chapter 10.

Conflict and Contradiction

Neo-Marxists also tend to hold one other assumption in their analysis of capitalist society: the presence of conflicts and contradictions. For neo-Marxists, the class structure of capitalist society ensures the existence of persistent and inevitable conflicts between different classes over a range of different issues. Class conflict is normal and expected.

The concept of contradiction relates to more structural features of the system. In the *Dictionary of Marxist Thought* Ben Fine states that a contradiction involves a "situation which allows the satisfaction of one end only at the cost of another" (1983: 93). For example, there would be a contradiction created when people with capital invested in manufacturing seek to reduce their costs of production and thus increase profits by replacing workers with machines. As more and more capitalists do this, more and more workers are replaced and become unemployed. As more and more workers become unemployed, their capacity to purchase the various goods that capitalists produce diminishes – which is a fundamental contradiction in a system based on the production and sale of commodities. The logical pursuit of the objectives of the system – an increase in profits – leads to a situation that is detrimental to the overall economic structure.

Neo-Marxism and Structural Functionalism: One Similarity
A neo-Marxist might argue that the key to understanding the operation and functions of most institutional orders and institutions is to be
found in how they contribute to the maintenance of the overall system
and thus serve the interests of the dominant class. A fundamental,
logical similarity between this approach and the approach of structural
functionalism is that both tend to examine social institutions and
orders in terms of their functions. Both approaches share common
assumptions about society and the relationship between the individual and society. Both of them tend to be macro approaches, meaning
that they focus attention on the larger social structure, its character,
and its features. Neither of them tends to concentrate on the individual human actor or agent.

But there is a big, and essential, difference between the two theories as well. The difference appears most clearly in answer to the question, "In whose interests do the institutions of a society operate?" The
structural functionalist answers, "In the interests of the entire society
and all its members." The neo-Marxist says, "In the interests of the
dominant class." Obviously, despite the similarity, sociologists choos-
ing one of these approaches over the other will ask different kinds of
questions and study different issues in the attempt to understand the
structures, processes, and dynamics of society.

The Symbolic Interactionist Perspective

Just as Weber might have been critical of both Marx and Durkheim for
focusing too much on structure and not enough on the individual,
there is a stream of thought in modern sociology that is critical of the
macro approach because it ignores a number of fundamental issues,
including how and why individuals come to act as they do on a daily
basis.

This approach, commonly referred to as symbolic interactionism,
accepts a definition of sociology more akin to the thought of Weber than
to that of any other classical thinker. Symbolic interactionism tends to
focus on understanding the micro elements, the face-to-face, everyday actions and interactions of individuals. The major twentieth-
century influences on the development of symbolic interactionism are
Max Weber, George Herbert Mead, and Charles Horton Cooley. Following them, Herbert Blumer (1969) synthesized their ideas into a systematic statement of the symbolic interactionist approach.

Society and the Individual

A useful starting point for understanding the approach or, to use Blumer's own term, perspective of symbolic interactionism is to consider how symbolic interactionists view humans.

The approach emphasizes the unique human capacity for abstract reasoning and thought. Because of our large, complex brain we have the capacity for a variety of intellectual processes, including reflective intelligence, abstract reasoning, and symbolic thought – abilities that are crucial for the development of the human mind. In turn, the human mind is important because it determines the everyday interactions and actions that make up our social existence. For an example we can compare a non-human animal's instinctual response to a stimulus to a human response. If I shout "yo" at a beaver swimming in a pond, I know what will happen – the animal will slap its tail on the water and dive. The stimulus is received and the response is immediate and instinctual. That is, the response is inborn and unlearned and does not require any conscious thought on behalf of the beaver. If I shout "yo" at a university student crossing a parking lot I cannot be sure what the response will be, because the student will first of all try to figure out what the stimulus was; then, using his or her mind, the student will attempt to interpret what the shout means before responding. The response, assuming the student chooses not to ignore me, will ultimately depend on an interpretation of what my "yo" means. Is it a form of greeting? Do I know Tibetan and am I simply pleased with something that has happened? Am I in fact even directing the stimulus at that student, or at someone else? The essential point is that there is a direct connection between stimulus and response in instinctual behaviour, while in the case of human behaviour the mind intervenes.

Before they respond to a stimulus, human beings must first interpret that stimulus. They attach a meaning to it, and on the basis and within the context of that meaning they decide on an appropriate response. In the human world a stimulus could be a sound, a physical gesture, a written symbol, or even an object. The process of attaching meanings to these stimuli requires that the individual attempt to make sense out of it. An alien object, such as the Coke bottle in the movie *The Gods Must Be Crazy*, can, if it is not understood, lead to a series of unusual actions and interactions that could change the world of the interacting individual. The meanings we attach to various physical, visual, verbal, and written stimuli are fundamentally symbolic. In an important sense, then, our behaviour and interactions with others are always influenced by our use and understanding of symbols. There is a symbolic basis to all our social interactions.

For the symbolic interactionist, human society is made up of a series of interacting selves – that is, of interacting individuals whose behaviours and interactions are very much influenced by how they interpret the actions and intentions of people they are in social contact with. Society is not something that is external to and outside of the individual, but rather it is *created* by human beings as they go about their daily actions and interactions. Society is not a fixed fact that exists apart and separate from individuals; rather, it is the product of a variety of interacting individuals going about their daily lives. The essence of society is individuals sharing symbols and, on the basis of those shared symbols, interacting with each other.

Symbolic interactionists are not particularly concerned with the origins of those symbolic systems that prove so important in our daily lives. It is clearly the case that the human capacity for the use of symbols and language developed over many thousands of years of human history, but the key element is an appreciation of the role the shared symbols play in facilitating continuing interaction and thus social life and society itself. This perspective argues that people are active participants in the daily creation of those forms of interaction that we have come to call society. It is in regard to this issue – of whether society exists "out there," external to us – that the symbolic interactionist perspective is most clearly differentiated from functionalism and neo-Marxism.

Functionalists focus on the overall social structure, examining the social functions performed by various institutions and social practices. Neo-Marxists focus on the role of the economy in shaping and influencing the overall social structure. But symbolic interactionists examine the daily interactions of individuals to explain and facilitate understanding of how society works. Symbolic interactionists are interested in how people know what to do and how they act as they go about their everyday lives, and in what sorts of adjustments people make to facilitate the continued interactions that form the basis of society.

Both the functionalist and neo-Marxist approaches have developed criticisms of the symbolic interactionist perspective, which has never been as widely used (Ritzer, 1988: 316-17; Stryker, 1980: 145-46). Both of the major approaches argue that symbolic interactionism downplays the impact of larger social structures on the individual. A neo-Marxist might argue that symbolic interactionism ignores the key issues of class, domination, and power. Can we be sure, a neo-Marxist might ask, that the meanings attached to significant symbols do not come from and serve the interests of a dominant class? A social thinker influenced by Durkheim would be concerned about the extent to which central social forces, such as adherence to a set of norms and values, are ignored when the individual is understood to be quite freely interpreting stimuli almost at will.

The symbolic interactionist perspective does, however, alert us to the fact that while understanding social structures is important, we must not lose sight of the micro picture. Although we need, surely, to have an overall picture of the forest, nevertheless we must be aware that it is made up of individual trees, and we must understand both of these conditions.

Conclusion

When we study the development of sociological theory from its emergence in the middle of the nineteenth century through to the second half of the twentieth century, what we find is an impressive array of ideas, arguments, concepts, and propositions that were developed and mustered to guide sociologists as they attempt to explain the overall structures and organization of human society. As impressive and wide-ranging as these theories are, however, they have failed to address one of the central issues in human affairs – how to explain the nature and dynamics of sex and gender relations. Given the importance of these issues, it behooves us now to examine new directions in sociological theory that attempt to offer ways of explaining some of the most essential questions concerning human conduct and social organization.

Terms and Concepts

Organic analogy – as used in functionalist theory, a mode of analysis that compares society to a living organism. A living organism is assumed to have certain basic needs that must be met and problems that must be solved if it is to survive. The component structures of the organism, its organs and tissues, are understood to operate, work, or function in a way that solves the various problems and meets the various needs and thus allows the organism to survive. The analogy assumes we can understand society in a similar manner, that is, as a complex system made up of different parts, all of which meet some need or solve some problem for the whole system, thereby allowing it to survive.

System prerequisites – the basic needs that must be met and the problems that must be solved if the system is to survive. For example, if society is to survive the material needs of its members must be satisfied, its culture must be transmitted from generation to generation, the spiritual needs of its members addressed, biological reproduction facilitated, some system of social decision-making developed, and so on. These are the system prerequisites for a social system, because if they are not met there can be no social system.

Function – the need or problem that a part of a social system deals with. For instance, if people have certain basic spiritual needs, then the function of religion and the religious order is to deal with those needs. The social function of religion is the satisfaction of the spiritual needs of members of society. The function of an institution or social practice is usually understood in terms of its contribution to the maintenance of the overall system, that is, its "task(s)" or "job(s)" within the overall system.

Dysfunction – when a part or component of a system ceases to perform its function or begins to operate in a manner that is harmful to the overall system. For instance, in an organic system an infected organ may be said to be dysfunctional. In a social system an institution not performing its allotted function would be considered dysfunctional.

Social inequality – in structural functionalism, has three basic dimensions: (1) economic inequalities (commonly called class); (2) inequalities in social honour and prestige (occupational prestige); and (3) inequalities in power or authority (associated with a person's institutional position). These three different forms of social inequality may very well arise out of completely different sources and need not be related.

Social change – in structural functionalism, tends to be slow, evolutionary, and orderly, unless there are catastrophic events. Although structural functionalists view the normal condition of society as being stable and characterized by social order, they recognize that social change does occur. There are several possible causes of social change, including shifts in values and norms, adjustments to the overall social structure necessitated by dysfunctioning components, and external factors and forces.

Alienation – in Marxian theory, a loss of control over the processes, products, and relations of material production. The concept is based on the assumption that the essential defining characteristic of human beings is their ability to labour and produce satisfaction for their material wants and needs. Humans express and realize their true humanity through their productive activity, and loss of control of the various aspects of this activity is a loss of an important part of their humanity. True freedom is deemed to involve control over the most important human activity: material production.

Dominant ideology – in Marxian and neo-Marxian theory, those sets of ideas, ideals, beliefs, and values promoted and advocated by the dominant class, which serve to justify the existing order and the position of the dominant class. Dominant ideologies can be complex sets of beliefs and ideals that permeate the entire culture and influence the operation of many different institutional orders. There are debates about how successful the use of a dominant ideology can be in the face of alternative ideologies that might arise from subordinate classes.

Contradiction – as commonly associated with Marxian and neo-Marxian theory, the structural incompatibility of certain features or processes within a society. For example, within capitalist society there is a contradiction between automation and economic stability. As individual capitalists automate production to improve their individual profit margins, they replace workers with machines, thus driving up the rate of unemployment. As a result, with more and more workers unemployed there are fewer and fewer people in a position to buy the commodities that capitalists produce, and the overall result is less economic activity and a loss of profits.

8

CLASSICAL SOCIOLOGY'S LACUNA: THEORIZING SEX AND GENDER

What dimensions or aspects of your life and experiences have been among the most important in terms of their impact on the development of your character and personality, general behaviour, and outlook on life? While there are many possible answers, it has become apparent to many that sex and gender are among the most important. When we examine human societies, what is one of the most important aspects of social relations that we are interested in? For many of us the answer is the manner by which sex and gender relations are organized, that is, how women and girls, men and boys are categorized, expected to behave, do behave, and are treated. As soon as we start to think systematically about questions relating to sex and gender, it becomes clear that sex and gender attributes and behaviours are a fundamental aspect of human existence. If you are still not convinced, think about the following questions for a moment. What does it mean in your society to be a woman? What is your conception of feminine? What traits do you attribute to femininity? How should girls, adolescents, young women, middle-aged women, and elderly women act? Would you rather be female or male? Why? What does it mean to be a man? What does it mean to be masculine? Should all men be masculine? Why?

One of the major reasons for questioning the appropriateness and pedagogical usefulness of the existing approaches in sociology is their inability to deal adequately with these important questions relating to sex and gender. Existing social theories have tended not to pay systematic attention to the impact of these fundamental dimensions of human existence on our social and individual being and on how societies are organized and structured. In some ways the history of the modern world is a history of a changing world with changing relationships between men and women; but the nature of these relationships and the changes in them have not been systematically included in the traditional social science theories.

A logical question is, why not? A Canadian theorist, Mary O'Brien, uses the term *malestream thought* to characterize the nature of much of the theoretical thinking that has dominated Western social science and philosophical thinking (1981: 5, 62). She has made the important and accurate argument that much of the thinking that informs our efforts to understand and explain the world has been dominated by a male perspective, so that we have ignored the voice of women as well as the central issue of sex and gender relations.

The situation, however, is well on its way to being rectified. It is no exaggeration to state that the emergence of new streams of feminist theory over the past thirty years represents *the* most important development in sociological theory this century. The creativity and vitality of feminist scholarship, research, theorizing, and political activity has resulted in the emergence and development of a very complex and diverse literature. It is impossible to cover all the various streams of feminism that have emerged over the past three decades here. In her overview of feminist theorizing and theory, Rosemary Tong (1989: 1) identifies the seven major streams of contemporary feminist thought as: liberal, Marxist, radical, psychoanalytic, socialist, existentialist, and postmodern. In what follows no attempt will be made to cover all these streams of thought, since we focus only on the three or four varieties of feminist theorizing that have had the greatest impact on sociological theory. Prior to examining some tenets of liberal, Marxist, radical, and socialist feminist explanations we must make sure we understand the concepts we are employing and must also briefly examine an approach that remains firmly rooted in popular culture and common-sense knowledge and that receives more attention in the mass media than any of the sociologically oriented approaches – biologically oriented explanations of sex and gender. First let us review our definitions.

Since much confusion surrounds the terms "sex" and "gender," it is necessary to revisit some definitions. When sociologists use the term "sex" they are referring to biological attributes. Caplan and Caplan provide a definition that is acceptable to most sociologists: "We shall use *sex* to refer to the biological sex of the individual – whether a person is born physically female or male. Sex is determined by the genes" (1994: 4). In virtually all human societies a person's sex, that is, the nature of their genetically determined reproductive and associated organs, has had a great deal to do with how their lives have unfolded and been lived. However, an equally important factor in the development of our personalities and behaviours is our gender. By *gender* we mean the personality and behavioural characteristics that are assumed to go with biological sex. Caplan and Caplan (1994: 4-5) once more provide an excellent summary:

> We shall use *gender* to refer to the social role of being a woman or being a man. Gender means "being feminine" or "being masculine," standards that look different in different societies. Gender is composed of a whole list of features that the society in question labels as appropriate for, or typical of one sex (but not the other, or more than the other), including feelings, attitudes, behavior, interests, clothing, and so on.

If we are interested in understanding human behaviour, a key question must be: what determines the characteristics of sex and gender related behaviour? As we noted above, the mass media and many people in society seem to be wedded to the idea that sex and gender behaviours are biologically or genetically predetermined and there is nothing we can possibly do about the fact that "Boys will be boys." As social scientists we must ask ourselves if this position has any credibility in the light of the evidence.

Biological Theories

Sociologists readily admit that most of our sexual characteristics are genetically determined. What we are less willing to acknowledge is that clearcut personality and behavioural characteristics are attached to having certain sexual and reproductive organs. The essential question for sociologists, however, is: Are gender differences genetically determined? The Caplans note that the question as to "how much of our masculine or feminine behaviour is unavoidably determined by our physical sex – underlies most of the controversies in the science of sex and gender" (5). If we can be sure of one thing, it is the fact that the media are always quick to cover issues relating to sex and gender. The cover story for the January 20, 1992, edition of *Time* was entitled "Sizing Up the Sexes." The bold print under the title reads, "Scientists are discovering that gender differences have as much to do with the biology of the brain as with the way we were raised" (*Time*, January 20, 1992: 36). Not to be outdone, about a month later *Newsweek* ran a story on the relationship between genetics and sexual orientation under the title "Born or Bred?" Even a cursory examination of how the mass media cover issues relating to sex, gender, and biology tends to turn up stories with a similar orientation. Headlines and stories such as "Boys found better at math" (*Regina Leader Post*, May 28, 1986), "Researchers find link between genetic inheritance and aggression" (*Globe and Mail*, October 23, 1993), "Brain Studies yield clues on Gays" (*Globe and Mail*, November 17, 1994) and "Packing of nerve cells differs in men, women" (*ibid.*) typify the current of thought that attempts to use or find biological explanations for gender behaviour. It is worthwhile noting that some media stories present as fact issues and claims still very much open in terms of scientific debate. A January 27, 1995, story in the *Globe and Mail* fails to discuss how the research was conducted, who paid for it, how the subjects were chosen, what the tests actually involved, and so on, yet the story concludes as a matter of fact that "The sexes differ in cognitive abilities, which included memory and judgment."

Basic Biology and Biological Explanations

The physiological development of our sex organs is determined by information carried in the genes that compose the twenty-three pairs of chromosomes that humans normally possess. There is continuing debate and ongoing research into just how many genes our chromosomes may carry, with speculation that the number may be as high as 50,000 or even 100,000. At present, science has identified over 3,000. Each gene is composed of a large molecule of a substance most of us refer to as DNA. Genes influence the structures and functioning of cells through the manufacture of proteins, which in turn act on cells. When a human egg and sperm unite to form a fertilized egg each contributes twenty-three chromosomes. Prior to fertilization the egg's twenty-three chromosomes include a sex chromosome, usually designated as the "X" chromosome. The sperm, on the other hand, as a result of random chance when it was formed, contains either an "X" or a "Y" sex chromosome. If the sperm happens to contain an "X" chromosome the fertilized egg will normally become female, with forty-six chromosomes including an "XX." If the sperm contains a "Y" sex chromosome the fertilized egg will contain forty-six chromosomes including an "XY" sex chromosome and it will normally develop into a male.

The developing embryo shows no noticeable sexual differentiation for about the first six to ten weeks of growth. After that time, the fertilized egg begins to show a difference. Depending on the chromosome structure, the formerly undifferentiated gonads begin to develop into either ovaries or testes. After this differentiation occurs a new physiological dynamic begins to develop as the ovaries and testes begin to produce different sex hormones. In the male the presence of androgens leads to a change in the manner by which the sex organs develop, resulting in the formation of the typical male reproductive apparatus. The female fetus continues a development trajectory initiated at fertilization. Since many issues relating to sex and gender relations are potentially politically sensitive, it is worth noting that even biologically based explanations of the developmental trajectories of female and male embryos have resulted in controversy. In her excellent study of theories of female and male development Anne Fausto-Sterling (1985: 81) points out that some of the so-called scientific literature seems to be predicated on sexist assumptions since female development was often cast in terms of females "lacking" a hormone or as female development occurring in the "absence" of something. Why not argue that the female developmental trajectory is normal, and the presence of a chemical substance leads to abnormalities in the developmental trajectory of males?

The issue of the impact of hormones on the development of the human organism once again becomes an important issue when we turn our attention to puberty. At this point in the physiological maturation process the presence of ovaries and testes results in the production of different types and levels of hormones. In females the ovaries typically begin to produce increased levels of estrogens and progesterones, while the testicles' production of androgens increases. It should be noted that the so-called sex hormones are in fact present in both females and males, and, as Rose, Lewontin, and Kamin (1985: 151) suggest, it is the ratio of the various hormones to each other that differs. In any event, it is clear that the typical physiological changes we observe during puberty are largely the result of significant changes in the amounts and types of hormones.

From the perspective of the sociologist, the key issue is not the presence of physiological sexual differences (they obviously exist) but rather what these sex differences have to do with personality, character, and social behaviour. When thinking about sexual differences we must heed those who have argued that an emphasis on sexual differences tends to hide the simple fact that females and males are more alike in terms of basic physiology than they are different (Epstein, 1988: 39-41; Renzetti and Curran, 1992: 28). Assuming there is basic compatibility in blood types and such, the majority of organs can be transplanted from females to males and vice versa. Still, we are confronted with the type of media stories cited above, ancient mythologies about what little girls and boys are made of, and much common-sense "knowledge" concerning what is "natural" when it comes to female and feminine or male and masculine behaviour.

The question of how physiological differences might influence personality, character, and social behaviours seems to have many answers. An abundant literature suggests a variety of hormone-based explanations for what is often referred to as male aggressiveness and female passivity. The conclusion these arguments often have pointed to is that the male dominance characteristic of patriarchal societies is natural. In criticizing an advocate of this position Rose, Lewontin, and Kamin (1985: 154) note that the argument holds that "there is an unbroken line between androgen binding sites in the brain, rough and tumble play in male infants, and the male domination of state, industry and the nuclear family." They also state that the counterpart to this argument about male dominance and testosterone concerns female passivity and the naturalness of mothering, an argument they, along with Tavris and Wade (1984: 162-63), convincingly reject on the basis of empirical evidence. Indeed, after examining the entire hormonal basis of behaviour, Rose, Lewontin, and Kamin (1985: 156) draw the following conclusion:

> All the evidence is that human infants, with their plastic, adaptive brains and ready capacity to learn, develop social expectation concerning their own gender identity, and the activities appropriate to that gender, irrespective of their genetic sex and largely independent of any simple relationship to their hormone levels (which can at any rate be themselves be substantially modified in level by social expectations and anticipations). Psychocultural expectations profoundly shape a person's gender development in ways that do not reduce to body chemistry.

Other biological or physiological explanations for different gender characteristics and behaviours have stressed the structures of the brain. Caplan and Caplan (1994: 32) undertake a detailed consideration of the arguments concerning apparent differences in the spatial abilities of females and males. They conclude that "Most studies actually yield no difference at all," and further, when there are differences they are usually very small and appear near or after adolescence with great overlap between male and female scores. The implication of this position is that such differences emerge only after many years of socialization. Fausto-Sterling reviews a wider literature dealing with a variety of brain functions ranging from IQ to mathematical ability. Her conclusion is that the effort "bears witness to the extensive yet futile attempts to derive biological explanations for alleged sex differences in cognition." She goes on to note that "such biological explanations fail because they base themselves on an inaccurate understanding of biology's role in human development." She concludes that "unidirectional models of biological control of human behaviour misconstrue the facts of biology" (1985: 60).

The work of Caplan and Caplan, Epstein, Rose, Lewontin, and Kamin, and Fausto-Sterling all points to the need to consider the social context of our sex and gender development and behaviour. In a section appropriately titled "Sex Differences: The Interaction of Nature and Environment," Renzetti and Curran summarize their findings:

> In other words, biology rather than *determining* who we are as males and females, instead establishes for us the broad limits of *human potential*. How each of us eventually thinks and behaves as a man or a woman is a product of the inescapable interaction between the potential and the opportunities and experiences to which we are exposed in our social environments. That these environments are diverse and that humans as a species exhibit great adaptability account for the wide variations in behaviors and personalities not only *between* the sexes, but also *within* each sex. (1992: 37; emphasis in original)

If we accept the arguments and evidence that our social environment plays an important role in structuring our sex and gender behaviours, we must once again return to sociological theory to better understand the dynamics involved. The remaining sections of this chapter will consider how various sociological feminist theories have sought to understand and explain sex and gender relations and behaviour. Since structural functionalism represents the dominant mode of theorizing for much of the past half-century we will first review how this approach might address the issues of sex and gender relations.

Structural Functionalist Thought

Although it is not necessary to restate the basic tenets of structural functionalist theory in detail, we should recall the importance of societal value systems and normative orientations in this stream of social theory. Structural functionalists maintain that every human society has a complex set of value systems and normative orientations at its core or centre. As we know, according to this theoretical perspective these sets of ideas, ideals, and beliefs are important because they provide the basis of social stability and integration, while also influencing the overall shape and character of the entire social structure. A complex society's value systems and normative orientations will typically contain an enormous amount of knowledge, information, common-sense wisdom, not to mention mythology and lore. Structural functionalists tend not to be excessively concerned with the origins of these belief systems, as it is generally assumed they have evolved and developed over the history of a society with input from a variety of sources ranging from the religious to the secular and even the academic. Daniel Rossides suggests that it is appropriate to think about "any given structure of values, ideas and practices as having emerged haphazardly during the course of history, much if not most of it, without conscious intent or design" (1968: 183). A central aspect or dimension of most societies' value systems and normative orientations are ideas and beliefs about sex, sex roles, gender, and gender behaviours.

It is clear, then, that ideas about sex and gender become an important part of the overall stock of knowledge that children acquire through the socialization process they are constantly exposed to in the various institutions to which they belong. In the family, in the education system, in religious institutions, via the media, and through their peers, children are constantly socialized according to the prevailing ideas about sex and gender roles and behaviours. Literally from the time of their birth, females and males both learn about being female and feminine, male and masculine. The knowledge we acquire through the ongoing, ever-present socialization process becomes a part of our personality and influences our attitudes, actions, and behaviour.

In discussing this approach to understanding sex and gender socialization, Epstein (1988: 104) uses Robert Merton's concept of "status-set." A status-set is similar to a role set (see Chapter 3) in that it refers to a set or cluster of statuses an individual may occupy at any one time. Epstein explains how this concept might be employed in understanding the perpetuation of sex and gender relations:

> Prevailing notions of properly feminine and masculine statuses lead to sex-typed status-sets in societies: A male-typed status-set might be father-husband-steel worker-veteran; a female status-set, wife-mother-primary school teacher-volunteer community worker. Although women and men share some common statuses, such as U.S. citizen, member of a political party, and high school graduate, these statuses do not carry precise normative expectations regarding behavior (that is, what the associated role is), or they may be defined differently for men and women. A male political party member might run for office, whereas a female political party member would be expected to work for the male's campaign.

Sex and gender behavioural attributes, then, are to be explained and understood as emerging out of females and males being socialized to accept and incorporate into their behavioural repertoires and personalities certain ideas about what it means to be female and feminine and male and masculine. It is the society's value system that defines sex and gender roles and these are passed on via socialization. In classical functionalist thought no particular concern was paid to the origins of these values or to their negative or positive impact on females and males.

According to functionalist thought, the acceptance of a value system and set of normative orientations by the majority of a society's members is a prerequisite for a smoothly functioning and orderly social structure. As long as there is a general acceptance of the socially sanctioned and prescribed sex and gender behaviours, and as long as these beliefs are effectively transmitted via the socialization process, there should be a measure of stability when it comes to sex and gender relations. While there is debate concerning the degree to which sex and gender relations in Western industrial societies were ever marked by stability and order, some have argued that by the 1950s, just when the traditional nuclear family was reaching its zenith, it was also beginning to crumble.

John Conway argues that despite being idealized in the media and other institutions the golden days of the nuclear family were not all that golden. For one thing, as he points out, there were few roles available to many women. Conway notes that the traditional Western industrial nuclear family, which he describes as "dads at work and mom at home with the kids," left few choices for women (1993: 13-14). Indeed, "For women who wanted a choice, there was none, and the socialization process ensured that few wanted to be anything other than wives and mothers" (15). Epstein (1988: 107) points out that by the 1970s a growing body of literature and research had begun to demonstrate that the sex and gender roles and behaviours that accompanied the "Happy Days" of the 1950s were not all that positive for women. She writes: "It was widely recognized that the norms that defined women's roles were those regarded as expressive, nurturant, service-oriented, and ancillary to men's both in personality and behavior, in contrast to the norms for men's roles, which were clustered around instrumental, dominant and goal-oriented qualities." Epstein notes that as early as 1963 Betty Friedan had objected to the fact that the typical feminine roles prescribed in the Parsonian view of the family had a negative impact on women, "narrowing women's horizons by isolating them in the home," and as a result these roles "created psychological problems for women and wasted their talents" (108). As was the case in the study of the family, the dysfunctional impact of the existing sex and gender roles and scripts was instrumental in new and more critical analytical approaches that accompanied the re-emergence of the women's movement in the 1960s. The first of these new approaches, liberal feminism, represents a critique of functionalist thought more or less from within.

Liberal Feminism

In their excellent summary of the development of feminist theory, Patricia Madoo Lengermann and Jill Niebrugge-Brantley (1988) note that women have been protesting their social position for centuries, although much of this activity has not been preserved on the printed page. In spite of this, in recent centuries there is an impressive record of scholarship dealing with the position of women in Western society. For instance, the eighteenth-century writings of Mary Wollstonecraft along with those of John Stuart Mill and Harriet Taylor Mill in the nineteenth century mark the beginning of the systematic development of a stream of feminism called liberal feminism.

The liberal-feminist approach has much in common with structural functionalism. Among the essential points of similarity is a stress on the role of values, norms, and ideas in the structuring of society and its inequalities. Although they use a different term to describe the approach and are not within this tradition, Pat Armstrong and Hugh Armstrong (1984) provide an excellent description of it. According to Armstrong and Armstrong, liberal-feminist ideas underlie many of the positions and publications of government departments and government-sponsored agencies. In their discussion of feminism, Lengermann and Niebrugge-Brantley identify Jessie Bernard as a key representative of this approach, while Rosemarie Tong (1989) notes that Betty Friedan is often classified as a liberal feminist.

The essence of the liberal, and functionalist, approach is its acceptance of the basic structures of Western society as appropriate, while recognizing the existence of a dysfunctional element: the emergence of sexist ideas in the society's value system. Those sexist ideas refer to the beliefs or values that attribute behavioural characteristics or personality attributes purely on the basis of biological sex. When this happens people are more or less automatically streamed into jobs, careers, and roles on the basis of gender rather than ability. Many women face insurmountable barriers in attempting to enter so-called non-traditional occupations and roles.

For women, the situation of not having a fair chance to develop all their abilities and potentials by being streamed into traditional roles and behaviours is clearly not in accordance with the premises of freedom and opportunity for all. For society, a major potential talent pool made up of half of the society is lost. For example, how many potential scientists have been denied an opportunity to contribute to the search for a cure for cancer as a result of women's systematic exclusion from particular jobs?

As Armstrong and Armstrong point out, this approach places a great deal of emphasis on socialization. Values, norms, beliefs, and behaviours are passed on from one generation to another through the process of socialization. Because the essence of the problem is located in the society's value and belief system, changes have to be made in that system. Sexist ideas and behaviours have to be confronted and altered. New non-sexist ideas have to be disseminated through the socialization process, while some cases will call for resocialization.

In liberal-feminist thought, the general picture is far from hopeless. Because liberal feminists accept the basic soundness of the current social structures, they conclude that all that is really needed is some "fine-tuning." The society's belief system and moral codes have become corrupted with sexist ideas; but the current institutional arrangements are strong enough to ensure that the required reforms and adjustments can be made and that these changes will lead to the eventual development of egalitarian relations between men and women.

Marxian Feminism

Much has been written about the relevance and usefulness of Marx and the concepts he developed for our understanding of sex and gender (Tong, 1989; Donovan, 1992). While opinions on this issue vary, one thing is quite clear – for Marx, sex and gender relations were not of primary significance in understanding the overall structures and dynamics of human society. In Marx's work we find systematic accounts of many key sociological issues, including the essential character of human beings, the nature and operation of the capitalist economic order, the nature of human consciousness, the dynamics of political power, and so on; however, we find little explicit treatment of sex and gender. There is, however, one original work dating to the era that Josephine Donovan refers to as "first wave" Marxism.

Engels and the Origin of the Family

Frederick Engels (1820-95) was a close collaborator and life-long supporter and friend of Karl Marx. In 1884, one year after Marx died, Engels published *The Origins of the Family, Private Property and the*

State, in which he attempted to provide the basis of a materialist approach to the development of the family. The study draws heavily on the work of a nineteenth-century anthropologist, Lewis H. Morgan. Engels argues that as human society develops and evolves we witness the development and evolution of different forms of familial organization. During the earliest period of human history, referred to as a stage of "savagery," sexual and reproductive relations were organized on the basis of group marriages. The second major stage, barbarism, was marked by the development of pottery, the domestication of animals, and the cultivation of cereal grains. By the end of the period, the smelting of iron and the use of an alphabet had come into being. During this second stage of development group marriages gave way to paired families.

Engels notes that the development of paired families and of restrictions concerning who could marry whom was in part due to the biological problems associated with close biological relatives reproducing ([1884], 1972: 47). There were, however, other reasons for the definitive emergence of monogamy – reasons that, Engels argues, were social and economic. As human society evolved there was an increasing social surplus; that is, there was an increasing difference between the total wealth produced in society and the wealth required for subsistence – for keeping the population alive and reproducing. Subsistence living implies a "hand-to-mouth" existence with no surplus that can be stored and used later. As humans became more productive, a surplus developed and the basis for a class structure emerged, because with a surplus comes the possibility of someone or some group controlling that surplus and thereby acquiring a measure of economic power. At a certain moment men began to appropriate and control the economic surplus, and as a result they came to have more power. Accompanying this process was the development of a concern, among those men who controlled the society's economic surplus, with the disposition of the surplus. They wanted to both protect their material wealth on a day-to-day basis and arrange for its intergenerational transfer: the disposition of the wealth after death. Engels argues that men established a system of monogamy and patriarchy in order to control the disposition of their wealth. By controlling women and attempting to ensure that women only had sexual relations with their designated husbands, men could be sure that their wives bore only their own children and confident that those children would be legitimate heirs to their properties.

According to Engels, the development of a social surplus and the subsequent appropriation of that surplus as private property provided the basis for the emergence of both a system of social class and a system of patriarchy. The root cause of class and patriarchal domination is to be found in the economic structures and processes of the capitalist system. Given that, the elimination of class and male domination can only come through the transformation of class relations. And because men's domination of women is fundamentally rooted in men's desire to provide legitimate and true heirs for their private productive property, Engels argues, the abolition of private productive property will logically mean that there will be no more need for men to oppress women ([1884], 1972: 71).

Debates concerning the strengths, weaknesses, and relevance of Engels's arguments have been legion (see Sayers, Evans and Redclift, 1987). The emergence in the 1960s of yet another surge in the ongoing struggles of women for equality and the creation of an egalitarian society produced a renewed interest in the potential insights of the work of Marx and Engels. Among the first to plumb the works of Marx for insights into the nature of contemporary sex and gender roles was Margaret Benston. In a 1969 essay entitled "The Political Economy of Women's Liberation" Benston argued that to understand fully the dynamics of sex and gender relations we must look more closely at the nature of housework and its relationship to material production in capitalist society.

Benston's analysis of the relationship between housework and the position of women in society draws on the distinction in Marxian economic theory between use value and exchange value. Commodities or items that have a use to somebody are said to embody use value. If you are hungry and I make you a sandwich and give it to you at no charge, the sandwich can be said to have use value only. Exchange value refers to the amount of value that can be received for an item or commodity if it is exchanged for money or traded for another commodity. If I prepare and give away my sandwiches they are said only to have use value; on the other hand, if I sell them (exchange them for money) they are said to have exchange value. Since capitalist market economies are based on production for sale and profit, commodities produced that embody exchange value are more highly prized and are deemed to be more socially important.

The work that women typically do in the home is unpaid and involves the preparation of meals, child care, house-cleaning, and other family service and support work. Benston argues that this work results in the creation of use values for family members, but no exchange value is produced since women do not charge or get paid for what they produce. Housework is, Benston argues, a form of pre-capitalist work. The problem for women is that the labour they engage in at home is undervalued and not deemed socially important because no exchange value is produced. As a result both women and the work they do are deemed less important than is the profit-producing work of men. Benston notes that in terms of the perpetuation of the capitalist system the work that women do in the home is essential since it involves the consumption of various commodities the capitalist system produces for sale. In addition, by providing a stable and healthy home life they make it possible for men to continue to work and produce surplus value. Women also are available to enter the work force during times of need, composing a reserve army of labour, a concept we will discuss later.

The key issue Benston raises – the relationship between women's work in the household and the overall nature of sex and gender relations in the society – became a topic of considerable debate during the 1970s. Peggy Morton (1972) drew our attention to a new issue involved in connecting women and their domestic labour to the larger society when she argued that women in fact produce one of the most important commodities involved in capitalist production – labour power. Morton does not disagree with the claim that women produce use values that are not sold on the market; she argued that what is important, however, is the fact that women also produce the essential commodity that capitalists require if they are to appropriate surplus value – labour power. As we know, within the Marxian approach labour power is the essential commodity, being as it is the source of surplus value and thus profits. According to this argument one of the key social roles the family plays is making it possible for workers to return to work day after day, week after week, month after month, and even year after year by providing them with a place where they get proper nutrition and can rest and relax and get their "batteries re-charged." Others, including Mariarosa Dalla Costa (1972) and Wally Seccombe (1974), supported this position, even emphasizing in stronger terms the role of housework in the production of surplus value in capitalist society. The question of the precise nature of the relationship between domestic labour and the production of surplus value became the topic of what has become known as the domestic labour debate, the details of which need not concern us here. (For an excellent summary of the various positions, see Armstrong and Armstrong, 1990: ch. 5.)

What is important about the debate over the precise nature of domestic labour (housework) in capitalist society is that it pointed out some important weaknesses in Marxian theory in regard to understanding sex and gender relations. Armstrong and Armstrong 1990: 88) note that at a certain point many interested in more fully understanding the nature of sex and gender relations "became increasingly disillusioned by a domestic labour debate that seemed to have reached a dead end." The dead end related less to the role of domestic labour than to the fact that too little attention was being devoted to the question of why it is that domestic labour is predominantly the domain of women. One answer to this question came out of what is commonly called radical feminism.

Radical Feminism

Among the most powerful of the feminist treatises of the last few decades is Shulamith Firestone's *The Dialectic of Sex: The Case for Feminist Revolution* (1970). Firestone maintains that men and women must be understood as being members of separate and distinctive classes. For Firestone, the basis of class is biological and, as in the Marxian analysis, one class has historically been dominant and exploitative. Firestone argues that men have dominated and exploited women largely because of the biological role that women play in species reproduction. The fact that women give birth is at the root of the problem. The biological processes of childbirth are such that women are forced to depend on men for long periods of time, and this dependency has resulted in the emergence of the larger patterns of domination and subordination characteristic of patriarchal society.

The central theme of Firestone's work, that the systematic oppression of women is one of the central characteristics of patriarchal capitalist society, has been taken up by other feminist thinkers, although many of them have disagreed with Firestone's specific explanation. For instance, the work in Lydia Sargent's book (1981) and in a reader edited by Annette Kuhn and AnneMarie Wolpe (1978) illustrates diverse explanations of women's oppression. Among the many innovative theoretical approaches are the efforts by scholars such as Michèle Barrett (1980) and Heidi Hartmann (1981) to develop a feminist analysis borrowing from the traditions of both Marxian and radical feminism. Such writers have worked at developing a mode of analysis that directs attention to the structural characteristics of capitalist society and the patriarchal system as they have developed within the context of Western society. The work of scholars such as Barrett and Hartmann is generally referred to as socialist feminism, which will be examined below.

Yet another, more recent, discussion in feminist thought has centred on the question of "diversity and commonality" (see, for instance, Code, "Feminist Theory," in Burt, Code, and Dorney, 1993). While feminists of various streams have "rallied around a common cause in their opposition to patriarchy," celebrating the sisterhood of all women, the idea of "difference" has also become prominent as new theories of race have been added to the older theories of gender. It has been argued that women have "failed to take into account the effects of institutionalized racism" and that factors of ethnic, racial, and sexual diversity have to be more adequately taken into account. As Canadian theorist Lorraine Code puts it, "The historical goal of achieving equality for women has to be refined and redefined if it is to retain any legitimacy as a feminist project" (Burt, Code, and Dorney, 1993: 48). For some feminists an adequate understanding of the nature of sex and gender relations, a precondition to the creation of egalitarian relations, was not possible as long as our thinking was confined to the logic of functionalism, Marxism, or any of the biologically oriented approaches. New and innovative directions were required. Some of these feminists were unwilling to jettison Marxism totally, although they did argue that traditional Marxism was of limited value. The outcome of these developments was what we call socialist feminism.

Socialist Feminism: Hartmann and Barrett

In her important essay, "The Unhappy Marriage of Marxism and Feminism: Toward a More Progressive Union," Heidi Hartmann lays out the rationale for the development of a new analytical approach that incorporates insights from and builds on the strengths of both Marxism and feminism. She notes that while Marxism provided potentially powerful analytical tools, it is essentially flawed: "while Marxist analysis provides essential insight into the laws of historical development, and those of capital in particular, the categories of Marxism are sex blind" (1986: 2). On the other hand, "feminist analysis by itself is inadequate because it has been blind to history and insufficiently materialist." Her proposed solution was a "more progressive union of Marxism and feminism" (3). The analytical fruit of this more progressive union would be a mode of analysis that simultaneously examined the structures and dynamics of both capitalism and patriarchy. Such an analytical approach would allow us to understand the dynamics of class exploitation that Marxian analysis holds is a key feature of capitalism and also the dynamics of sex and gender-based exploitation and domination that feminists see as integral to patriarchy. Since feminists and Marxists are not supposed merely to analyse and engage in intellectual debates about inequality, oppression, and exploitation, a new theoretical orientation such as this would offer something more practical. Hartmann explains: "As feminist socialists we must organize a practice which addresses both the struggle against patriarchy and the struggle against capitalism" (33).

The essential project that Hartmann outlines is very much the same as that attempted by Michèle Barrett in *Women's Oppression Today: Problems in Marxist Feminist Analysis*. Barrett offers a more detailed outline of the analytical logic of a socialist feminist approach and is critical of traditional Marxian, liberal-feminist, and radical feminist analyses because they fail to provide an adequate way of understanding and explaining the nature of women's oppression in complex relations that comprise capitalist society. An adequate analytical approach must take into account "the economic organization of households and its accompanying familial ideology, the division of labour and its accompanying relations of production" (1985: 40).

Barrett musters a convincing set of arguments against any form of biological determinism, radical feminist or otherwise. She then engages in an examination of the concept of ideology that is critical in her analysis. Barrett is careful not to suggest that ideology can be used in any simplistic manner, yet she maintains it is central to understanding the structuring of notions of sexuality and gender in capitalist society. After examining the role of the educational system in transmitting ideology, she looks at the dynamics of family life. Barrett is critical of the concept of "the family" because it tends to be ahistorical and ideological, meaning that as capitalism has developed there have been various forms of family organization and to postulate the nuclear family as the norm is to impose an unrealistic model or standard on everyone. "The family" is an ideological concept because it includes ideas about what the "normal" sex and gender relations are supposed to be. Important to her understanding of family relations is what she terms the "ideology of familialism," which involves, among other things, "ideologies of domesticity and maternity for women, of breadwinning and responsibility for man" (206-07). Such powerful ideological formulations of the "normal" family with associated sex and gender roles become a part of the dominant ideology and they come to impact the thinking, character, and lives of people.

Barrett's analysis of the operation and dynamics of families and households makes it clear that the institution and the assumptions about sex and gender behaviours contained therein do not operate in the best interest of women. She explicitly asks who seems to benefit from the nature of patriarchal family relations and the attendant sex and gender relations? Her answer is, as we have stated, not most women and not the working class, though perhaps working-class men get some benefits. As for the ruling class, she concludes that they seem to gain the most from the operation of these social structures, though even in this case the benefits are not exactly unambiguous (222-23). Barrett also examines the role of the state in maintaining and reinforcing the structures and dynamics of the patriarchal family, noting that throughout history there is evidence that the state has participated in creating social conditions and regulations that foster the oppression of women.

Barrett and Hartmann both draw our attention to an important analytical problem when it comes to understanding sex and gender issues. Can sex and gender relations in our society be understood purely within the context of the patriarchal system, with no reference to the fact that we live in a capitalist society? Or, are sex and gender relations in our society to be understood primarily as the outcome of the operation and dynamics of the capitalist system, and thus if that system were changed would we tend to see the emergence of more egalitarian sex and gender relations? Or must we, as Barrett and Hartmann suggest, turn our analytical attention to understanding both capitalism and patriarchy and the intersections between the two?

Conclusion

In this chapter we have reviewed some of the approaches developed to allow us to better understand the complex issues associated with the important topic of sex and gender relations. We examined biologically based explanations and the research that claimed to support them, but found them inadequate. The fact that structural functionalist theory sees the issues of sex and gender as merely aspects of how a society's value system and normative orientations are organized suggests that this approach is not capable of making this a primary issue in its theorizing and explanations of human conduct. As Armstrong and Armstrong (1990: 45) point out, those adopting this general approach "have not provided a systematic explanation of how or why ideas and behavioural patterns develop or how and why they change." Moreover, as Armstrong and Armstrong further indicate, it is also problematic to assume that value systems and normative orientations represent "a neutral set of beliefs uniting society" because sometimes these ideas and beliefs serve to justify various relations of domination and power (41). On the other hand, the tendency of theorists influenced by Marxian thought to focus on material production, economic processes, and class relations has resulted in this stream of thought downplaying the issues of sex and gender or just adding them on as a secondary issue.

After examining the mainstream efforts to address the questions surrounding sex and gender relations we turned to feminist theory. It is imperative that sociologists account for the challenges and incorporate the insights of feminist theory into future theorizing. We need to adopt new modes of theorizing about human society that take us beyond the limitations of orthodox functionalism and orthodox Marxism and include the various elements of sex and gender relations in all our thinking about every aspect of human conduct and social organization. Fortunately, the basis for such an approach exists in the various streams of feminist theory, although much work remains to be done.

Terms and Concepts

Feminism – a complex term used to describe diverse sets of beliefs, political practices, social practices, social movements, and sociological theories. As used here it refers to a set of underlying assumptions and principles that recognize the historical subordination and oppression of women; it seeks to explain this phenomenon and provide alternative non-oppressive modes of social organization.

Liberal feminism – a stream of feminist thought that focuses on inequalities between men and women. Liberal feminists primarily locate their explanation of women's inequalities in a dysfunctioning of the existing social institutions. Liberal feminists argue that sexist ideas and beliefs are a central cause of women's inequalities and that these can be corrected through the introduction of non-sexist ideas, values, and norms and intensive resocialization without any major or radical change to the basic institutional orders.

Marxian feminism – tends to see the inequality and exploitation of women as an historical process and part of the overall system of class exploitation of capitalist society. Although there are a variety of different streams of Marxian feminism, they all tend to view the position of women as a special case of subordination understandable only within the context of capitalist society, and thus they focus more on class exploitation and domination than on the exploitation and domination of women *per se*. They generally argue that once the capitalist relations of class domination and exploitation are eliminated, the stage will be set for the emancipation of women.

Radical feminism – describes an extremely diverse set of thinkers who argue that neither liberal nor Marxian feminism really understands the basis of women's oppression. Although there are radically different positions, ranging from biologically based arguments to others closer to Marxian feminism, radical feminists stress the need to understand that women's oppression predates capitalism and has continued to exist in non-capitalist societies; therefore, it cannot be simply a matter of sexist ideas or an offshoot of class domination. Radical feminists call for a systematic empirical and theoretical rethinking of all dimensions of human relations, with the issues of sexual and gender differences at the centre of this process. We must, they argue, begin with sex and gender relations and not merely add them on as we think about human relations and social structures. No existing theory has done this.

PART III

Applying Sociological
Theories and Concepts

The promise of the sociological imagination goes well beyond being forced to learn new concepts and wrestle with abstract theoretical ideas and debates. The promise of the sociological imagination is that these concepts and theories must somehow assist in your ongoing efforts to understand yourself, others, and the social world around you. For that to happen, you must be able to take the concepts and theories we have been discussing and apply them to real issues and events. No introductory book or course will fully develop your sociological imagination or even introduce you adequately to the complexities of the discipline. All we can hope to do is illustrate how sociologists view and understand the social world.

In this section you will be introduced to several important social issues. In each case you will be asked to think about these issues in several different ways, using different theoretical perspectives. No effort will be made to convince you that one approach is necessarily better or more adequate – that judgement is left up to you. The issues to be considered in the following chapters are: (1) social inequality; (2) the nature of political power; (3) deviance and social control; and (4) the nature of family relations.

9

EXPLAINING SOCIAL INEQUALITY

"The social inequalities that characterize Canadian society are as stark and deeply rooted as you will find anywhere in the world."

Many Canadians would disagree with this statement, because a part of the common-sense stock of knowledge of our society maintains that while there are some people who are rich and some who are poor, Canada is, after all, an egalitarian society. Before we jump to the conclusion that there is a significant degree of equality in Canadian society we should look at some empirical data.

Social Inequality in Canada

Income Inequality

According to *Maclean's* magazine (October 14, 1991), one of the richest men in Canada makes $426,190 an hour. His personal-dividend account grew by about $4.4 million a week. In February, 1987, the Financial Post's *Moneywise* magazine reported on the richest people in Canada and estimated the top individual's family worth at $6.3 billion. Second on the list was a family whose wealth, though a staggering $100 million less, still amounted to $6.2 billion. The next three families on the list were all worth more than $1 billion. The last family on the list of fifty was not exactly in dire straits, with a family worth of about $100 million. On March 30, 1995, the *Globe and Mail* reported that a leading Canadian corporation had paid one of its executives a $2.5 million bonus on top of his base salary of slightly over $500,000 and an existing bonus of over $233,000.

The April 13, 1987, issue of the *Financial Post* contained a report on the income levels of Canada's top corporate executives. Data were available only on those Canadian companies with shares listed on stock exchanges in the United States, where the freedom of information laws make it possible to find out salary levels. The list, though far from complete, paints a solid picture of a group of Canadians who all experienced quite a good year. The list of twenty-seven names with corporate affiliations included incomes ranging from $503,946 to the top income of over $2 million. These data make it clear that some people in Canada have significant incomes and established fortunes; but if we look at other data it becomes just as clear that many more Canadians live on much more modest incomes. The 1992 *Canadian Global Almanac* provides information on the salaries of more "average Canadians." It notes that in 1988 the average income for self-employed doctors was slightly over $113,000, as compared to nearly $41,000 for teachers and professors and about $29,000 for provincial government workers. In 1988 people fishing for a living averaged about $22,500 per year while pensioners received only $14,259. The average for all occupations was $22,377. According to a *Globe and Mail* article, the average family income in Canada declined by $3,025 between 1989 and 1993, when it was $43,225. The same story notes that the average income for those families in the lowest 20 per cent of the population was just $10,657 a year.

In 1988 the Special Senate Committee on Poverty, in its eighteenth annual report, indicated that 19.3 per cent of Canadian families had income levels below the poverty line – a figure representing about 1,348,000 families. In total, about 5.4 million people in Canada were living below the poverty line. The Senate's definition of poverty is based on a measure of disposable income and amounts to about 50 per cent of the average income for families of two or more.

The inequalities in income that these different data sources point to are also apparent in data on the general distribution of income in Canada. A Statistics Canada publication, *Income Distribution by Size in Canada 1988* (Catalogue 23-207), divides the population of Canada into five quintiles and presents an estimate of the amount of the society's total income that each quintile receives. The combined data for individuals and families illustrate substantial inequalities in income in Canada.

Quintiles	% of income received
Lowest	4.6
Second	10.4
Middle	16.9
Fourth	24.9
Highest	43.2

Thus, while the lowest 20 per cent of the population received less than 5 per cent of the income, the highest 20 per cent received about 43 per cent. The bottom two groups together – or 40 per cent of the population – only received 15 per cent of all income.

Canadian society, then, is indeed characterized by significant structural inequalities in income. In Canada there are rich folk, there are poor folk, and there are folk in the middle. However, these data, while describing certain features of Canadian society, do not explain the phenomenon of inequality. A logical question that follows the presentation of such data is "Why?" Why do some people in Canada have incomes in excess of a million dollars a year while a significant number of others live below the poverty line? Why does the top 20 per cent of the population receive over 43 per cent of the country's income while the bottom 20 per cent receives less than 5 per cent? How do we explain income inequalities in our society?

Prestige or Status Inequality
In addition to the structural economic inequalities in Canadian society, there are also what sociologists call *prestige inequalities*. There is a tradition in sociology of using the terms "status," "prestige," and "honour" interchangeably. Because in this book we consistently use the term "status" in a different context – to refer to positions within an institution or group – we will use the word "prestige" for the purposes of examining structures of inequality. What, then, do we mean by the term?

The *Modern Dictionary of Sociology* defines prestige in terms of social recognition, respect, and even admiration and deference (Theodorson and Theodorson, 1969: 312). In their *Dictionary of Sociology*, Abercrombie, Hill, and Turner (1988: 194) note that the concept of prestige has a long tradition in American sociological studies of occupational rankings. They indicate that a consistent pattern has emerged when people in capitalist societies are asked to rank different occupations according to "social standing or desirability." It seems that people in Western societies agree that some jobs are more prestigious than others. Sociological researchers have found that many people think that there is more prestige attached to being a judge, priest, and even university professor than there is to being a construction worker, janitor, or trapper.

If we accept that there are certain commonly held ideas in our society about the prestige, honour, or social recognition attached to various occupations and positions, we can also argue that a person in a given occupation might be located above or below another person in a different occupation. The questions that emerge from this type of research relate to the general importance and role that such a ranking plays in the society's structures of inequality. There is significant disagreement about the basis and role of these apparent prestige-related inequalities.

Power

In addition to economic and prestige inequalities, sociologists have found substantial evidence indicating an unequal distribution of power in society. The very fact that you have bought and are reading this book may in itself be an indication of a power difference. In all likelihood you purchased this book and are reading it because you have to, whether you like it or not – that is, because someone told you to get it and read it. The fact that instructors can influence your behaviour in this way means they have power over you. This particular concept of *power* refers to different relations between individuals within an institution, yet the concept can also be used to refer to larger social processes at a macro level, as in the case of power vested in the government to make certain decisions that have an impact on the lives of most if not all members of the society. These two "levels" of power indicate that although social scientists frequently use the concept of power, they do so in different ways. As a result the concept is often subject to confusion and misunderstanding.

The definition of power most widely adopted in sociology is based on the classical definition provided by Weber, who noted that power means the ability of an individual or a number of individuals to realize their will in a communal action even when that will is resisted by others (Weber, 1946: 180). Weber's use of the term "communal action" implies that power tends to be related to social collectivities such as groups and classes more than to individual situations. This raises the further issue of how we understand power at the micro level of an individual within an institution. If we are to understand the connection between the macro and micro dimensions of power, we must first consider how different theoretical perspectives have handled the issue.

The "Discovery" of Class in North America

When we examine the extent of the inequalities in our society, some obvious questions should come to mind. Why do these significant differences in income levels exist? Why are some jobs, occupations, or positions considered more prestigious than others? Why are people not equal in terms of the power they exercise?

The issue of social and economic inequality was not a pressing concern for most North American social thinkers until midway through this century. While there were exceptions, such as the work of Thorstein Veblen, the idea that North America consisted of open and basically classless societies was a pervasive aspect of the world view held by most academics and non-academics alike. Other societies, such as those in Europe, were viewed as having traditions of class inequalities, but the United States in particular was a part of the New World where all individuals were supposed to have an equal opportunity to better themselves. According to this belief system, people were able to determine, to a large extent, what their lives would be like. As Harold Kerbo (1983) points out, the founders of American sociology ignored the issue of social inequality until the trauma of the Great Depression forced social scientists to undertake investigations that began to question the mythology of the United States as a classless society.

During the 1930s and 1940s two different types of studies pointed to the existence of social and economic inequalities in the United States. The first important empirical investigation of inequality, by Robert and Helen Lynd, found significant differences in the economic and social positions of Americans.

Middletown: The Economic Basis of Class
Robert and Helen Lynd conducted a detailed investigation of the patterns and structures of inequality in an Indiana city they thought was typical of the United States in the mid-1920s. They called the city "Middletown," which was also the title of the 1929 published account of their work.

The Lynds used a variety of techniques to gather data on the social structure and patterns of interaction and behaviour in the city. They found not only that Middletown was a class-divided city, but also that class position was one of the most important factors influencing an individual's life chances there. They concluded that there were essentially two classes: the working class, made up of about 70 per cent of the population; and the business class, made up of the remaining 30 per cent.

A key aspect of their initial study was its historical dimension. The Lynds collected as much data as they could on Middletown as it had existed in 1890, about thirty-five years before their study, to provide an indication of what was happening to the overall structures of the society. On the basis of their data they concluded that the class structure of Middletown was becoming more pronounced. The Middletown of the 1920s was considerably more industrialized, and the development of industry had altered the previous class structure. The working class had grown in size. In 1890 Middletown had been more of a typical pioneer city, with considerable equality of opportunity for people to improve their situation providing they had the initiative and were willing to work hard. As American society became more industrialized, the amount of capital required to engage in business grew rapidly. By 1920 the situation had developed to the point that it took more capital than most individuals could muster to engage in any industrial or manufacturing enterprises. As a result, the majority of people found themselves in the working class.

The Lynds later returned to the city and produced a second important study of social inequality in the United States, *Middletown in Transition* (1937). The second book painted a slightly different picture of the class structure, although the two basic classes remained the same. The class structure had become somewhat more complex, because Middletown had developed a more substantial industrial base and a considerably larger service sector. As a result the Lynds concluded that there were essentially six classes:

> *Group I.* Wealthy owners of large local businesses. Manufacturers, bankers, local heads of major corporations.
> *Group II.* Smaller local manufacturers, merchants, professionals. High-paid salaried officials in local and national businesses.
> *Group III.* Medium-sized and smaller local businesses, professionals, white-collar workers, clerical workers, civil servants.
> *Group IV.* Aristocracy of local labour. Supervisors, highly skilled craft workers, and trades people.
> *Group V.* Working class. Average and typical blue-collar workers in skilled and unskilled jobs. Average wage-earners.
> *Group VI.* Marginated people. Seasonally employed, unemployed.

The work of the Lynds provided firm evidence that despite the views held and espoused by many Americans, especially politicians and the wealthy, there was indeed a class structure in the United States. Their research, by concentrating on the economic basis of class, tended to push the analysis of social inequality in the direction of a Marxian theory – although there were many U.S. sociologists who were not at all interested in that mode of analysis.

W. Lloyd Warner and Associates: Prestige as Social Class

In the early 1930s a group of sociologists led by W. Lloyd Warner began a series of community studies destined to have an enormous impact on the study of social inequality in the United States. Warner and his associates produced a large number of different studies in addition to a manual that presented their method of analysing social inequality in a formal manner (see Warner, 1949). An approach that we will call stratification analysis developed out of this work.

This *stratification analysis* refers to an approach to the study of social inequality that assumes that society is layered or divided into strata. The strata or layers are made up of people who share a common characteristic or attribute such as income or social prestige and honour. Thinkers adopting this approach tend to see the strata or layers in society as forming a ladder or continuum on which people are placed higher or lower, depending on how much of some measurable "characteristic," "attribute," "possession," or "quality" they possess. Because many different criteria could be used to define strata, it was important to define as precisely as possible just what the basis of the stratification system was.

Warner and his associates studied the city of Newburyport, Massachusetts, which they called Yankee City. They, too, were interested in the issue of inequality, although their studies were based on a different set of assumptions from that of the work of the Lynds. The approach Warner adopted assumed that the most important types of inequality were related to social status, and so the Yankee City studies were geared to investigating inequalities in prestige rather than the economic dimensions of social inequality.

The assumption that a society's value system is the basis of its stratification system was compatible with the basic tenets of structural functionalism – the dominant theoretical orientation at this time – and as a result the work of Warner and his associates became well known and accepted. Based on their investigation of people's beliefs, attitudes, patterns of social interaction, and consciousness of inequalities, the Warner group identified six distinct classes in Yankee City: the upper-upper class; the lower-upper class; the upper-middle class; the lower-middle class; the upper-lower class; the lower-lower class.

The Warner researchers used a number of different research methods to arrive at this schema. As Dennis Gilbert and Joseph Kahl (1987) note, their main method became known as "evaluated participation." This method attempts to place families and individuals in one of the classes on the basis of their reputations, patterns of social interactions, community participation, and memberships in formal networks and associations. Warner and his group eventually developed another system for determining class position, a system they hoped would be easier to administer than the evaluated participation approach. The second method was based on four major factors: an individual's occupation, source of income, house type, and dwelling area. They established an index or ranking of occupations, income sources, house types, and dwelling areas based on the standards and values of the community being studied, and ranked individuals and families according to their combined standing in these four scales. On the basis of these criteria the group argued that the class structure of Yankee City, and North America in general, looked like this:

- Upper-upper: old established families. Biggest houses, in exclusive areas. Strong sense of lineage and belonging to this class.
- Lower-upper: newer wealth. Less secure in income, identity, and sense of lineage. Manners and habits less polished and "natural."
- Upper-middle: business people and professionals. Individuals and families in affluent areas, self-maintained houses (no gardeners and servants). Value education and community participation and service.
- Lower-middle: smaller business, white-collar salaried semi-professions (such as teachers), supervisors in factories. Own modest middle-class houses in middle-class areas. Churchgoers and lodge members.
- Upper-lower: blue-collar and clerical workers. Own or rent small and average houses in working-class areas. Hardworking and respectable people who stay out of trouble.
- Lower-lower: marginally and seasonally employed. Spend time on relief of various kinds. Less respectable than upper-lower workers. Seldom own houses. Rent in poorest areas of town.

The arguments developed by Warner and his associates became widely accepted, although some scholars disagreed that the study of social prestige was an appropriate mode of understanding class. Perhaps the most serious criticism was that the approach tended to ignore the relationship between status inequalities and power structures and economic position. The Warner approach focused on social and community beliefs and values as related to the amount of prestige attached to an occupation and source of income, while it ignored the actual amount of income. The approach was based on subjective appraisals of an individual's social position. The Lynds had advocated an alternate position, arguing that an individual's or family's position within the actual economic processes determined class position. From the very beginning of their studies of inequality, American sociologists were unable to agree on the basis and nature of social class.

The Structural Functionalists:
Parsons, Davis, and Moore

The work of the Lynds and the Warner group was significant because the studies clearly demonstrated the existence of structured patterns of inequality in American society. Despite the widespread popular belief that the United States was a society without classes, in their own ways the Lynds and the Warner group demonstrated that there were indeed classes, and that class was an important part of social structure. Although there were important differences in how they understood the term "class" and what formed the basis of class differences, American sociologists subsequently had to address the issue of class. That issue was taken up by three well-known and important sociologists, Talcott Parsons, Kingsley Davis, and Wilbert E. Moore.

Talcott Parsons
Talcott Parsons first addressed the issue of social stratification in 1940 and continued to explore the issue in his subsequent work. Not surprisingly, his explanation of social inequalities follows the overall logic of the structural functionalist perspective.

Given that structural functionalism assumes that every society has at its core a complex set of values, norms, beliefs, ideas, and ideals that give the society its shape and character and serve as a major source of social stability and order, it follows that certain individual qualities or attributes will be highly valued and that others will be less valued. For example, in a particular society at a specific historical moment physical strength and endurance may be valued, while in another society at another moment in history people with intellectual prowess may be highly valued. Yet another society may consider the possession of material wealth to be most important and desirable.

As a result, in almost all societies certain people have come to attain a higher status, honour, or prestige than others. The opposite is also true, that there are some people whose characteristics and attributes are the opposite of those considered desirable or valued highly, and as a result those people are ranked lower in the social hierarchy. It is inevitable that there will be a system of status or prestige stratification. This hierarchy leads to structured inequalities in wealth and power. People who rank high on the prestige scale can use that position to acquire, enjoy, and maintain economic rewards and power.

Parsons's explanation of social stratification has become less important than other aspects of his work. However, as Peter Hamilton argues,

Parsons's line of thinking was important because of the direction it gave to structural functionalist thinking on the issue (1983: 88). Parsons continually argued that we must examine the functions that social phenomena play for the entire social system. The logic of this argument was adopted by Kingsley Davis and Wilbert E. Moore, who undertook an alternative way of analysing the function of social differentiation in a social system.

Kingsley Davis and Wilbert E. Moore

The seminal Davis and Moore essay, "Some Principles of Stratification," first published in 1945, has become the classical statement of the fundamentals of a structural functionalist explanation of social inequality. As the essay's title suggests, the authors developed an approach to why systems of stratification exist in most societies. They argued that modern complex societies are characterized by the existence of complicated and specialized institutions that contain various positions. That is, the institutions include a division of labour, with different roles attached to various positions. The reason why complex societies have stratification systems is related to the nature of these different roles or tasks.

As Davis and Moore pointed out, an examination of the different positions within most major complex institutions indicates that the positions are not all the same. They differ in a number of ways. Some of them are more important than others in terms of both the functioning of the institutions and, by implication, societal stability and survival. Some institutional positions are more pleasant than others, and some require special skills and training. If the institution is to operate at maximum efficiency, competent, committed, and qualified individuals must be attracted into the important, difficult, and less pleasant jobs. For example, within the structures of a modern university the job of president is usually considered to be important, difficult, and even – because it may on occasion involve firing or disciplining employees – unpleasant.

If the institutions that make up society are to function to the maximum benefit of society, some means of motivating individuals to take on the important, unpleasant, and difficult jobs must be developed. It is also important to develop a means of encouraging individuals to acquire the special skills and training that some of these jobs require. The question is, how can society motivate people to take on important, sometimes unpleasant jobs that may require the acquisition of special skills and training? The answer, according to Davis and Moore, is to develop a system of rewards.

Society has at its disposal, they argued, a number of different rewards it can allocate to entice or motivate individuals to take on the difficult and important jobs and acquire the necessary skills and training. Although Davis and Moore did not specify in detail what those rewards are, they did note that there are three different kinds of rewards. These relate to what they call things that contribute to "sustenance and comfort," things that contribute to "humor and diversion," and things that contribute to "self-respect and ego expansion" (1945: 65).

The Davis and Moore argument stimulated a major debate among social scientists, which eventually produced a further refinement of the precise nature of the rewards society allocates to individuals. The key for us here is their contribution to the study of social stratification: they systematically laid out what they thought were the reasons for and causes of social stratification. Their conclusion is quite simple: by providing a basis for motivating individuals to take important, difficult jobs that require the acquisition of special skills and training, social stratification performs a function for society. Not only is a system of social stratification functional for society, in all likelihood it is necessary and inevitable. In essence, Davis and Moore argued that without a system of unequal rewards, society would not be able to motivate people to take on those difficult and specialized jobs that are so important to society.

Davis and Moore Elaborated: Society's Reward System
After Davis and Moore presented their theory, an exchange took place between Davis and Melvin M. Tumin (Tumin [1953], 1974; Davis [1953], 1974). Others, such as Richard Simpson (1956) and Dennis Wrong (1959), also contributed to the ongoing discussion. Wrong's intervention raised a central issue in the developing functionalist approach, namely, what are the precise rewards that society has to allocate or offer? Wrong referred to power, prestige, and wealth as the central elements of the reward system, taking up a position that became an essential aspect of the emerging functionalist approach to social stratification.

In 1957 another functionalist, Bernard Barber, published a book that became a classic in the field. In *Social Stratification* Barber used arguments based on the work of both Parsons and Davis and Moore, pointing out that social stratification performs an integrative function. First, he suggested that the process of rewarding people for upholding or representing the values and norms of the community really serves to reinforce those very same values and norms. Second, he pointed out that a system of differential rewards is necessary to motivate people. Barber emphasized that prestige is the primary reward, with the other rewards being somehow related.

The precise nature of the connections between the various rewards was more fully developed in the following decade. In 1967 Melvin M. Tumin produced an important study in the prestigious "Foundations of Modern Sociology Series." Tumin's book, *Social Stratification: The Forms and Functions of Inequality*, presented a systematic account of the revisions that had been made to the functionalist theory of stratification. One of his most important points related to the system of rewards (Tumin, 1967: 40). The rewards that individuals receive can be classified, he suggested, under three general headings. First are the rewards related to property and material wealth. Second are those associated with power in society, which allow certain people to secure their will even when that will is opposed by others. Third are the rewards associated with psychic gratification or, to use language familiar to us by now, prestige and honour.

In the functionalist perspective, wealth, power, and prestige are the three essential rewards that, first, society allocates to those who excel in conduct that is socially desirable, and that, second, are used as motivation to ensure that some people are willing to perform socially important tasks that may be difficult, unpleasant, and require special skills and training. In their introduction to a book of readings on social stratification in Canada, James Curtis and William Scott (1979) made explicit reference to these three rewards, and their book includes sections examining each of the rewards. In his important analysis of social stratification in the United States, *The American Class System*, Daniel Rossides explicitly referred to the three dimensions of social stratification, which he refers to as class, prestige, and power. The position that the stratification system of Western society involves three dimensions or components has become a widely accepted tenet of functionalist theory, and Rossides's advice that these "areas" of inequality be considered analytically separate has been heeded (Rossides, 1976: 33).

The Dimensions of Social Stratification

Wealth and Income as Social Class

The first dimension of the stratification system relates to social divisions based on economic criteria. Within the functionalist perspective the terms "class" and "social class" are generally used when discussing the economic differences in people's lives. Although functionalist class analysis includes a large number of different positions, here we will focus on one example.

In *The American Class System*, Rossides used "class" to refer to social positions determined by economic criteria and forming recognizable groupings within the stratification system. Using economic criteria as the main determinant of a person's class position, supported by associated characteristics related to education and overall style of living, Rossides argued that there are five classes in America.

1. Upper class: very high incomes. Old established wealth and money. Owners of major corporations. 1-3 per cent of population.
2. Upper-middle class: high income. Upper-level professionals. Highest level of civil service and military. Corporate executives and owners of medium-sized national businesses. 10-15 per cent of population
3. Lower-middle class: average incomes and above. Small business owners. Lower-level professional, white-collar workers, small farmers, civil servants. Some modest personal savings. 30-35 per cent of population.
4. Working class: average incomes and below. Skilled and unskilled blue-collar workers in factories, mines, stores, and service industries. 40-45 per cent of population.
5. Lower class: income close to or below poverty level. Unemployed or seasonally and marginally employed. Some on social security. 20-25 per cent of population.

Rossides's criteria, which are quite general, tend to relate to income and how that income is earned. There is no implied relationship between the classes, other than the fact that the people at the top of the class system have or earn more income than those at the bottom; as a result the groupings exhibit different personal and lifestyle characteristics. Although Rossides does not make the argument, a more "pure" functionalist might argue that those near the top are in all likelihood being rewarded for the tasks they perform for society. According to this theory, the jobs of the high-income earners and the wealthy are by and large not only more important but also more difficult: they require special skills and training.

Prestige

There is a long tradition in North American sociology of viewing prestige or social honour as central to stratification analysis. The work of Parsons exemplifies this tradition. In more recent functionalist analysis prestige has come to be viewed as an analytically separate dimension of stratification, one of the rewards society has at its disposal. This argument holds that the status or prestige reward becomes built into the society's value system, and as a result we all come to know that being a Supreme Court justice or university president has more honour and prestige attached to it than being a logger or garbage handler. According to the logic of this theory, some of us are then willing to take on the "difficult, important jobs" and even stay in school for many years, in part because we know one day we will have a position that rewards us with social status or prestige. In their efforts to better understand the specifics of how social honour or prestige fits into the stratification system, sociologists have generally concentrated on *occupational prestige*, that is, the generally accepted social attitudes and values concerning different jobs and occupations.

In the United States, researchers have been interested in occupational prestige for at least four decades. In 1947 the National Opinion Research Center conducted a study of how Americans rated various occupations in terms of their prestige. The NORC investigation set the stage for a series of other works in the United States and Canada, and this research further developed our understanding of occupational prestige.

The various assessments of occupational prestige have all adopted a more or less similar approach. People are interviewed and asked to rank a variety of different occupations according to how they perceive the social standing or position of the occupation. On the basis of these various rankings, researchers look to find patterns and, given these patterns, establish a ranking of occupations. Significantly, the studies conducted in both the United States and Canada indicated a shared perception among the citizenry about the social standing of various occupations and led to a series of scales ranking various occupations according to prestige.

Rossides introduced a reproduction of part of the 1963 NORC occupational prestige ratings from the United States. Among the highest-rated occupations in this scale were U.S. Supreme Court justice, scientist, governor, and college professor. Among the lowest were janitor, soda fountain clerk, garbage collector, and shoe shiner (1976: 244-45).

Two major studies were conducted in Canada, one by Peter Pineo and John Porter (1967) and the other by Bernard Blishen (1967). In his study Blishen ranked 320 different occupations. In the top ten positions of this socio-economic index he placed chemical engineers, dentists, college professors, physicians and surgeons, geologists, mining engineers, lawyers, civil engineers, architects, and veterinarians. The bottom ten positions included spinners and twisters, weavers, teamsters, labourers, winders and reelers, sectionmen and trackmen, labourers in textiles, shoemakers, fish canners, and trappers (1967: 42, 50)

In addition to ranking occupations in a more or less systematic manner, sociologists have also examined other forms of stratification. Peter Pineo (1980) reported on how Canadians rank individuals from various national and ethnic groups. Similar studies have been conducted in the United States, with similar results (Ogmundson, 1990: 241).

The first two dimensions of the stratification system raise important questions. Can we conceive of an individual whose income and thus class position might be high, yet whose prestige position is much lower? Conversely, is it possible to think about an individual with a relatively low income, and thus a lower class position, but with a very high level of social honour or prestige? For instance, where on the scale of prestige would you place a wealthy individual widely recognized as a slum landlord, as compared to a member of the local clergy?

As important as occupational prestige or social honour may be, like income or wealth these elements are not the only rewards society has at its disposal. Some people relish the prestige attached to their positions, while others are more interested in what comes with a high income. Possibly, still others are satisfied with the power that comes with their position in the social scale.

Power

For centuries the issue of how to define and understand power in society has been at the centre of considerable debate within the social sciences. The question of power has been a particular thorn in the side of the functionalist tradition, because the discussion of power inevitably leads to the argument that power is concentrated in the hands of a ruling class, and this is a view that many functionalist sociologists have wanted to distance themselves from (Aron, 1966: 201).

In any case, in attempting to deal with the complex issue of power, functionalists tend to differentiate between personal or individual power and social or political power. The first level, that of the individual, emphasizes a person's position within a particular institution or set of statuses. The second level, that of society as a whole, emphasizes power as it occurs in the political system.

At the second, broader social level, power tends to be understood as political power, or, as Tumin stated, it relates to the ability to influence general social policy (1967: 41-42). The institutional order we call the political or the polity is the setting for decisions concerning general social policy and debates concerning broad social issues. Within the structural functionalist approach, one of the essential functions of the polity is the establishment of collective goals and objectives that influence and have an impact on the entire social structure (Dobriner, 1969: 122).

Authority

In functionalist thought, authority refers to the concept of *legitimate influence*, in which influence is understood as the capacity to affect the thinking and actions of another person or social grouping (Barber, 1957: 234).

In this sense, authority is seen as a relatively benign and necessary form of power. It is benign because it flows from or is located within formally established and socially sanctioned structures and relations. Functionalists tend to argue that authority is necessary in a modern industrial society because the complexity of most institutional orders requires a division of labour. In other words, complex institutions include job or task specializations, with some roles or positions being responsible for co-ordinating the overall operation of the institution. For example, according to functionalist thought, institutions like modern Western universities, with their intricate divisions of labour, require hierarchical decision-making. Functionalists would argue that for a university to perform its functions for society, some measure of authority must be granted to various positions to ensure that administrators administrate, teachers teach, cleaners clean, and students do their work. They apply the same logic to a variety of other institutions, from the family order to the economy.

Authority is not only necessary for the smooth operation of institutions but is also an important part of the social reward system. Some people find that the authority associated with a difficult position is a key part of their reward for undertaking that job. Functionalists could argue that one of the reasons why people are willing to take on difficult and important jobs requiring the acquisition of special skills and arduous training is because they know that eventually they will be rewarded with a measure of personal power (Tumin, 1967: 40-41). For functionalists, authority is the institutional dimension of power and the reward system; as such, it is necessary for institutional functioning, and in that sense its role is not particularly difficult to understand (Parsons, 1966: 249).

Within the functionalist approach there is broad acceptance of the necessity for the stratification or layering of relations of authority in complex societies. Bernard Barber states that because there are role differences and role specialization, some degree of stratification based on the authority of position is inevitable (1957: 232). But functionalists also maintain that the element of stratification does not mean society as a whole must be authoritarian or undemocratic. It is possible to have a society that has differential amounts of individual power and is also open, egalitarian, and democratic. Their explanation for this has to do with their particular understanding of the nature of the polity and political power.

Marxist Theories of Class

The structural functionalist approach, which was dominant in North American sociology from the mid-1930s through the 1960s, created a new subfield or subdiscipline – the study of stratification – through its varied attempts to answer the questions raised by social inequality. Although the different positions taken up were often subtle and complex, the structural functionalists did share a general set of premises and assumptions in their interpretations of the whys and hows of social stratification.

In the 1960s an alternative approach emerged as scholars began a systematic re-evaluation and re-examination of the ideas and theories of Marx. Through that process some of them hoped to separate or distance Marx's ideas and theories from their association with political regimes like the ones that had developed in the Soviet Union and Eastern Europe. Many neo-Marxists believed that Marx's name had become associated with governments that had nothing in common with Marx's original commitment to social criticism of capitalist society and the creation of a truly humane, free, and democratic society.

The broad stream of thought referred to as neo-Marxism encompasses a great many different theorists and thinkers who emphasized and focused on different aspects of Marx's work. Despite having some differences, the theorists' approaches have enough in common so that, as a way of beginning the process of understanding this mode of analysis, we can paint a general picture of their basic assumptions.

Marx's View of Class
There is perhaps no more important concept for Marxist and neo-Marxist social analysis than the concept of class. The reasons for this are closely related to the general analytical approach taken up by the thinkers who have followed a Marxian approach.

Marx, and later his followers, approached the study of society by adopting a materialist approach. An essential tenet of both the classical and contemporary versions of Marxism is the assumption that the most important human social activity is material production; and all Marxists insist that the most appropriate point of departure for social analysis is an investigation of the society's economic order. A society's economic basis is itself determined by the stage of development reached by that society's productive forces (its level of technological and scientific development) and its social relations of production (the patterns of ownership and control of the productive forces).

The Two Major Classes

Marx examined the social relations of production in the most advanced capitalist society of his day, Britain, investigating the patterns of ownership and control of the society's productive resources. He concluded that capitalist societies are by definition class societies. In a capitalist society, he found, there are some people who own and control the factories, mines, mills, and other productive resources, and these people receive income and make a living by virtue of that ownership of productive property. But not everyone in capitalist society owns a share of the society's productive resources. Indeed, most people survive only by selling the one thing they do own, something they can sell again and again, day after day, month after month, year after year: their capacity to work, known as their labour power.

The people who own the society's productive resources (or at least hold some share in them) are usually not in a position to operate those resources themselves. They require the help of others, and that help is supplied by wage labourers. Both groups – those who own society's productive resources and those who do not – exist in a symbiotic relationship: each needs the other in order to survive. Those selling labour power require someone who needs to purchase labour power, and those wanting to purchase labour power require someone who offers labour power for sale. The key to Marx's understanding of class is his analysis of the relationship between these two classes.

Marx used several different terms to refer to these two main social groups. He referred to the owners of society's productive resources as the capitalist class, the bourgeoisie, the owning class, and capital. He referred to the others who sell their labour power as the working class, the proletariat, or labour. In addition, when Marx wrote of ownership of property he was not referring to personal property such as houses, clothing, or other purely personal items; rather, he meant the productive resources of society, which are by definition part of the economic infrastructure that produces and distributes wealth.

Surplus Value and Exploitation

For neo-Marxists, a key question is: What is the essential nature of the relationship between the capitalist class and the working class? For Marx the answer was: it is a relationship of exploitation. The capitalists, by virtue of their ownership of a portion of society's productive resources, are in a structural position to exploit the working class, and they do so because of how the entire economic system works. The key to Marx's explanation of why and how the capitalist class exploits the working class is found in the concept of surplus value and his understanding of the key dynamic of capitalist society.

Capitalism is, Marx contended, a system predicated on the assumption that the most important goal in life for those with money is to use that money to make more money. In a capitalist society those with wealth do not merely "sit on their laurels" and enjoy what they have; rather, they take their wealth and invest it with the objective of eventually accumulating even more wealth. For Marx, the central dynamic of capitalism is the accumulation of wealth on an expanding scale.

To understand the essence of Marx's analysis of class relations, we must bear in mind that he was examining an industrial capitalist society in which the most effective way for an individual with money to make more money was to invest in some form of industrial production. Marx argued that investing in industrial production involves the purchase of certain commodities with the ultimate objective of turning a profit. The key to the process, he maintained, was to be found in the nature of the commodities purchased by the capitalist class.

When people with capital invest their money in an industrial enterprise, they purchase several different kinds of commodities. First, they must acquire a factory within which production can occur. Next, they must acquire raw materials that can form the basis of the manufacturing process, and they need machines and technology they can use to process the raw materials into a final product. But, according to Marx, if investors just purchase these three types of commodities they find that rather than making money they lose money, because raw materials and machines sitting in a factory cannot by themselves produce profits. Before they can create the basis for profits, investors must purchase the additional, and most vital, commodity required in the productive process: labour power. To make a profit the owner of capital must bring together the raw materials, machines, and labour power in a factory. Once they have assembled these commodities, the capitalists produce and sell new commodities (the factory output) and thereby make more money.

For Marx, a major interest was the precise nature of the process by which industrial capitalists were able to make money by hiring workers to run their factories. Who actually produced the wealth that the owners were able to claim as profits? His answer to the question might be easier to understand through an example. Assume for a moment that I am in possession of a substantial sum of money and I want to invest it so I will make more money. Further, I have determined that an investment opportunity exists in the manufacture of a new style of jogging shoe. I go out and invest by purchasing all the necessary raw materials, a factory, and the necessary machinery and technology. I find out that the total daily costs of my raw materials will be $40, and the payments on my factory and depreciation on my machines will cost another $20 a day.

Lastly, I hire students to work in my factory. The agreement I make with them specifies that I must pay them $10 an hour for an eight-hour day. Suppose that in eight hours of work they create eight pairs of shoes. At the end of eight hours they get $80 and I get the eight pairs of shoes. If I go out and sell the eight pairs of shoes for $10 each and realize a total return of $80, I will be losing money, because at that price I have not been able to recover my costs of production.

We live in a capitalist society, so I am not involved in the productive process just because I want to provide people with jobs; I am involved because I want to make money, and if I am not making money I will shut my factory down, sell the assets, and invest somewhere else. So let's assume a different outcome, one that will enable me to continue in production. Assume that I sell the shoes for $20 each. After I sell the shoes I have $160. Given the total daily costs of my raw materials and the payments on my factory and depreciation on my machines, at the end of the day my balance sheet looks like the following table:

Total value of commodities produced:	
8 pairs of shoes @ $20 each	$160
Total costs of production:	
Wages for labour power	$80
Raw material costs	40
Depreciation and factory costs	20
Total	$140
Subtract from total value of commodities produced	$160
the total costs of production	-140
Equals surplus value appropriated by capital	$20

The origin and disposition of the surplus that arises out of this productive process were, for Marx, the key to understanding the nature of class in a capitalist society. Marx used the term *surplus value* to describe this amount, arguing that although surplus value is in fact produced by the working class through their productive activity, it ends up being appropriated by the capitalist class. The production of surplus value by the working class and its appropriation by the capitalist class form the basis of class exploitation. The working class is exploited because they work and labour to produce and create wealth, which is subsequently claimed and appropriated by another class.

Marx concluded, then, that capitalism is, by definition, a class society and relations of exploitation are a basic and fundamental characteristic of this class structure. The two classes must be understood in terms of the different structural positions they occupy in the economic institutions. The method of defining and understanding these classes is quite different from the method used in stratification theory. It is not that the owners necessarily have or make more money that puts them in a different class position; it is their different structural position in the economic order.

Other Classes in Marx's Schema

Although Marx believed that understanding the relationship between the capitalist class and the working class was essential to understanding the overall dynamics of the system, he never claimed these were the only classes. In fact, there has been a good deal of debate among those interested in Marx's analysis about just how many other classes he thought there were. The last volume of his major work, *Capital*, breaks off just when he was about to begin to engage in a systematic analysis of the class structure of his society. At that point he refers to four major classes. In addition to what have sometimes been called the two great classes, Marx also referred to the landlords and the petty bourgeoisie.

The landlords essentially represent a remnant of the previous mode of economic organization, feudalism, although they had been an important part of the processes involved in the initial development of capitalism. The petty bourgeoisie are in a structural location between the capitalist class and the working class. Like the major capitalist class the petty bourgeoisie own productive resources, but the magnitude or size of those resources is limited, and they are able to operate those productive resources themselves or with the aid of unpaid labour (such as family labour). The capacity to engage in some productive activity without the employment of paid wage labour is an essential characteristic of the petite bourgeoisie and an important difference between them and the major capitalist class. Also, unlike the working class, the petite bourgeoisie do not have to sell their labour power in order to make a living. Their income comes from the small productive resources they own; however, the fact that they are able to operate these resources themselves, without paid labour, means that, unlike the capitalist class, they do not directly exploit the working class.

How Many Classes?

No attempt at class analysis has caused as much debate and controversy as Marx's. There are a number of reasons for this, one of them related to the political implications of his analysis. Marx concluded that class relations involve more than an unequal distribution of wealth: they also involve relations of domination, subordination, exploitation, and even a lack of real freedom for the subordinate classes. The other reason Marx's analysis has stimulated a lot of debate is because it was unfinished – interrupted by his death in 1883.

At no point in any of his works do we find an adequate theory of class. As Bertell Ollman (1968) pointed out, there are a number of seemingly contradictory statements about class scattered throughout Marx's work. A common theme is the argument that the basis of a person's class position must be understood in terms of the social organization of material production. Class positions are determined by structural positions in the economic order; however, there is some confusion relating to the question of the number of classes in a capitalist society. Statements can be found in Marx that there are two, four, and even more than ten classes – the last kind of statement being found in historically specific analyses such as those dealing with the political events in France in the early 1850s (Marx [1852], 1972). In those historical works he referred to many different subclasses within the major capitalist, petty-bourgeois, and working classes. Marx used the term *fraction* to refer to internal class divisions based on economic interests. For example, he argued that the capitalist class is subdivided into industrialists, bankers, financiers, and large-scale merchants. He argued that in the end class analysis is meaningful only when it is carried out in the context of a specific historical social structure. Marx was interested in understanding class structures and dynamics in real historical circumstances and not in producing abstract schemas and theories.

What do we make of Marx's seeming confusion? There are two possibilities. One is simply that he was confused and could not decide how many classes there were. The other is that he was examining classes at different levels of abstraction, and when he worked at a very abstract level, as in writing *Capital*, he was only trying to provide a theoretical view of the most general features of capitalist society. At this high level of abstraction his discussion of class was limited to an enunciation of the general principles upon which class membership is based. In other more historical and empirical works he elaborated on those abstract principles, painting in the actual details of an historically situated, concrete society. Performing social analysis at this lower level of abstraction, that is, of a particular society at a specific moment in time, led him to make refinements to his general and abstract theory. He still understood classes primarily in terms of people's position in the economic structures, but he then tried to account for and describe specific historically determined internal divisions within the various classes.

In either case, as far as providing a solid and well-developed basis for subsequent class analysis, the legacy of Marx was laced with a good deal of confusion. For this reason, Western scholars interested in re-examining Marx and separating his approach from the stultified dogma of "official Marxism" began to revise and update his approach to class.

Neo-Marxism and Class Analysis

The decades of the 1970s and 1980s saw the emergence of a number of new approaches in the study of class from within the Marxian tradition. The neo-Marxist approach accepted many of the basic premises and assumptions of Marx's overall approach, although also arguing that revisions were necessary to make his analysis relevant to late twentieth-century capitalist society (Baran and Sweezy, 1966). Significantly, many of the scholars attempting to revise Marx disagreed with one another, and as a result a variety of schools or approaches emerged within the general approach that we are calling neo-Marxism. Among the central issues of contention and disagreement was the question of how the class structure of capitalist society had changed in the hundred or more years since Marx had studied it – or of what the concept of class meant in advanced capitalist society.

Classes and Class Fractions

One of the many attempts to further elaborate on and develop the legacy of Marx involved the rethinking of Marx's notion of class fractions. In *Marx and History*, D. Ross Gandy provided a concise summary of an updated Marxian understanding of class. Gandy noted that a Marxist understanding of class involves the explicit recognition that nowhere does Marx himself provide a systematic account of class. He also suggested that a Marxist conception of class must locate and define classes in terms of positions within the economic structures and processes (1979: 96).

Central to the Marxian approach is the recognition of the existence of three main classes in an industrial capitalist society. In typical Marxian fashion, Gandy used the terms "bourgeoisie," "petty bourgeoisie," and "proletariat" to refer to the three major classes in capitalist society. He stated the importance of recognizing the existence of these classes, but he also argued for the importance of recognizing internal divisions within them. Within the bourgeoisie, for example, Gandy saw key differences between people with investments in different sectors of the economy such as industrial production, finance, banking, and merchandising. Each of those fractions has different economic interests and concerns that can lead to situations of conflict. For instance, with the issue of rent controls the different sectors of the capitalist class may take up different positions. An industrialist may be in favour of rent controls because they decrease the cost of living for workers, thus producing less upward pressure on wages. An investor in real estate would undoubtedly be opposed to rent controls.

Similarly, within the ranks of the petty bourgeoisie there are many different economic positions or fractions – farmers, small merchants, independent artisans, self-employed professionals – that must be accounted for in any class analysis.

The last major class, the working class or proletariat, can also be divided internally, and the many different occupations and levels of skills must be accounted for in class analysis. Gandy noted the potential for the emergence of divisions within the proletariat between workers in different areas of production.

Gandy also discussed the role of additional classes in society. In addition to the three major classes, he noted that social analysis must take into account the existence of people not directly involved in productive activities. What he refers to as vagabonds, beggars, thieves, and others making a living more or less illegally are commonly referred to as the *lumpenproletariat*, and they, too, have to be accounted for because they play a role in society.

The potential role of the lumpenproletariat raises a central point in Marxian class analysis. Marx was first and foremost a revolutionary. He was interested in understanding society so it could be changed in a manner that would allow the vast majority who he believed laboured under exploitative and alienating conditions to be truly free. For Marx, class analysis had as its objective an understanding of the political and material interests of different classes. Such an analysis would make it possible to determine which classes and groupings had an interest in changing the existing social order – and thus to understand what kinds of political positions and actions the various classes might adopt. Social criticism aimed at social change remains a vital aspect of neo-Marxist social analysis.

C.H. Anderson's Subclasses

Not all scholars working within the Marxian tradition used the notion of class fractions in their efforts to elaborate on Marx's analysis of class.

In *The Political Economy of Social Class* (1974) C.H. Anderson argued for the need to refine Marx's rather simplistic schema. He maintained that class distinctions are based on the ownership of productive property and on the income source, but he also suggested that what occurs in an advanced capitalist society is the emergence of new classes, including a new working class composed of white-collar workers. These members of the working class are different from the traditional Marxian industrial working class. While they do sell their capacity to work in order to make a living, they also work in production-related scientific and technical jobs as opposed to directly productive ones on the factory floor (Anderson, 1974: 125). Anderson also referred to a service-producing class made up, for example, of workers involved in providing health and educational services. Finally, he discussed the class position of those directly tied to the capitalist class, whose income is dependent on providing various services to that class. In this class, which he called subcapitalist, Anderson included lawyers, accountants, and financial managers.

In his approach Anderson developed an analysis that involved the examination of the emergence of new classes in industrial capitalist society. He did not really provide an adequate explanation of the precise basis for those new subclasses, but his work pointed in a new direction that was to be explored by a number of other scholars.

Nicos Poulantzas and Non-Productive Labour

The work of Nicos Poulantzas (1936-79) is commonly associated with a stream of Marxian thought referred to as French structuralism. Poulantzas (1975) argued that the major development in the class structure of capitalist society since Marx's time was the emergence not of a new working class but of a new petty bourgeoisie. He insisted on the necessity of defining the working class strictly in terms of the concept of exploitation. The working class are those people who produce actual commodities and in so doing produce surplus value; therefore they are exploited by capital in the process of production. It is not the selling of labour power that determines class but whether or not a person engages in the production of surplus value. That is, class depends on whether a person engages in what Poulantzas refers to as *productive labour*, defined as the labour that is involved in physical production of commodities. It is as a result of doing productive labour that a person is directly exploited by the capitalist class.

For Poulantzas, some of the workers Anderson had discussed, such as managers, teachers, health workers, and commercial and service workers, are not members of the working class. These people do not produce commodities and therefore do not produce surplus value and are not exploited in a manner similar to the productive workers. Because these others do not fit into any of the traditional Marxian classes, Poulantzas suggested that they could be best understood as composing a new class, the new petty bourgeoisie. He suggested that there are four basic classes plus various class fractions in a capitalist society. But his arguments were not widely accepted.

E.O. Wright and Contradictory Class Locations

Erik Olin Wright was one of many to develop a critique of Poulantzas. In addition, he developed an alternative way of understanding the class structures of advanced capitalist society. Wright's revision of Marx was more radical, that is, it went deeper and more to the core, than the work of either Anderson or Poulantzas. Interestingly, after developing this alternative approach during the late 1970s Wright became engaged in a process of self-criticism that led to the rejection of his initial arguments (Wright, 1985).

Wright's first published efforts to reformulate Marx were based on a re-examination of the basis of class (see Wright, 1978). He argued that class membership is primarily determined by three factors: control over investment and resources; control over the actual physical production of commodities; and control over the labour power of others. On the basis of these factors he postulated that there were three major classes in capitalist society: the traditional Marxian bourgeoisie (controls all three factors); the proletariat (controls none of the three); and the petty bourgeoisie (controls some investments/resources and some production but not the labour power of others). What was important about Wright's argument was his contention that between the major classes were smaller classes occupying what he called *contradictory class locations*: groupings that do not fit into any of the major classes. Wright suggested there were at least three major contradictory class locations.

Between the bourgeoisie and the petty bourgeoisie Wright located a class of small employers. This class position represents those who own enough productive resources to require the hiring of wage labour to operate their enterprises, but whose holdings are not equivalent to that of large-scale capital, which dominates the economy. Small employers represent a distinctive class because they have economic and political interests that are distinct from any of the other major classes, although at certain times and on certain issues they might form alliances with other classes. Small employers form a contradictory class position between the bourgeoisie and the petty bourgeoisie.

Wright suggested that there are two additional contradictory class locations, one between the bourgeoisie (capital) and the working class and the other between the working class and the petty bourgeoisie. He locates managers, supervisors, and technocrats between capital and the working class. This class position involves control over the actual process of production on a daily basis, but no fundamental control over investment decisions. People in this class do not share exactly any of the features of the other classes and warrant being recognized as a distinctive class. Finally, Wright suggested that people who work sometimes for themselves and sometimes as wage labourers should be understood as occupying a contradictory class location between the petty bourgeoisie and the working class. Wright's work stimulated considerable response and debate as part of a continuing neo-Marxist effort to develop an adequate approach to class in advanced capitalist society.

Although the work of Gandy, Anderson, Poulantzas, and Wright represents only a small sample of the positions taken up in the neo-Marxist literature, these few sketches should help to illustrate the nature of the discussion of class within the Marxist tradition. Above all, neo-Marxists understand class in terms of people's positions in society's economic structures and not in terms of stratified positions in a continuum. In addition, the theoretical approach of neo-Marxism also sees class as being systematically related to even larger patterns and processes of domination and subordination.

The Study of Social Inequality in Canada: New Directions in Class Analysis

For the past several decades the study of social inequality in Canada has been an important element in Canadian sociology. A number of scholars have engaged in an analysis of social class in Canada, and their diverse work illustrates the relationship between abstract debate and the actual practice of sociological analysis. Not only have some of these theorists attempted to further develop the existing approaches, but also in some cases they have worked to synthesize ideas from different perspectives.

John Porter's Vertical Mosaic

In 1965 John Porter's *The Vertical Mosaic: An Analysis of Social Class and Power in Canada* appeared, and the over-600-page book soon became a classic in Canadian sociology. Its basic approach is more in the tradition of elite theory than class analysis. Porter suggested that the development of capitalism during the twentieth century had changed the nature of the system Marx studied and that, as a result of developments such as institutional specialization, power not property should become the focus of studies of inequality.

Porter argued that we recognize people with power as forming elites and those without power as forming the non-elites (1965: 27). Because the elites form the group with power, they are important factors in shaping and influencing the general development and character of society. Porter used this basic tenet of elite theory to study the major elites he found to be controlling Canadian society. He investigated their family backgrounds, attitudes and values, social connections, education backgrounds, religious affiliations, and ethnic and national backgrounds. His findings proved surprising to many Canadians.

Porter suggested that there are five important elites in Canada: economic, political, bureaucratic, ideological, and labour. These elites represent people in the key decision-making or power positions in key institutions in Canada. The economic elite is made up of the major decision-makers in the corporate sector. The political elite is composed of federal cabinet ministers, provincial premiers, and top members of the judiciary in Canada. The bureaucratic elite is composed of the top decision-makers in the federal public service and administrative structures. The ideological elite includes those in control of the mass media, as well as top decision-makers in the educational sector and the major churches. The labour elite is made up of top labour leaders, that is, the heads of major unions and labour federations.

The data that Porter presented illustrate two important facts about these elites. First, with the possible exception of the labour elite, the membership of the various elites is drawn from a narrow sector of the population. In essence, Porter concluded that the majority of elite members were white Anglo-Saxon men with middle-class and upper-class backgrounds. Second, there seems to be a pattern of systematic interaction among elite members – not only with members of their own elite but also with member of other elites. The general picture is of a society dominated and run by a relatively small number of powerful people who have common backgrounds, values, and education and who are not representative of most Canadians.

Porter's work remains extremely important for several reasons, not the least of which is the response it stimulated from other scholars.

Wallace Clement: From Elite Theory to Class Analysis

Exactly ten years after *The Vertical Mosaic* came out, the results of research that in part updated Porter's study were published. In *The Canadian Corporate Elite: An Analysis of Economic Power*, Wallace Clement continued to look at the roles of power and class in Canada, but what was different about Clement's work was his greater focus on the issue of economic power and his use of both class and elite analysis. He examined both those in command or in positions of power in the major corporations in Canada and the role of the media and of the elite that controls the media. Clement noted that economic power was becoming more and more concentrated; as a result the role of the economic elite was becoming more and more important. Clement also discussed the existence of divisions within the economic elite: between the people who controlled Canadian corporations (the indigenous elite) and the ones who controlled branch plants of multinational corporations in Canada (the comprador elite).

Like Porter, Clement found that there is anything but open recruitment into the corporate or economic elite. The elite tends to be drawn from specific class, ethnic, national, religious, and regional backgrounds. There were still important similarities in educational background and continuing interactions at both formal and informal levels. By formal levels of interaction, Clement was referring to the tendency for various elite members to sit on each other's corporate boards of directors.

Clement became one of Canada's most productive scholars. His second book, *Continental Corporate Power* (1977), was dedicated to John and Marion Porter and studied the economic and corporate linkages between Canada and the United States. Later, in a collection of essays called *The Challenge of Class Analysis* (1988), Clement made it clear that in his opinion some form of class analysis continues to be an essential part of any adequate sociological approach to Canadian society. Clement's approach to class, as shown in these essays, is very much influenced by the neo-Marxist approach. He defined class largely in terms of property, noting that there continue be two major classes in Canada, capitalists and workers, along with a declining petty bourgeoisie (1988: 171). Clement also noted that within these classes there are fractions or economic divisions, although he said the precise nature of these divisions would only become apparent when researchers engaged in concrete, historical investigation of the dynamics of class in Canada.

Similarly, the argument that the Marxian legacy is still the most appropriate approach to class analysis continues to inform the work of a number of other Canadian scholars, although not all of them explicitly adopt a Marxian framework.

The Canadian Class Structure: Forcese and Veltmeyer

The fact that Dennis Forcese's *The Canadian Class Structure* has gone through several updatings since its original publication in 1975 attests to its importance and acceptance by Canadian social scientists. Forcese argues that social inequality is a fundamental fact of life in Canada, although he does not explicitly spell out what theoretical approach he thinks is most appropriate. His analysis is that social class has to do with wealth, prestige, and power – and the resources those elements command (1975: 13). He notes that measuring social class is a difficult task, but that wealth seems to be the key factor (15). Wealth, he further argues, is tied to occupation and property; but because meaningful class analysis must take place at the micro level, we must also take into account local dimensions, city/farm relations, regionalism, ethnicity, and gender.

Forcese demonstrates that the reality of class is manifested in issues as diverse as the level of our health care, our daily quality of life, how we are affected by the processes of crime and the operation of the justice system, and our quality of living or working conditions as well as our religious and political attitudes and level of education. Forcese suggests that a Marxian approach is a good point of departure; but by presenting a wealth of important data he also illustrates the complexity of class, warning us not to adopt a simple abstract schema. His book reminds us that class analysis is ultimately about the real world and therefore must proceed on the basis of an approach that is capable of recognizing the complexities of that world.

While Forcese tends to use but not elaborate on the theoretical boundaries of a Marxian approach, Henry Veltmeyer explicitly attempts to present a systematic neo-Marxist approach to social class. In *Canadian Class Structure* (1986) Veltmeyer presents a systematic revision of Marx, arguing that class position is determined by whether a person, first, owns property or the means of production, second, sells labour power, and, third, controls the labour power of others. A fourth determinant is a person's source of livelihood (1986: 16). On the basis of these economic criteria Veltmeyer suggests that there are three major economic classes: the bourgeoisie or capitalist class, the petty bourgeoisie or middle class, and the proletariat or working class (21). In addition, he suggests that we must recognize the existence of internal class sectors or subclasses. In Canada this means dividing the bourgeoisie into the monopoly and lieutenant sectors and the petty bourgeoisie into the small business, independent producer, managerial, and professional sectors. Finally, the working class can be divided into the semi-professional, office, service, and productive sectors (25).

In addition to these major classes, which are defined primarily by economic criteria, Veltmeyer notes that some members of the working class, such as older and younger workers, are often not in the labour force at particular moments. As well, there is a major marginalized class called, in Marxian fashion, the lumpenproletariat. This group is made up of those more or less permanently out of the labour force, on relief, and otherwise destitute.

Throughout his book Veltmeyer makes clear that for him the real purpose of class analysis is to assist in the process of understanding and explaining the dynamics of Canadian society. He indicates that a correct analysis of economic classes can form an important part of how we come to understand the real lives of real people (1986: 107).

Toward a Synthesis: Hunter and Grabb

Alfred A. Hunter's *Class Tells: On Social Inequality in Canada* (1981) illustrates an important direction for class analysis in Canada. The book outlines the major competing theoretical perspectives in the areas of class and stratification analysis. It also presents a massive amount of empirical data on economic, gender, and ethnic inequality in Canada. By examining issues such as the role of merit in determining income level and the relationship between inequality and education, Hunter demonstrates how social inequality influences virtually every dimension of our lives. The book also contains an overview of the historical emergence of class in Canada and the relationship between class and political activities.

As the title implies, one of Hunter's major points is the fact that class does indeed *tell*, that is, it influences virtually every aspect of our being. Although Hunter summarizes the major perspectives, he does not overtly embrace or adopt either a Marxian or structural functionalist approach; but in his conclusion, having demonstrated the importance and persuasiveness of structured inequality, he does use some concepts usually associated with the neo-Marxist perspective. He reminds us that structured inequality is a dynamic and changing phenomenon and that the historical record shows that some classes come into being while others fade away and become less important. Hunter's study implies that no matter what approach we use, we must be capable of dealing with the complexities of economic, gender, and ethnic inequalities.

One of the most ambitious attempts to develop a fresh approach to the study of social inequality is found in the work of Edward Grabb. In *Theories of Social Inequality* (1990) Grabb presents a systematic overview of various classical and contemporary perspectives. After introducing students of society to these debates Grabb argues that the study of economic inequality must be integrated with an analysis of power and domination. He suggests that once we do this we will realize that control over economic matters is but one aspect of inequality. In addition to economic power and control, we must account for political power and domination as well as ideological power and domination.

Grabb does not argue for a three-dimensional system, as in orthodox functionalism; it is clear that he is interested in the phenomenon of social domination and power as it unfolds through a class system in a capitalist society that is, at its core, based on three classes. For Grabb the three classes are the upper class, a heterogeneous middle class, and a working class, although he does not provide a detailed account of the basis of his class positions. Grabb ends his book by reminding us of the importance of moving beyond economic analysis to understanding the nature of gender inequalities as well other structured inequalities that are related to ethnic and national considerations.

Toward an Alternative Materialist Approach

If we assume that the most appropriate mode of analysis for understanding the class structures of our society is one that directs our attention to the economic structures, it makes sense to look to both Marx and Weber for insights into how to conceptualize and understand class. In recent years two important groups of authors have attempted to use both Marx and Weber as the basis for an understanding of class in capitalist society (Clegg, Boreham, and Dow, 1986; Bilton *et al.*, 1987).

The class structure of capitalist society is understandable in terms of the organization of material production and distribution. A central characteristic of capitalist economic structures is the role of the market in the distribution of wealth. People's claim to a share of society's wealth is fundamentally determined by their positions within the structures of the market. Their positions within the structures of the market in turn depend on the resources they bring to the market. Some people come to the market in possession of wealth and capital, and as a result they become the owners of the major productive resources of society. Such people can be designated as the corporate ruling or upper class (Clegg, Boreham, and Dow, 1986: ch. 5; Bilton *et al.*, 1987: 55). This class enjoys economic power and is able to accumulate the major share of the social surplus. While there can be important divisions within the ranks of this class – between, for example, those who control the banking sector and those who dominate the manufacturing sector – we cannot specify the nature of such divisions except by examining a specific society.

The other major class that shares in the ownership of society's productive capacities is the petty bourgeoisie. According to Stewart Clegg and his co-authors it is more useful to distinguish the petty bourgeoisie from the corporate ruling class by the scale of operation involved than by the strict Marxian distinction between those who employ and those who do not employ labour. Clegg, Boreham, and

Dow suggest that the petty bourgeoisie can be best understood as those employing less than ten employees, arguing that such a number indicates a scale of enterprise that results in a different capacity to claim social surplus and thus accumulate wealth.

In addition to the corporate ruling or upper class and the petty bourgeoisie, there is the new middle class. Clegg, Boreham, and Dow suggest that this is a heterogeneous class made up of numerous different occupational positions. The common thread is that all these structural positions tend to help the corporate ruling class or some sections of the petty bourgeoisie realize or claim their portion of the social surplus. In addition, the middle class facilitates the reproduction of the conditions necessary for continued social stability. Tony Bilton and his co-authors note the existence of a middle class broadly made up of those who bring non-manual skills to the market. As a result these people are in a position to claim greater economic rewards than those who bring manual skills to the market; they can thereby increase their chances of claiming economic benefits.

Both the Clegg and Bilton books note that in capitalist society one of the largest classes is the working class. In the abstract Clegg, Boreham, and Dow refer to the working class as the sellers of labour power who produce the economic wealth in society. According to Bilton and his co-authors, the working class is comprised of non-owners of wealth who bring mostly manual skills to the market. Again, both books agree that there will be internal splits and differences based on factors such as the level of skills and the specific occupation, but all such splits and internal divisions must be examined within the context of a particular society.

What these scholars are attempting to do is provide a conceptual map or guide to assist in the understanding of class in modern capitalist society. The precise nature of the classes – their internal divisions, histories, patterns of development, and relationships with each other and the state – is a central issue that must be addressed. But this central issue has to be addressed in the context of an analysis of a specific society.

In the end these conceptions of class structure will prove to be useful only if we can apply them to the concrete investigation of class formation and struggle in a particular society. After all, the final test of the adequacy of any theoretical construction is its usefulness in facilitating empirical and historical analysis. We must always ask ourselves, to what extent does this theory help us make sense of the complexities of class in our society? The challenge for students, then, is to take these ideas and apply them to the study of class in their own society.

Terms and Concepts

Stratification theory – associated with the functionalist perspective, assumes that individuals in society are layered or arranged in strata. According to the stratification theorists, there are three quite distinct dimensions of the stratification system: class, status, and power.

Class – based largely on income (amount or source), a category of people who share similar economic characteristics. The relationship between different classes is usually understood in terms of a layering situation in which one class has more income and is placed higher in a hierarchy while another class has less income and is ranked lower. There is no implied antagonistic relationship between and among classes. The terms lower, middle, upper-middle, upper, and so on are typically used.

Status – perhaps more appropriately called social prestige or honour; not necessarily related to class, although it is often associated with an occupation. Surveys have shown that people rank some occupations with quite low incomes as more prestigious and carrying more social honour, and therefore as more desirable than others with higher incomes. Members of the clergy are typically cited as examples of people with high status but low incomes.

Power – when viewed at the individual level, power is associated with a person's position in a particular institution. To function properly many institutions contain a division of labour, and not all positions within the institution contain equal amounts of authority and power. Some people will accept a position because of the power and authority it carries.

Surplus value – in Marxian theory, the difference between the total costs of producing a commodity and the amount that the capitalist gets for the commodity. If the total costs (including labour costs, raw materials, depreciation on machinery, and factory costs) of producing a car were $10,000 and the company producing the car sold it for $12,000, the difference ($2,000) is the surplus value. According to the Marxian perspective, because this wealth was produced by the workers who actually made the car but goes to the owners of the company, the appropriation of this surplus wealth is the basis of class exploitation.

Exploitation – used to describe the process by which the owning or capitalist class appropriates wealth produced by the working class. According to the Marxian perspective, the real producers of wealth are those who actually engage in productive activities in the mines, mills, and factories. It is the labour power of the working class that produces the commodities; however, the workers receive only a portion of the wealth they produce in the form of wages, while the difference between the total costs of production and the amount the capitalists get for the commodity (surplus value) is appropriated by capital. The appropriation of surplus value is the basis of class exploitation.

Capitalist class – usually associated with Marxian class analysis; those who, in a capitalist society, own and control the society's productive and distributive resources, that is, the factories, mills, mines, as well as the financial and distributive capacities. Other terms are also used, including bourgeoisie, capital, and owning class.

Working class – as opposed to the capitalist class, the term used within Marxian theory to refer to those who do not own and control any productive and distributive resources within capitalist society. In order to make a living the working class, or proletariat, is forced to sell its labour power, and within the productive process these workers end up being both alienated and exploited. In Marx's view the proletariat was the class with an interest in radical social change and thus in ending the exploitation and alienation inherent in the capitalist relations of production.

Fraction – originally used by Marx in the context of class analysis: an internal division within a major class based on some economic criterion. For example, the bourgeoisie might be subdivided into an industrial fraction (ownership of major industrial enterprises), a resource-capital fraction (major investors in resource and extractive industries), a financial fraction (banking, insurance, and financial services), and a commercial fraction (both wholesale and retail businesses). Similarly, the petty bourgeoisie and the capitalist class might be internally divided.

Petite bourgeoisie – along with the capitalist class and the working class, the third major class in a classical Marxian class schema. The petty bourgeoisie are owners of some productive resources, but unlike the capitalist class the resources they own are so small that they tend not to require hired labour to operate them. Unlike the working class the petty bourgeoisie do not sell their labour power. The classical example of the petty bourgeoisie is farmers who own the productive resources and produce goods with their own and unpaid family labour.

Lumpenproletariat – as used by Marx, those people who are in a sense outside the normal productive arrangements in society. Made up of people without regular incomes who live off crime or by begging, or by wandering about with no systematic role in society. The political role of the lumpenproletariat was worrisome to Marx because they could not be counted on by the proletariat to assist in ending class rule, alienation, and exploitation in capitalist society.

10

THE POLITY
AND POLITICAL POWER

Although the study of the polity – of the structures, operation, and processes of government and social decision-making – is usually deemed to be within the purview of political science, sociologists have always maintained a keen interest in the issue. The study of the polity is more than the study of political parties and voting patterns. It includes the social decision-making process – a process that has an impact on every member of a society.

Complex modern industrial societies have developed or evolved formal mechanisms and political structures to facilitate social decision-making. In most Western societies these structures are among the most visible, complex, and formal institutions. The polity is often formally structured and organized on the basis of codified rules and procedures called constitutions; and these constitutions are really just sets of rules and regulations that govern the structures and processes of social decision-making. Most often sociologists leave the study of the formal constitutional arrangements and processes to the political scientists and focus instead on the functions of the polity and the social dynamics of the decision-making process.

The polity performs a series of essential social tasks. The process of social decision-making includes setting a number of general and specific social goals, priorities, and initiatives. Social policy can include everything from domestic issues such as the availability of unemployment insurance and abortion to spending on education. Social policy issues can also include matters as different as international relations and the funding of space research programs. The polity or the political order is particularly important for the members of a society because the decisions made within political institutions touch on the lives of virtually everyone. When a decision is made within one of the educational institutions, it usually has an impact only on those immediately

231

involved with that institution. Similarly, when a religious institution changes its policy on an issue such as abortion, not everyone in the society is necessarily affected. The situation is different when important decisions are made within the political order. When the government decides to implement free trade or a comprehensive goods and services tax, for example, every member of the society feels the effect. Given the far-reaching impact of decisions made within the political order, it is not surprising that the study of the polity is an important part of the discipline of sociology.

As we have seen, when sociologists attempt to understand and explain social phenomena, they often use different theoretical perspectives. In the field of political sociology we can identify at least three general frameworks: (1) the pluralist approach, commonly adopted by structural functionalists; (2) a class analysis model associated with some version of a Marxian orientation; and (3) some version of elite theory. In recent years scholars influenced by feminist theory have also been turning their attention to the polity, so we will examine some of these developments as well. We will begin by examining the basic tenets of the pluralist approach.

Pluralism

When structural functionalists undertake an analysis of the operations of the political order in Western societies, they tend to adopt an approach that is commonly called *pluralism*. The pluralist perspective appeals to them because it maintains that social systems such as ours – and the political structures within them – are basically stable, democratic, and open (Rossides, 1968: 157; Tumin, 1967: 45-46). Functionalists argue that the development of a democratic, pluralist political system has been the essential means of preventing individual inequalities from being translated into systematic social or political inequalities. What is unique about Western capitalist societies, they would argue, is the fact that although such societies recognize the necessity and functional value of individual inequalities, they do not allow those individual inequalities to affect the overall process of social decision-making.

According to Tumin, the essential features of a pluralist, democratic political order are the opportunities that all members of a society have to use formally established electoral procedures to select the personnel who operate the political institutions. In addition, all members of society can compete to influence the decision-making process between elections through actions such as lobbying the decision-makers (Tumin, 1967: 44-45). The most important aspect of Western democracies, a pluralist functionalist would argue, is the extent to which all members of society have an opportunity to participate in attempting to influence the policies of the government through these activities. The income levels or class positions of individuals may well vary considerably. The amount of status an individual enjoys may vary according to occupation, ethnic group, or gender. But when it comes to the social decision-making process, all people are equal. In all liberal democratic societies the creed is "one person, one vote," and thus on election day all are essentially equal: the people with high income and the people on social assistance are equal in the polling booth. The same basic structural situation exists in the area of lobbying, because regardless of a person's class or status position, all are equal in having the right to make their opinions known to the decision-makers.

In an open and democratic society the citizens tend to know what the government or other parts of the polity are doing. If a decision that carries broad social implications is about to be made, all of the people interested should know about it, because a key part of a democratic polity is a free press and an informed citizenry. If people feel strongly about an issue, they have the right to contact members of Parliament, the Senate, the cabinet, or the head of the government to express their opinions. There are no rules preventing any person, regardless of income level or status, from engaging in this activity. The element of lobbying – the opportunity to approach people who have been democratically elected to operate the political institutions – is another of the structures that makes it possible to have a society in which there are individual differences in wealth, status, and authority.

Although in theory all individuals have the opportunity to influence the polity through the electoral process and lobbying, the pluralist approach tends to pay more attention to the activities of organized groups in the political process than it does to the actions of individuals. People tend to find that they can be more influential if they organize themselves and act collectively, and thus it is common in liberal democratic societies to see the emergence of organized groups representing different sectors and interests in society. The groups that emerge may represent interests grounded in the institutional orders, from the economic to the religious, the educational, or the family. Among those groups, we typically find parent-teacher associations, church associations, anti-poverty organizations, university alumni associations, environmentalists, business interests (large and small), women's organizations, and labour unions. The continuing debates in

North America over the issue of abortion represent a situation in which many different interest groups representing many different viewpoints and sectors of society have competed to influence the policies and actions of the government.

An essential feature of political decision-making in liberal democratic societies, pluralists argue, is the extent to which the outcomes tend not to systematically favour any particular individual or group. As individuals and groups compete with each other to influence the decision-making process, over time, supposedly, no one group wins all the time or loses all the time. The phrase "you win some, you lose some, and some are draws" summarizes the expectations of this approach. Indeed, the term "pluralism" itself draws attention to the sense of having more than one interest group competing for political influence. Political power and influence are scattered throughout the society in the myriad of interest groups and individuals competing through elections and lobbying tactics to influence the social decision-making process.

The concept of pluralism, then, is used to explain the nature of political processes in liberal democratic societies. These societies are characterized by a stratification system in which there are individual inequalities in income (class), status (prestige), and power (authority). These inequalities are, structural functionalists maintain, both necessary and inevitable. But their existence does not mean that these societies are undemocratic and authoritarian. The strength of the liberal democratic system is to be found in the political structures that have developed and evolved. These political institutions have proved capable of facilitating a political process that allows all individuals an opportunity to influence the political decision-making process and thus ensure that individual inequalities cannot be translated into systematic inequalities at the level of social decision-making.

Power and the Ruling Class: The Marxian Perspective

For Marx and those following his mode of analysis, the relationship between capital and labour involves relations of exploitation, domination, and subordination. The capitalist class is the class with *economic power*. The capitalist class is in a structural position to make society's major economic decisions and ultimately to determine whether economic expansion or contraction occurs – to determine whether jobs are created as plants are built and expanded or if jobs are lost as plants are closed or relocated. Neo-Marxists also argue that the class possessing economic power is able to translate that power into political and ideological power. In short, the class with economic power is in reality a ruling class because of its capacity to convert its economic power into other kinds of power.

Political Power: The Realm of the State

Given Marx's concern with understanding the patterns of domination in capitalist society, it is not surprising that political power and the state were issues of concern to him for his entire adult life. His early works were devoted to a critique of the conception of the state developed by the German philosopher Georg Wilhelm Frederick Hegel (Marx [1844], 1970). He first began to undertake a more systematic analysis of the state in *The German Ideology*, co-authored with Engels in 1845-46.

Marx and Engels first discussed the position of the institutions we call the state by using or applying the materialist perspective they were in the process of developing. After repeated statements outlining the basic premises of their materialist approach, Marx and Engels identified the state as an institutional order distinct from though related to other social structures such as the economy and civil society. In their analysis, *civil society* refers to a variety of institutional orders, including the family and religion. While they did not specify the precise nature of the relationship of the state to the economy, the state is clearly linked, they argued, to the structure of class relations. Indeed, Marx and Engels noted that all struggles involving political power are really nothing more than an expression or manifestation of class struggles.

In their subsequent polemical works, such as *The Communist Manifesto* (1848), Marx and Engels further developed this point, suggesting that the state is really nothing more than a structure that directly serves the interests of the capitalist class and its fractions (Marx and Engels, 1952: 43-44). The implication is that the capitalist class somehow directly controls and manages the state, ensuring that the state looks after its interests.

In other works Marx presents a more complex picture of the relationship of the state to the capitalist class. In *The Eighteenth Brumaire of Louis Bonaparte* (1852), Marx presented a picture of the state as having considerable autonomy from the capitalist class, yet in the long run serving its interests. Again, in the first volume of *Capital* (1867), he pictured the state as autonomous though still, over the long run, serving the interests of the capitalist class. What he did not, however, systematically present in any of these works is an argument about how the state comes to serve the capitalist class, or how the capitalist class controls and dominates the state and the political process.

Revising Marx: Neo-Marxism on the State

One of the first substantial efforts by neo-Marxists to understand the state in capitalist society is found in the work of Ralph Miliband. In 1969 Miliband published *The State in Capitalist Society*, in which he attempted to accomplish two objectives: to offer a critique of the pluralist approach; and to develop the outline of a neo-Marxist alternative. Miliband argued that the various branches or agencies of the state, such as the government, the administrative arm, the military, and even state agencies, tend to be staffed, at their upper decision-making levels at least, by personnel drawn from the business and propertied class as well as the professional middle class. The class background, educational training, and general value orientations of these people lead them to believe that the proper role of government is to oversee the maintenance of social, economic, and political stability and thus the existence of the status quo. Miliband argued that the overwhelming economic power wielded by members of the capitalist class makes it possible for them to dominate the electoral and lobbying processes. In addition to these factors he examined the role played by ideology in the larger political processes, arguing that the vast majority of people in command positions in the state tend to accept capitalist society as the most appropriate if not the best of all worlds; as a result, they work for the continuance and stability of the system. The end result of all these processes and structures, Miliband argued, is a political system controlled and dominated in a variety of ways by the economically dominant class. In the final analysis, according to Miliband, the capitalist class is able, in a number of ways, to influence the state and ensure that it continues to act in their own long-term interests.

The Poulantzas Challenge

About the same time that Miliband was working on his book, Nicos Poulantzas was developing an alternate neo-Marxist approach. This approach was quite different, stressing the logic and functioning of the structures of capitalist society and not the personal and personnel connections between capital and the state, which had been Miliband's focus. When used in this context, personal connections between the capitalist class and the state would involve the capitalist class promoting candidates for state positions that share its ideology and value system, with common educational backgrounds and social connections. Personnel connections would involve members of the capitalist class actually occupying positions of power in the state system.

The Poulantzas approach became associated with a particular

variation of neo-Marxism called French structuralism, and it bore a strong resemblance to more orthodox functionalist thought. The key was Poulantzas's assumption that because capitalism is a class-based society it is in constant danger of breaking down due to class-based conflict and tension. In such a society some means of providing social stability is essential if the society is to continue to exist and operate relatively smoothly. For Poulantzas, the role or function of the state is to provide a basis of social order. The state, he argued, is a powerful factor of cohesion that attempts to bind together the conflict and contradiction that riddle society (1972: 246). The essential reason why the state acts in the interests of the dominant or capitalist class is because some institution must perform this function or the society will disintegrate.

Poulantzas explicitly criticized Miliband for dwelling on personal and personnel connections (1972: 246). For Poulantzas, the capitalist class itself tends to be divided into internal fractions that can have differing economic interests and political agendas. Given this situation, the possibility of instability exists if one of the fractions directly controls the state and uses it to secure its narrow interests. The state must be capable of accommodating the various demands of the various fractions or segments of the dominant class, all the while overseeing as much as possible the smooth functioning of the whole system. A key issue for Poulantzas is the question of state autonomy. He argued that the state in capitalist society is relatively autonomous of the capitalist class, yet the logic of the structures results in the state functioning to stabilize the system.

The differences in the positions developed by Miliband and Poulantzas resulted in a series of journal articles that turned into a debate between the two. What is important for our purposes is that this debate ultimately produced and stimulated a number of different directions and approaches within the neo-Marxist school. Many of those differences are still apparent today in the neo-Marxist literature, although there is some indication of a move toward less abstract approaches that allow for the analysis of actual historical and concrete events.

Neo-Marxist Theory and Social Research

As the debate among neo-Marxists continued, many new positions emerged. These positions or approaches were quite varied in their degree of sophistication and theoretical complexity (Knuttila, 1992; Jessop, 1982; Carnoy, 1984). One of the interesting outcomes was a demand that critical or neo-Marxist approaches must be capable of stimulating actual social analysis if they are to be useful in the process of social criticism (Skocpol, 1985). The arguments of Albert Szymanski are especially illustrative of efforts to develop an approach that has the possibility of being used in historical and empirical research and analysis.

In his 1978 book *The Capitalist State and the Politics of Class*, Szymanski discussed the state in capitalist society while avoiding the problems associated with relying on the personal/personnel linkages of Miliband and the abstract functionalism of Poulantzas and others. Szymanski argued that in a liberal democratic state there are mechanisms of power through which individuals and members of classes can attempt to influence or control the state (1978: 24-25). He noted that there are two different types of mechanisms of power that individuals belonging to various classes could use to try to influence the operation and decisions of the state: direct and indirect. His argument was not that the pluralist approach is completely wrong; it is just that it only addresses a couple of the means through which the state can be influenced. Among the direct mechanisms are:

- direct participation in the operation of the state by individuals and members of classes;
- the lobbying process;
- the policy formation process; for instance, various "think tank" organizations that offer policy advice to governments; by establishing or funding such organizations, classes and individuals can influence the state.

In addition to these direct mechanisms of power, Szymanski outlined four indirect modes of controlling the state:

- the ideological environment. State officials are constrained in their actions and policy initiatives by the overall ideological environment. Those making decisions within the state are always aware of and concerned with public opinion, and they simply will not take actions that would be deemed to represent a violation of some aspect of the dominant ideology. Ideological power is a mechanism of political power, because by influencing public opinion people can indirectly influence the state.
- economic power. The state operates as part of a set of social structures that depend on the economy for their existence. Without a healthy and expanding economy the entire social structure, including the state, will encounter difficulty. A growing economy provides the elected state representatives

with a better chance of re-election, not to mention an expanding tax base. The capitalist class makes the major economic decisions relating to investments and economic growth or decline, and if the state undertakes actions deemed to be against the interests of capital, capital can close plants and curtail investment and thereby cause instability in the economic basis of society.

- the financing of the electoral process. To win elections, politicians need substantial amounts of money, and through financial contributions, or the withholding of same, the policies and actions of parties and candidates can be influenced.
- the presence of the military as a mechanism of last resort. Usually a conservative force dedicated to the status quo, the military will defend the existing order should its ultimate stability be threatened. Szymanski argues that the military has close ties to the dominant class.

In his discussion of specific linkages or mechanisms of power through which the state can be influenced, Szymanski was attempting to avoid the functionalist logic of Poulantzas by providing concrete examples of the means by which the capitalist class could influence the state. In a constitutional liberal democratic society these mechanisms of power had theoretically become available to all citizens; but it was clear that the capacity to use them requires economic power and resources. Given the fact that neo-Marxists assumed that economic power and resources are largely in the hands of the capitalist class, they maintained that there is an unequal distribution of economic power.

The kind of work done by Miliband, Poulantzas, and Szymanski indicates, first, that in more recent years neo-Marxists have attempted to develop an alternative to the functionalist and pluralist approach to the study of the polity in capitalist society. Second, it shows that, given the various positions within the neo-Marxist camp, not all of those who have disagreed with the functionalist and pluralist approaches have agreed among themselves about exactly what approach to take. As a result, various schools or streams of thought have developed within the Marxian tradition.

Classical Elite Theory

Alongside the structural functionalist, Marxist, and feminist theories there has been one other major approach in Western sociology that has focused explicitly on the issue of social inequality. Although elite theory is not as important in terms of its use by contemporary sociologists, it does warrant a brief introduction. Among the first of the classical elite thinkers was Vilfredo Pareto.

Vilfredo Pareto

Although Pareto (1848-1923), an Italian born in Paris, was trained in engineering and mathematics, he later turned to the social sciences and eventually developed a complex theory of society. A part of his theory sought to explain the persistence of social and economic inequalities. His major sociological work, translated as *The Mind and Society: A Treatise on General Sociology*, was published in Italy in 1916.

Pareto argued that the social and economic inequalities that had always characterized all human societies are due to the simple fact that the human beings who make up society are not themselves equal. Pareto developed a complex series of arguments to explain the basis of human inequalities. The essence of his position is that individual inequalities are based on the biologically determined distribution of personal attributes, abilities, talents, and aptitudes. Not all individuals are equally endowed in terms of their capacities and propensities. When unequally endowed individuals engage in the competitive situations that typically characterize human social existence, some will always tend to exhibit superior traits and over time they will emerge as a special group, which Pareto called the elite (1976: 248).

The superior performers assume control of the realm of human affairs or conduct in which they operate. Pareto argued that there are two different kinds of elites, the governing and non-governing. The governing elite is composed of those directly involved in politics and political rule, while the non-governing are superior performers not directly involved in politics. The majority of the population, however, are not in either of the elites, and they make up what Pareto refers to as the "lower stratum," "lower classes," and "the commonality" (1976: 158, 249). The elites constitute a minority that rules over the majority – what elite theorists call the masses. This is as it should be, since members of the elite hold their positions by virtue of their special abilities.

The basic fact that human individuals are unequal led Pareto to pose fundamental questions about the logic and possibility of democracy. Indeed, if we follow Pareto's elitist approach to its logical conclusion, democracy, which implies the rule of the masses, is an undesirable state. It is not surprising, then, that the Italian dictator Mussolini found Pareto's ideas attractive (Coser, 1977: 406).

Another Italian social theorist, Gaetano Mosca (1858-1941), took Pareto's core ideas one step further. In his major work, *The Ruling Class* (1896), Mosca developed a less biologically based explanation of why there are elites. But he nevertheless retained a strong element of the biological argument for individual superiority, which from the perspective of a sociologist means his arguments are highly flawed. The most powerful statement of elite theory that contained an explicitly sociological thrust would be developed by Robert Michels.

Robert Michels

Robert Michels (1876-1936) was a German-born academic who spent most of his adult life in Italy, where he became familiar with the arguments of Pareto and Mosca. Michels, too, was interested in the same phenomenon, that is, the tendency for human society and all other forms of human organization to become dominated and governed by small groups of people. He was interested in how and why elites always emerged.

Michels is best known for his study of the internal operation of the social democratic party in Germany. In *Political Parties* (1911) he reached disturbing conclusions for all who value and cherish the democratic ideal, because he argued that there is something inherent in organizations and organizational activity that leads to the emergence of elites.

According to Michels, if individuals or groups want to have an impact on any aspect of a modern complex society they must first organize themselves. This is so because of the very nature of a modern society. All of the various groups attempting to gain power and influence in society are themselves highly organized, and to compete with them requires a sophisticated degree of organization. But the need for organization brings with it certain problems and dynamics. The existence of large and complex organizations brings on problems related to the logistics of organizing large mass meetings, communicating with a mass membership, and organizing debates in the presence of hundreds or even thousands of members. Even in an organization formally committed to democratic procedures these logistical problems give rise to an interesting tendency: after an organization struggles with these logistical problems for a while it becomes apparent that it needs some form of delegation of authority and decision-making rights to function properly or to the highest degree of effectiveness. There is, Michels argued, an organizational imperative or logic that leads to the emergence of delegation of authority, which in turn leads to a specialization of tasks. Once this process begins the organization is well on its way to becoming dominated by an elite.

Michels argued that once the specialization of internal tasks develops and the delegation of authority begins, a universal process takes place. The people specializing in various tasks tend to become "experts" in their areas and very soon they come to assume leadership positions within various parts of the organization. These specialists and leaders increasingly make decisions on their own, and they become more and more separated from the majority of the members, that is, from the masses. A further dynamic or process develops as well. As the leaders and specialists carry out their tasks, their personalities and behavioural patterns are changed by their experiences. Those who see themselves as representing the masses tend to become involved in meetings with representatives from other organizations; they travel to various centres to meet government officials and other powerful individuals. As the process carries on, these specialists and leaders increasingly come to constitute an elite that gradually assumes control of the organization.

These tendencies, Michels said, are exacerbated by apathetic tendencies among the masses. Many of those not directly involved in decision-making have a desire to be led. As a result the masses not only go along with their organization being taken over by an elite, but they also want it – although Michels gave no adequate explanation of why the masses would possess this characteristic.

For Michels, the tendency for elites to emerge is so strong that it can be referred to as a law: the "Iron Law of Oligarchy." In a forceful and much quoted summary of his argument, he stated, "It is organization which gives birth to the domination of the elected over the electors, of the mandataries over the mandators, of the delegates over the delegators. Who says organization, says oligarchy" (1962: 365).

Beyond Class Politics: Feminism and the State*

Thus far we have examined two major analytical approaches to the study of the polity in capitalist society. In the case of the pluralist and structural functionalist approach, the polity is seen as a part of a social decision-making process in which there are no dominant forces, interests, or players who consistently get their way at least in the long run. According the various Marxian positions, the state in capitalist society is either instrumentally, structurally, or through mechanisms of power "connected" to the capitalist class and as a result the state tends to work in the interests of that class. As a result of its ability to influence the state, the capitalist class is truly a ruling class, having both economic and political power. As we have seen, however, the adequacy of

---

* Material in this section is from Murray Knuttila, "The State and Social Issues: Theoretical Considerations," in Les Samuelson, ed., *Power and Resistance: Critical Thinking about Canadian Social Issues* (Halifax: Fernwood, 1994).

functionalism and Marxism have been very much questioned in recent years, and this applies to their understanding of the state as well.

The most important and systematic critique of the analytical and explanatory capacities of the approaches discussed above has come from thinkers, scholars, and activists associated with various schools of feminist thought. As new questions were posed concerning the nature and role of the state, especially as it relates to sex and gender relations, the existing approaches were found wanting in two related, but different aspects. First, convincing arguments supported by overwhelming evidence showed that the state played a central role in the subordination of women and the domination of men. This evidence then led to the second important development, namely, demands that the existing theoretical frameworks that had informed the study of the state be radically rethought so as to account for the role of the state in maintaining a society based on patriarchal and heterosexual relations. Let us first look at the literature that illustrated the role of the state in maintaining unequal sex and gender relations.

An early work that argued that the state played an important role in sex and gender relations was Mary McIntosh's 1978 essay, "The State and the Oppression of Women." McIntosh claimed that the state is involved in the oppression of women through its support of the household system, which in capitalist society is intimately linked to the accumulating of capital. Her thesis holds that the household is the site of the production and reproduction of *the* essential commodity in the production and appropriation of surplus value in capitalist society – labour power. Further, she argued that the state plays a central role in the maintenance of the specific household form in which women produce and reproduce labour power and thus the state oppresses women through various measures that serve to maintain patriarchal family relations in its efforts to provide the conditions that are necessary for the maintenance and continuation of the system.

Numerous feminist writers elaborated on these themes. As we have seen, Michèle Barrett (1985) warned us not to try and explain the persistence of patterns of male dominance and the patriarchal family just in terms of economic factors, arguing that we need to consider the role of ideology. In a powerful essay, "Masculine Dominance and the State," Varda Burstyn (1985) questions the value of a Marxian-based concept of class in addressing sex and gender oppression. Indeed, she argues that we need to develop the concept of "gender class" to understand the full extent of the oppression of women, which is not just a matter of women in capitalist society being oppressed but rather is part of a larger transhistorical pattern of sexual oppression. Burstyn suggests that the state has played a central role in both economic class domination and gender class domination. Further, she maintains that the state has acted to enforce these dual patterns of domination because state structures have tended to be dominated by men.

A somewhat different argument was developed by Jane Ursel (1986), who advocated the development of an analytic approach that recognized the importance of both material production and biological reproduction is determining the shape and character of human society. Ursel argued in effect that the concept of capitalism as understood in Marxian analysis is useful for understanding the nature of material production in Western society, while the concept of patriarchy is most appropriate for an analysis of reproduction. She notes that the state has played a central role in facilitating the continuance of the various modes of material production and biological reproduction, and thus the state has served the interests of those who benefit from the class-based relations of production in capitalist society and the sexual oppression of patriarchal society.

Two important articles, Norene Pupo's "Preserving Patriarchy: Women, The Family and The State" (1988) and Jane Jenson's "Gender and Reproduction, or Babies and the State" (1992), illustrate the complexities of the relationship between the state and sex and gender relations. Pupo examines the rise and role of what we might term family-related legislation in Canada, noting its contradictory nature. She writes:

> Through its vast system of laws, regulations, and the institutional structure of the welfare state, the state shapes both personal and social lives. Historically women have both welcomed and resisted the encroachment of the state in the family home. The state at once is regarded as a source of protection and justice and as the basis of inequality. Such contradictions are inherent in a state under capitalism. (229)

She goes on to note that the while the actions and policies of the state may appear to be liberating, "in the long run it reproduces patriarchal relations."

A similar analysis of the sometimes contradictory nature of state policies and actions is found in Jane Jenson's work. Jenson reviews some of the efforts of feminists who opted to use a Marxian approach to the state to understand the oppression of women, though the major portion of the article is devoted to presenting valuable comparative data drawn from the experiences of women in France and England. On the basis of this data she concludes that it is not possible for her to make generalized theoretical statements. However, "Beginning with the logic of the capitalist state's location in any conjuncture, and mapping the articulation of power relations such as those of class and gender in the politics of any social formation, it is possible to understand the ways in which the state contributes to the oppression of women" (229). Then Jenson makes a very important point: "Moreover, it also points to the space for resistance."

The notion that people have opportunities to resist is central, as is the argument that there are even opportunities to use the contradictions in the system in a positive way. This argument is developed by two Canadian scholars, Pat and Hugh Armstrong, who have contributed greatly to the advancement of feminist scholarship. The Armstrongs note that "more and more feminists have come to realize that the state is not simply an instrument of class or male rule: that it can indeed work for the benefit of at least some women" (1990: 114). They go on to reiterate the idea that the state remains very complex and contradictory.

In *Toward A Feminist Theory of the State* (1989), Catharine Mackinnon focuses on the negative impact many state actions have for women. In her discussion of the actions and logic of the liberal state in capitalist society Mackinnon notes that "the state, through law, institutionalizes male power over women through institutionalizing the male point of view in law. Its first state act is to see women from the standpoint of male dominance; its next act is to treat them that way" (169). She later concludes with a powerful claim: "However autonomous of class the liberal state may appear, it is not autonomous of sex. Male power is systemic. Coercive, legitimized and epistemic, it *is* the regime" (170; emphasis in original).

Though we have barely scratched the surface in terms of the available literature that empirically illustrates the role that the state plays in sex and gender oppression, an important point made by R.W. Connell (1990: 519) should now be clear:

This adds up to a convincing picture of the state as an active player in gender politics. Nobody acquainted with the facts revealed in this research can any longer accept the silence about gender in the traditional state theory, whether liberal, socialist or conservative.

As Connell then goes on to argue, concepts of sex and gender must be included from the beginning in all theorizing and thinking about the modern state. The task of theorizing and understanding that sex and gender relations are integral to the polity and the state means that we must break with existing approaches.

Terms and Concepts

Pluralism – argues that Western liberal democracies are among the best political systems because they recognize that there are different interests in society that must be given an opportunity to influence government. Pluralists argue that a democratic electoral system and an open process of decision-making that allows for group lobbying are the most appropriate systems for ensuring a democratic decision-making process. It is assumed that all groups and interests in society have a more or less equal opportunity to influence the government through electoral and lobbying activities.

State system/polity – as used in sociological theory, all the institutions, organizations, and agencies connected with the political processes in societies with formally organized political institutions. In Western liberal democracies the state system or polity includes not only the formal elected apparatus of government, but also the appointed officials, all arms of the state bureaucracy, the judiciary, police and military, and the various national and international agencies.

Instrumentalist view of state – used to describe a neo-Marxist view of the state in capitalist society that stresses the personal and personnel connections between the capitalist class and the state. According to the logic of the instrumentalist view, the capitalist class is able to control and direct the activities of the state because the people operating the state either come directly from the capitalist class or share the values, ideologies, and objectives of the capitalist class. The state is seen as an "instrument" of the capitalist class because of such direct connections.

Structuralist view of state – a neo-Marxist approach to the state that is critical of the supposed simplicity of the instrumentalist approach. The structuralist position draws on a kind of functionalist logic and focuses on what the state must do to maintain the capitalist system. It argues that the state's major role is in attempting to prevent the conflicts and contradictions from destroying the system, and its operations are defined by the logic and structures of the system, not the connections that state personnel have to the capitalist class. For example, the fact that the state needs tax revenues to operate means that state managers, no matter what personal political affiliations they have, must attempt to ensure that profits remain high and the economy healthy because economic slowdown might mean no re-election. The structural importance of maintaining "business confidence" – of preventing cap-italists from moving their production to another country and attempt-ing to ensure continued investment – is a pressure that leads to the state acting in a manner that pleases the capitalist class.

Mechanisms of power – as opposed to pluralism, instrumentalism, or structuralism, stresses the need to understand that there are a number of different means that can be employed to influence the state in capitalist society. In a liberal democratic system there are both direct (personnel and personal connections, lobbying, and impacting policy formation) and indirect (using economic power, ideological power, and political funding) mechanisms of power. Although all classes and indi-viduals are able to use these mechanisms of power, the class with over-whelming economic power is best placed and for this reason is better able to exercise the various mechanisms of power.

Elite theory – emphasizes, in several different streams, that society always has been and always will be controlled by a small group called the elite. The elite is composed of those individuals who are superior performers in some area of human endeavour. Eventually these supe-rior performers rise to positions of power, authority, and control, and the masses of people are content to have these superior performers "run the show." Some elite theorists such as Pareto argued that there was a biological reason for elite superiority, while others such as Michels looked for an organizational basis for the emergence of elites. The focus for all elite theorists is the small group that controls and runs society and holds wealth and power.

11

DEVIANCE AND SOCIAL CONTROL

Have you ever done anything that someone in a position of authority or power considered wrong? The chances are very great that for most of us an honest answer to this question is "Yes." According to sociological wisdom, when we act in a manner that contravenes the dominant norms that govern a given society or social situation we are engaging in deviant behaviour. There are a great many different sociological definitions of deviance, including: (1) "any social behavior that departs from that regarded as normal or socially acceptable within a society or social context" (Jary and Jary, 1991: 120); (2) "behavior which fails to conform with the accepted norms and standards of a social group or system" (Martin, 1976: 21); and (3) "behaviour which violates institutionalized expectations, that is, expectations which are shared and recognized as legitimate within a social system" (Cohen, 1959: 462). As you think about these definitions a fundamental sociological proposition regarding deviance should become apparent – deviance tends to be socially defined and constructed. As we know from our discussion of culture, values, and norms, when it comes to human behaviour, there are enormous variations in what we might consider normal and appropriate.

In sociology, deviance and deviant behaviour are generally distinguished from crime and criminal behaviour. As we know from our discussion of norms, folkways, and mores, sometimes norms (especially mores) become codified into laws and legal codes. A crime is generally considered to be a violation of a criminal law or a formal, legally sanctioned social norm. Crimes are sometimes categorized as being against property, violent, white-collar, and victim-less. Criminal behaviour tends to be subject to penalties and sanctions as specified or laid out in the laws and legal codes. As is the case with deviance and deviant behaviour, crime and criminal behaviour are socially constructed. A specific behaviour can be made a crime simply by changing the laws and legal codes.

Implicit in sociological definitions of deviance and crime is the notion of social control. Who or what social institution or agency defines what is normal and acceptable or abnormal, unacceptable, and therefore deviant? Who or what social institutions or agencies determine what sanctions are appropriate for a particular case of deviant behaviour? As Jary and Jary put it, "the question of by whom, and how, deviance is labeled becomes crucial to its explanation (1991: 120). Similar questions emerge when we consider the legal system, crime, and criminal behaviour. The issues of who makes laws, how laws are made, how they are enforced, and who determines and implements punishments and sanctions are essential if we want to understand the social phenomenon of crime. By now the reader should be sensitive to the fact that when sociologists raise who, what, why, and how questions, they will look to theory, in particular sociological theory, for the answers.

Biological Explanations

On October 22, 1993, the *Globe and Mail* ran a story about a family whose male members demonstrated a propensity toward violence and aggressive behaviour under the banner, "Researchers find link between genetic inheritance and aggression." The story reports that a study of one particular family's history had found that the presence or absence of a particular enzyme seemed to influence the behaviour of some males. The intimation that there is a biological basis and explanation for deviant or criminal behaviour is an ancient idea. Early in the twentieth century Cesare Lombroso popularized the idea that criminal behaviour was inborn. He studied the physical features of prison inmates in order to identify the characteristics of the typical criminals. Among his list of typical characteristics were shifty eyes, high cheek bones, oversized ears, and scanty beards. Although there were some who apparently found this work interesting, it was soon pointed out that there was a problem in his investigative techniques because he had not compared the prison population to the general population. Were these characteristics indeed representative of only the prison population or were they common in the general population? When it was discovered that these so-called criminal characteristics were in fact quite common and present in many non-criminals, Lombroso's work became less credible.

Among the more interesting attempts to relate physical attributes to behaviour and intellectual attributes was the work of a physician named Franz Gall (1758-1828) and a student of his, Johann Spurzheim (1776-1832). Gall was initially interested in the relationship of a variety of physiological characteristics, such as the shape of the forehead and jaw, but later he focused on the overall shape and features of the skull. To Gall's credit, he did focus on the brain as the central organ in understanding human behaviour, but we now know that his claims that the various bumps and indentations of the skull were the key to understanding the brain were misguided and, shall we say, wrong-headed.

Other notable efforts to associate and explain deviant and criminal behaviour with physiological characteristics are found in the work of William Sheldon, who published a typology of human body types in 1940 and followed this study with an effort to determine the extent to which these general body types were represented among a small sample of youth in Boston defined as juvenile delinquents (1949). During the 1950s two researchers, Eleanor Glueck and Sheldon Glueck, conducted a follow-up study that tended to support Sheldon's conclusions; however, they were never able to point out any plausible causal connections between body type and deviant behaviour. It seems as if this is an idea that will not easily go away, because in 1985 yet another study claimed to find a relationship between biology and deviant behaviour. In *Crime and Human Nature*, James Q. Wilson and Richard J. Hernstein argue that there is a connection between physical attributes, what they term "intelligence," and personality traits that seems to predispose certain people to deviant and criminal behaviour.

For a sociologist, one of the difficulties of many of these types of analysis is the lack of causal mechanisms that actually explain the connections between these apparent individual differences and deviant or criminal behaviour. In a review of Wilson and Hernstein's book Christopher Jencks states: "*Crime and Human Nature* is a book about the way individual differences affect criminality in one particular kind of society, namely our own, not about the way societies can alter – or eliminate – the effects of individual difference" (1987: 38).

Jon Shepard presents an excellent summary of why sociologists tend not to accept biological explanations when he notes that such explanations tend to ignore culture and social learning, are often based on data gathered by questionable and flawed research methodologies, and are ideologically suspect in that they can be interpreted as justifying existing patterns of social inequality that might produce what is defined as deviant behaviour (Shepard, 1990: 151). As we have seen in the definitions above, sociologists insist that deviance must be studied in its social context; therefore, we must turn our attention to the role society has been deemed to play in fashioning and defining deviant behaviour.

Emile Durkheim

Given the fact that Emile Durkheim devoted the bulk of his intellectual life attempting to establish the legitimacy of sociological explanations for various social phenomena, it is appropriate to begin with his analysis of deviance and crime. As we know, Durkheim was very much concerned with the question of how to establish and maintain social order and stability. Durkheim emphasized the role that shared moral codes and values, sometimes referred to as "collective representations," played in shaping and influencing our social life and the overall characteristics of society (1964: xli). As long as the majority of individuals in a given society shared a belief system or a moral code, the society would tend to be stable and social order would prevail. Durkheim acknowledges, however, that it is impossible to conceive of a situation in which all members of a society totally share a belief system and agree on everything. In *The Rules of Sociological Method* Durkheim employs insights from the organic analogy in his chapter titled, "Rules for Distinguishing Between The Normal and The Pathological" in order to explain why such an occurrence need not be fatal for society. The arguments advanced could be summarized in the following fashion. Every normally functioning organism will experience periods during which there are temporary disturbances, morbidities, or occurrences that are potentially pathological and disruptive to the functioning of the whole. Such disturbances to the normal functioning of a healthy organism need not be fatal because compensations occur that typically return the organism to a normal healthy state. In society, the presence of individuals who do not share the beliefs and values of the majority might seem to be akin to a virus infecting normal tissue in an organism. However, their presence need not represent a radical threat to overall social order.

Durkheim goes on to define crime as a potentially pathological phenomenon in society; however, he notes that this is not necessarily the case because crime can be understood as being a normal part of every society:

> Crime is present not only in the majority of societies of one particular species but in all societies of all types. There is no society that is not confronted with the problem of criminality. (1964: 65)

Further, he argues that "crime is normal because a society exempt from it is utterly impossible" (67). Durkheim's definition of crime is as follows: "Crime, as we have shown elsewhere, consists of an act that offends certain very strong collective sentiments" (76).

Given the complex nature of our lives in an advanced industrial society, we cannot all possibly be and think alike, therefore, some individuals very likely will come to hold beliefs and opinions that contravene those dominant in society as a whole (69-70). The presence of sentiments, opinions, and patterns of behaviour that go against the grain of the dominant collective sentiments can actually result in social progress because such challenges to the status quo are "indispensable to the normal evolution of morality and law" (70). Durkheim is explicit about the fact that morality and law must change and evolve as the conditions of human life change. Referring to society's belief systems, which he calls collective sentiments, he writes:

> Nothing is good indefinitely and to an unlimited extent. The authority which the moral conscience enjoys must not be excessive: otherwise no one would dare criticize it; and it would too easily congeal into an immutable form. To make progress, individual originality must be able to express itself. In order that the originality of the idealist whose dreams transcend his century may find expression, it is necessary that the originality of the criminal, who is below the level of his time, shall also be possible. One does not occur without the other. (71)

There are of course limitations, and excessively high rates of serious crime might become a social pathology.

In *The Rules of Sociological Method* Durkheim argues that crime might actually serve a positive social function by facilitating the development and evolution of collective sentiments and thus preventing the ossification and stagnation of society. In *The Division of Labour in Society* he returns to the issue of crime. In this later work Durkheim once again illustrates why he is considered one of the founding figures in sociology, defining crime in the context of society: "In other words we must not say that an action shocks the common conscience because it is criminal, but rather that it is criminal because it shocks the common conscience. We do not reprove it because it is a crime, but it is a crime because we reprove it" (1964: 81). He goes on to argue that in order for society to continue to exist in a stable and orderly manner, violations of collective sentiments must be dealt with, that is, punished. The punishment of violators is really about affirming the collective sentiments and/or conscience. By punishing those who are deviant we reaffirm the validity of the values and norms that are the basis of social order. When discussing punishment Durkheim declares that "Its true function is to maintain social cohesion intact, while maintaining its vitality in the common conscience" (1964: 108).

What we find in the writing of Durkheim is an analysis of deviant and criminal behaviours that places an emphasis on the social context. Whether a behaviour or action is deviant and/or criminal will depend on the value system of the society, that is, on the collective conscience of the community and the extent to which those sentiments have been codified into law. According to Durkheim's analysis deviant behaviour can actually have several positive functions, including preventing social ossification by facilitating social change and development, and reinforcing social stability by having the beliefs of the collectivity reinforced when punishment is meted out to violators of the collective conscience. The general principles that informed Durkheim's work were influential in the subsequent development of functionalist thought.

Parsons and Merton

As was noted in Chapter 7, Talcott Parsons is generally recognized as the founder of twentieth-century American structural functionalism. While Parsons incorporated ideas from a wide array of sources in the formulation of his theories, Durkheim was one of the most important influences. A common thread throughout all of Parsons's writings is the central position that values and roles play both in guiding the actions of social actors and in stabilizing the overall social system. An integrated and stable social system requires that the individual actors within the system be adequately socialized, that is, they must be familiar with and accept the legitimacy of the society's value orientation. In one of his earlier major works, co-authored with Edward Shils, Parsons wrote: "Internalization of patterns of value is crucial in the integration of an actor in a role system" (Parsons and Shils, 1952: 156). According to Parsons and Shils, an individual characterized by "faulty internalization" of society's value system might tend (1) to withdraw from social interaction "or (2) to evade the fulfillment of expectations, or (3) to rebel by openly refusing to conform" (156-57). Deviance and deviant behaviour is thus something that develops or occurs when for, some reason, an individual is not properly socialized and as a result has not adequately internalized society's value system. Elsewhere Parsons and Shils had referred to this as a problem of "mal-integration" (151).

In his much denser theoretical work, *The Social System*, Parsons devoted considerable attention to the study of deviant behaviour and social control (see Parsons, 1951: ch. VII, "Deviant Behavior and the Mechanisms of Social Control"), although the basic logic of approach outlined earlier remained intact. He defines deviance "as a disturbance of the equilibrium of the interactive system" (250) and reminds us that "all social action is normatively oriented, and that the value-orientations embodied in these norms must to a degree be common to the actors in an institutionally integrated interactive system" (215). If an individual social actor (Parsons tends to use the term "ego") does not fully internalize the society's value orientations and as a result is not fully integrated into the social system, she or he might begin to manifest abnormal behaviours, which Parsons categorizes as compulsive in the performance of duties or status expectations, rebelliousness, or withdrawal (257). Whatever the type of abnormal or deviant behaviour that is manifest, its origins are to be found in an inadequate internalization of the dominant value system and the consequent lack of integration of the individual into the overall social system.

In his concluding remarks Parsons sounds remarkably like Durkheim: "The conformity-deviance 'dimension' or functional problem is inherent in social structures and systems of social action in a context of cultural values." He also states that "tendencies to deviance" are socially structured. Further, Parsons reiterates Durkheim's point about the role that deviance plays in social change and the need for society to have mechanisms of social control to ensure that deviant tendencies are maintained within acceptable bounds (320-21).

As important as are Parsons's insights for the development of the structural functionalist approach to deviance, it is the work of his student, Robert K. Merton, that has had the greatest impact. Originally written in 1938, Merton's celebrated essay "Social Structure and Anomie" has become one of the most often quoted and referenced works in the study of deviant behaviour. Merton begins with a critique of those theories of deviance that have sought to explain the phenomenon in biological terms. As a sociologist Merton finds such explanations unacceptable, and he definitively states that his approach will locate the primary causal processes that explain deviant behaviour in the social structure. He writes: "Our primary aim is to discover how some *social structures exert a definite pressure upon certain persons in the society to engage in non-conforming rather than conforming conduct*" (1968: 186; emphasis in original).

Two central concepts in Merton's analysis of deviant behaviour are culturally defined *goals* and the *means for achieving* these goals (186-87). Merton defines goals as the socially legitimized and sanctioned objectives for which we strive. The means for achieving these goals are simply the "allowable procedures for moving toward these objectives" (187). According to Merton there need not necessarily be a relationship between how much emphasis a culture places on given values and the actual or practical means available to individuals in their efforts to achieve goals. If some goal is highly valued while many people lack socially sanctioned or legitimate opportunities to achieve that goal, non-conformist or deviant behaviour may develop as individuals strive to achieve the valued goal. In Merton's words:

> It is when a system of cultural values extols, virtually above all else, certain *common* success-goals *for the population at large* while the social structure rigorously restricts or completely closes access to approved modes of reaching these goals *for a considerable part of the population*, that deviant behavior ensues on a large scale. (200; emphasis in original)

Merton went on to examine some typical types of deviant behaviour that might emerge under these circumstances. He briefly comments on conformist behaviour, which occurs when an individual accepts a culturally defined goal and has access to the means through which to achieve that goal; however, he points out that this is not really a form of deviant behaviour and therefore not of particular interest. He refers to the four major forms of deviant behaviour that arise from a disjunction between a socially emphasized goal and the lack of means to achieve it as being innovation, ritualism, retreatism, and rebellion.

Innovation is a behavioural pattern that occurs when an individual accepts the social values and goals but lacks the legitimate means of achieving a goal and turns to innovative, non-conformist, and deviant means to achieve it. Imagine a situation in which an individual accepts the idea that the accumulation of wealth is the supreme objective in life. If individuals lack access to the normal means of accumulating wealth, such as job or business opportunities, they might resort to innovative and deviant behaviours such as theft, fraud, or the sale of illegal substances in order to make money.

Ritualism is a form of adaptation that Merton notes might not be considered deviant, but since it is "departure from the cultural model" he suggests we treat is as such (204). The ritualist is an individual who comes to reject the goal, but ritualistically clings to socially sanctioned behaviours that typically lead to achieving that goal. The example Merton provides is of an individual who has given up on or is not interested in upward mobility in an organization, yet slavishly works away at his/her job just as hard as the upwardly mobile individual. The individual exhibiting ritualistic behaviour appears to be satisfied with what he or she has and is not seeking higher status, more power, or wealth like so many in capitalist society do.

The adaptation Merton calls *retreatism* might appear to be more akin to our typical understanding of deviant behaviour. The individual adopting this approach rejects both the culturally or socially sanctioned goal and the culturally and socially legitimized means of achieving the goal. The retreatist might typically be the "drop out." Merton provides some examples:

> In this category fall some of the adaptive activities of psychotics, autists, pariahs, outcasts, vagrants, vagabonds, tramps, chronic drunkards and drug addicts. They have relinquished culturally prescribed goals and their behaviour does not accord with institutional norms. (207)

Lastly there are Merton's rebels. *Rebellion* is a behavioural pattern that involves rejection of society's goals and means of achieving those goals; however, unlike those engaged in retreatism the rebel postulates an alternate system of goals and means. The rebel might end up producing a counter-culture, that is, postulating a new set of values, institutions, and social practices that will achieve those goals. The rebel might reject the competitive ethos of market society and the work ethic and practices that are supposed to facilitate monetary success in favour of a communal and co-operative value orientation and lifestyle.

Merton's ideas proved to be extremely important in the subsequent development of structural functionalist theory. Indeed, in his discussion of Merton's work, Edwin Schur states that "Virtually all subsequent theorizing about deviance has built on, or had to take account of, his major formulations" (1979: 138). Others, such as Albert Cohen, sought to extend Merton's concepts as they examined the role of subcultures in producing deviant behaviour.

Deviant Subcultures

If you ever enrol in a social problems or deviant behaviour course and study theories of deviance in some detail, you will discover that introductory books tend to simplify complex arguments. In what follows we will take several approaches that are in fact different and combine them. It is possible to do this because these approaches also share a number of common assumptions and propositions. For the student of sociology, these approaches are relatively easy to understand because they simply combine what we know about the impact of subcultures and socialization on human behaviour. The approaches we are combining are variously referred to as the cultural transmission approach, the subcultural approach, the social-bonding approach, the differential association approach, and modelling theory. They share a common focus, namely, the existence of subcultures characterized by values and norms that are significantly different from those of mainstream society. Individuals who are exposed to or a part of these subcultures become socialized or resocialized into these values and as a result begin to act in ways that are deviant from the mainstream culture.

While a great deal more could be said about how functionalists have explained deviance, these brief comments provide some indication of the general tenor of the arguments. The emphasis on values and deviation from established values differentiates this approach from the more class-oriented focus of Marxian or conflict theory.

Conflict Theory and the Study of Deviance

The manifold differences in the explanations for social phenomena offered by sociologists operating from the conflict or Marxian perspective as opposed to a structural functionalist approach become once again apparent when we examine some of the dimensions of a conflict-oriented explanation of deviance.

Needless to say, the conflict approach will be predicated on a materialist approach. In an essay titled "Toward a Marxian Theory of Deviance," Steven Spitzer notes that for the Marxian the crucial unit of analysis is the mode of production. He then spells out what the point of departure must be: "If we are to have a Marxian theory of deviance, therefore, deviance production must be understood in relationship to the specific forms of socio-economic organization" (1978: 351). The mode of production dominant in our society is, of course, capitalist, and thus an analysis of deviance must begin with an understanding of the socio-economic organization of capitalism.

Without repeating in detail what was said in Chapters 6 and 7 about the basic tenets of Marxian theory, we need to remind ourselves of the basic assumptions that inform such social analysis. The social relations of production that typically characterize the capitalist mode of production are predicated on patterns of ownership and control that generate a class system. Although there are ongoing debates among neo-Marxists concerning the precise nature of the class structure and the number of classes in advanced capitalist society, these scholars generally agree that a dominant class controls the major economic institutions and benefits from the operation of these institutions. The dominant class is typically made up of those who own and control the forces of production and who, as a result of this structural position, are able to draw off various amounts of social surplus in various forms, such as profit and rent. There is also general agreement that other classes are defined by different relationships to the forces of production. Members of the non-dominant class typically survive by selling their capacity to work, their labour power. These class relations tend to generate relations of power, domination, subordination, alienation, and conflict. According to neo-Marxian theory, the dominant class is able systematically to translate its economic power into ideological power and political power. Ideological power will, of course, allow the dominant class to influence definitions of normal and abnormal, acceptable and deviant behaviour. Control over the institutions of the polity give the dominant class a large measure of control over the codification of its values into law and the implementation and enforcement of those laws by the agencies of social control such as the police. The existence of a class structure in which the various classes are defined by different structural locations in the economic order will produce economic, ideological, and political conflict as different classes struggle to improve, enhance, and protect their economic and political interests.

Those adopting a neo-Marxian or conflict approach will tend to assume that the capitalist system is also characterized by a series of fundamental and radical contradictions. Not the least of these contradictions is the tendency for the dominant class to attempt to improve the economic productivity of its workers through the application of new technologies, while workers might resist technologies because they know that one of the costs of technological change is workers' jobs. As more and more workers are replaced by technology, the overall or aggregate capacity of the people in a society to buy the goods and services that capitalists offer on the market are reduced and thus there is a fundamental contradiction between technologically based economic change and the health of the economy as characterized by consumer activity. The end results of technological change can be rising unemployment, declining sales, and economic stagnation, all of which threaten the economic foundation of the society. Eventually these processes will result in a more polarized class structure, with growing pockets of poverty and misery amid potential plenty and opulence. Under such circumstances theft, violence, and other criminal behaviour are to be expected.

When the economic foundation of a society is characterized by class relations that tend to generate conflict, and when a dominant class has access to state and ideological power in order to maintain its position, the inevitable result will be conflict. And when there is conflict, those with power will likely seek to define those opposing their interest as abnormal, unreasonable, and deviant. Spitzer argues that those who steal from the rich, question the operation of the system, try to escape the relationships of alienation and despair via drugs, or question the sanctity of capitalism and the dominant ideologies that reinforce it become defined as problem populations (1978: 352-53). Schur points out that according to conflict theory those who might question the dominant values in society are not necessarily maladjusted because their opposition might arise from "systematic class oppression and arbitrary definition of 'their' behaviour as deviant" (1979: 143).

Whereas more "traditional" conflict or neo-Marxian theory focused on the role of class domination, conflict, and resistance, this theory could be revised to include the possibility of dealing with the conflicts and contradictions that arise from race, sex, and gender relations. While such a task will not be attempted here, it is possible to envision an analysis of how behaviours arising out of efforts to overcome sexual, gender, ethnic, or racial oppression come to be defined by the dominant ideology as deviant.

Conflict theory tends to focus much of its attention on social forms, modes, and agencies of control. Spitzer notes that state agencies use a variety of approaches in attempting to deal with deviant behaviour. Among them are efforts to absorb deviant populations into the general population by co-optation, thereby diffusing or normalizing their actions and criticisms of the system. He argues that efforts are also made to convert potential "troublemakers" by hiring them as police, guards, and social workers who then have responsibility for social control themselves. As he puts it: "If a large number of the controlled can be converted into a first line of defense, threats to the system of class rule can be transformed into resources for its support" (1978: 361). Other approaches include containment, that is, segregation or placing people into ghettos in order more effectively to manage them. Finally, as a last resort, there is outright repression and greater support for law enforcement and punishment, key elements of what Spitzer calls the "crime industry" (362).

It should be apparent by now that once again we can see that the functionalist and conflict perspectives offer radically different explanations for deviant behaviour and quite different answers to the questions posed at the beginning of this chapter. These two approaches, however, also share something in common once again – their focus on the macro picture, on how society (with its value system in one case and its ruling class and structures of power in the other) defines and creates deviance. There is, of course, an alternative approach that derives from symbolic interactionism.

Symbolic Interactionism and Deviance: Labelling Theory

As the reader will recall, the symbolic interactionist perspective focuses, by definition, on the everyday social interactions that make up the bulk of our lives. The approach examines how individuals in interactive situations interpret the behaviours and symbols of other actors and how these interpretations influence their interactive process. If I introduce myself and explain that I am nervous about meeting new people because I have just spent ten years in prison for murder, how will this information influence your reaction to me and our subsequent interaction? An interactionist would be more interested in answering that question than she or he would be in finding out why I committed the initial deviant act, why I was punished in the manner I was, what my punishment had to do with maintaining social order, and so forth. Interactionists always focus their attention on the interpretations and meanings that actors bring to an interactive situation and how this knowledge impacts on the interactive process. When they study deviance, symbolic interactionists will tend to focus their attention on the effects that being labelled a deviant has on interaction between the deviant and others once they know about the presence of a person labelled as deviant. The very title of Howard Becker's classic study using this approach is illustrative: *Outsiders: Studies in the Sociology of Deviance.*

Admittedly, these sketchy comments do not do justice to the interactionist approach. However, like all the material in this introductory volume, they are designed to whet the reader's appetite. Many of the studies of deviance that employ this approach are more exploratory than explanatory. It could be argued that the strength of the symbolic interactionist perspective is its capacity to explore the interesting, complex, and subtle nature of human interaction at the micro level and, therefore, that criticisms of its lack of explanatory power are misguided.

Conclusion

The primary purpose of this chapter has been to introduce the reader to some of the theories that sociologists have developed in their efforts to explain social deviance. When examining these alternate theories and explanations the reader should consider to what extent each approach is capable of explaining the empirical manifestations of deviant behaviour they encounter in their daily lives, including what they learn about from the mass media. In using theory we consider whether it is logical and also its capacity to allow us to make sense of the real world we confront on a daily basis.

Terms and Concepts

Deviance – social actions and behaviours that violate commonly acceptable, dominant, or mainstream values, norms, folkways, and mores. Sociologists will, depending on the theoretical orientation they adopt, explain and interpret deviance and deviant behaviour very differently.

Social Control – the mechanisms, agencies, and practices through which conformity to social accepted values, norms, and beliefs is enforced. Social control can be: (1) understood to be largely internal, involving individual acceptance of society's values and norms; or (2) seen as external, involving the use of formal state and other agencies of enforcement. Usually sociologists understand it to include both.

Subculture of deviance – commonly associated with a structural functionalist approach, characterized by values, norms, beliefs, and social practices that deviate from those of the mainstream or dominant culture. It is assumed that subcultures of deviance are perpetuated through socialization.

Merton's typology of individual adaptation – R.K. Merton argues that deviant behaviour very often occurs when there is a disjunction between an individual's acceptance of a cultural goal and her or his capacity to achieve that goal. The individual responses include: (1) innovation (acceptance of goal but lack of access to normal institutional means to achieve so alternate innovative means are developed); (2) ritualism (rejection of cultural goal but dogged maintenance of prescribed behaviours to reach goal); (3) retreatism (rejection of both goals and socially sanctioned behaviours to achieve them, which thus involves dropping out and existing at margins of society); (4) rebellion (rejection of cultural goals and means for achieving but involves the postulation of alternate goals and means).

Labelling Theory – associated with symbolic interactionist understanding of deviant behaviour, labelling theory focuses on the implications for interaction that follow from individuals being labelled in certain ways. Social labelling typically involves the ascription of positive or negative characteristics to an individual. Labelling theory might study the implications for subsequent social interaction that follow from an individual being labelled a murderer, a pedophile, or a Communist.

12

SOCIOLOGICAL APPROACHES TO THE STUDY OF FAMILIAL RELATIONS

As important as class is, it is only one aspect of inequality in our society. Indeed, we could argue that issues of class are not even the most important dimension of inequality, and that class distinctions pale when compared, for instance, to inequalities in relationships between men and women or inequalities based on differences of ethnicity or colour.

In this regard, an issue of central concern for both sociologists and the general public is the set of social relations and interactions we commonly refer to as "the family." By looking at how sociologists have analysed and explained familial relations and interactions we can learn a number of things. First, a discussion of how sociologists analyse something as common, everyday, and ordinary as familial relations provides us with an opportunity of seeing just how the sociological approach differs from the way we usually understand the world. Most Canadians have, by virtue of personal experience at least, some understanding of the nature and character of familial relations. But our common-sense understanding is not the same as a systematic view of the phenomenon, and as a result sociologists would maintain that such a view is inadequate.

The second benefit we can gain by studying familial relations is connected to the question of social theory. The precise differences, strengths, and weaknesses of the various theoretical positions become clearer when the theories are applied to specific issues. Sociologists using the major perspectives of structural functionalism and neo-Marxism, as well as those influenced by feminist thought, have developed an extensive literature on the family, and a quick overview of the basic arguments each position has put forth should allow us to develop our understanding of the issues of gender and familial relations.

While there are any number of other social issues or institutions that could be used to illustrate the nature of sociological analysis, familial relations are appropriate for discussion here for a number of reasons.

1. It has often been argued that some form of organized familial relations is a universal feature of human society. If some form of family is found in all societies, the study of families is surely of fundamental importance.
2. Concern for and an interest in familial relations pervade our society. Politicians, people in the media, representatives of organized religion, as well as social scientists and town gossips all articulate a professed interest in the structures, conditions, and future of families.
3. An understanding of familial relations is a necessary precondition for understanding the larger patterns of sex and gender relations in society. Much of what defines our femininity and masculinity is rooted in our families.
4. Families are important agents of socialization and are therefore important in the development of our overall personalities.

Thousands of books, articles, and collections deal with various aspects of familial relations. There are studies dealing with cross-cultural perspectives, marriage rites and family relations, different family forms, mate selection dynamics, the stages of family life, sexual relations in and out of marriage, marriage and family dissolution, and parenting. Here we are going to focus briefly on a narrow and particular aspect of the sociology of the family: the general structure and operation of the nuclear family in industrial capitalist society. We will see how these relations have been addressed by structural functionalists and neo-Marxists, keeping in mind our goal of seeing how sociological analysis works and how the adoption of a specific theoretical perspective influences the questions asked, the research performed, and, finally, the analysis produced.

Basic Definitions

There is much debate in sociology about whether it is appropriate to use the term "the family," because, strangely enough, in a complex industrial society such as ours there is no such thing as "the family." There are instead a number of different types or forms of family, including primary, secondary, single-parent, nuclear, and extended. To the extent that there is workable definition of *family*, it usually includes ideas such as a group of people related or connected by bloodline, marriage rite, or adoption who live together or view themselves as a unit and who perform caretaking services for others, especially the very young (for example, see Schaefer, 1989: 321; Robertson, 1981: 350).

Nuclear family generally refers to a couple who, along with any dependent, unmarried children, share a residence and form a social unit. This definition incorporates most of the features of the various definitions found in the literature. Nuclear families are differentiated from extended families by the fact that *extended families* typically include, in addition to the couple and any dependent children, other relatives such as grandparents, aunts, or uncles. We could define an extended family as three or more generations connected by either blood or marriage relationships forming a social unit and living together. As its name indicates, a *single-parent family* refers to an individual who, for whatever reason, is living with a child or a number of children.

In discussing families we often encounter the word "*kinship*," which refers to networks of people who define themselves as being related by virtue of ancestry, marriage, or adoption. *Marriage* generally refers to some socially or culturally sanctioned arrangement for sexual relationships and the care and rearing of the young. There are many historically and culturally specific rules and forms of marriage.

The Structural Functionalist Approach

The Nuclear Family in Industrial Society

Structural functionalists would say that to understand the position and role of the nuclear family within a developed industrial society such as Canada we must remind ourselves of the nature of the overall social structure. When functionalists examine any aspect or component of a society they begin by asking what is perhaps the most important sociological question: what function does the social phenomenon we are investigating perform for society and its members? It is a question predicated on an important basic assumption, namely, that most if not all social institutions and practices perform functions for society. What, then, are the functions of the family?

To answer this question we must remind ourselves that social systems face a number of problems that must be solved if they are to survive. Functionalists typically refer to these problems as system prerequisites, and they use the notion of system prerequisite as a basis for explaining the typical functions of the nuclear family in modern industrial society.

For the most part, functionalists agree that the functions of the family have changed over time. As industrial society emerged and developed, the entire social structure changed. In pre-industrial society the family was a pivotal institution, because within its confines a great amount of economic activity occurred, children and the young were educated, and in some cases political decisions were made. As society developed and evolved its various structures became more complex, complicated, and specialized. With the emergence of an industrial economy came new economic structures in the form of factories, a development that removed economic activity from the home. The demands of an industrial economy led to the widespread establishment of a formal educational system outside of the home. What in fact occurred was a significant and systematic narrowing and specialization of the functions that the family typically fulfilled. The end result of this evolutionary and developmental process was the typical nuclear family, which came to characterize industrial societies (Parsons, 1971).

The Functions of the Nuclear Family
Just as in structural functionalist theory there are several different "lists" of system prerequisites, in the functionalist literature on the family there are also a number of opinions on just how many central functions the family performs. F. Ivan Nye and Felix Berardo note that the family has been seen as performing at least seven essential functions for society and its individual members: producing economic goods and services, allocating status, educating the young, providing religious training, and offering recreation, protection, and affection (1973: 8). Adrian Wilson notes that all families tend to perform four core functions: facilitating reproduction and the regulation of sexual conduct, socializing the young, providing a site for the provision of material necessities, and providing emotional support (1985: 10). In their book on the family Bryan Strong and Christine DeVault state that the family performs four functions: the production and socialization of children, the facilitation of economic co-operation, the assignment of status and roles, and the provision of an environment for the development of intimate relationships (1986: 5-6). Lastly, Talcott Parsons and Robert Bales argue that the number of functions the family performs diminishes as society develops and evolves and that as a result the modern nuclear family has only two essential functions: the socialization and training of the young and the provision of an environment within which adults can maintain stable personalities (1955: 16). According to Parsons and Bales, the family provides for a socially acceptable and legitimate outlet for sexual energies and the fostering of relationships based on intimacy (19-20).

Although their lists of functions vary greatly, all of these scholars are making a similar point: that the family is best understood in terms of the functions it performs for society as a whole and for individual members of that society. The articulation of a list of functions, however, is just the beginning of the analysis of familial relations. When we understand something of the family's functions we can move on to try to find out precisely how the family performs those functions.

The Internal Dynamics of the Nuclear Family

Let's assume for a moment that we accept the argument that the essential functions of the nuclear family in our society are facilitating biological reproduction and the regulation of sexual conduct, the socializing of and caring for the young, and providing economic and emotional support for adults. We must then move on to studying how the family accomplishes these functions. In a functionalist analysis it becomes readily apparent that the family is like every other complex institution in society: it contains within it a division of labour. Given that the family is the institutional arrangement that provides for children's socialization and care and for some of the material needs (food, for example) of adults, it follows that some family member or members must look after the children and some other member or members must provide the food. The increasing specialization of the family's functions means that it is increasingly removed from economic activity, and the survival of the family unit and its members relies on someone working outside the family to bring in the resources required to provide the family's material necessities. That is, some members of the typical nuclear family must earn income to support the family unit. The next question is: how is the division of labour to be determined? Who provides internal services such as child care and socialization, and who engages in work outside the family to acquire the necessary resources for living (Zelditch, 1955)?

In a controversial argument Parsons suggests that the basis for the allocation of roles is at least partly biological. He notes that the fact that women bear and nurse children strongly predisposes them to roles within the family that have to do with the nurturing and care of the young. At the same time, men, by virtue of being exempted from the biological processes associated with birthing and nursing, come to specialize in roles that take them outside the family (Parsons, 1955: 22-23). Following this logic – although Parsons does not specifically make this argument – once these roles become established and accepted, the knowledge of these behavioural patterns becomes incorporated into the society's value system and normative orientations. Definitions of female and male roles become part of what young children learn through the socialization process, and thus girls and boys will begin to see and define themselves in terms of specific types of roles.

Expressive and Instrumental Roles

The work of Parsons and the other contributors to *Family, Socialization and Interaction Process* (1955) established the usage of the terms "expressive" and "instrumental" to describe the two essential roles within the nuclear family (see, for example, 22-23, 313-15). The *expressive roles* are associated with caring, nurturing, emotional support, family integration, and group harmony and are mostly internal to the family. *Instrumental roles* involve connecting the family to the larger social environment and typically include qualities associated with leadership, achievement, securing resources, or goal attainment. Instrumental roles can operate both within and outside the family, although they also connect the family to the external world (Leslie and Korman, 1985: 197; Bourricaud, 1981: 88).

The ideas of expressive and instrumental roles, when added to those concerning male and female roles, provide an analysis suggesting why it is that women and men do what they do within the family structure. Many functionalists would argue that the allocation of different roles for men and women becomes less of a biologically determined process and more of a cultural and social process. That is, the movement of women into expressive roles and men into instrumental roles is something that relates more to society's values and norms than to some biologically based destiny. Once certain ideas and conceptions concerning what it means to be male and masculine or female and feminine become entrenched in the value system, they are passed on from generation to generation through socialization, thus influencing the personality characteristics and decisions that men and women make about their lives.

Functionalists would argue, then, that the processes by which female and male personalities develop are intimately connected to the structures and functions of the family, through the division of labour, socialization, and the allocation of expressive and instrumental roles. Other complicating factors can enter the picture – for example, when prevailing religious beliefs specify appropriate roles for women and men. When the definitions of masculinity and femininity contained in religious belief systems reinforce the values that have developed in the family and the larger society, this means that yet another agent of socialization is at work. In addition, the broader values, norms, folkways, and mores of a society are also transmitted through agents of socialization such as the educational system and the mass media. As a result, children come to acquire from an early age a systematic understanding of what is appropriate for males and females. Definitions of what it means to be masculine and feminine become a key part of our character structures, and as a result they have a great impact on our actions and behaviours.

Family Dysfunctions

In 1965, in an article entitled "The Normal American Family," Parsons delineated the general patterns of the nuclear family as "normal." To the extent that such a portrayal was part of what C.W. Mills called the great American celebration, it failed to address the possible element of dysfunction in the nuclear family. We now know that problems were developing within the North American family even in the post-war period of prosperity and its accompanying "good life."

By the early 1970s the mass media were becoming aware that not all was well with the American family. For example, in October, 1971, the popular women's magazine *McCall's* included an article called "Why Good Marriages Fail." A major story in the March 12, 1973, *Newsweek* was "The Broken Family: Divorce U.S. Style." In the September, 1974, issue of *Redbook*, Margaret Mead contributed to the developing awareness of crisis in the American family with her article, "Too Many Divorces, Too Soon."

Added to the stories about more and more "normal families" dissolving was evidence that some of the relationships within the traditional nuclear family were dysfunctional, to say the least. The August, 1971, edition of *Psychology Today* contained the article, "Families Can Be Unhealthy for Children and Other Living Things" by Arlene Skolnick, an expert on family relations. The story was part of a process then under way that involved making public the so-called private issue of domestic violence. The decade of the 1980s brought the issue of domestic violence and sexual abuse into the realm of full public discourse, although even now there are still those who would deny its severity as a public issue. The first systematic revelations of this aspect of the nuclear family have caused considerable controversy.

In addition to the evidence of severe dysfunctioning, the typical nuclear family came under attack from other sources during the sixties and seventies. The emergence of a youth counter-culture with its "hippies" and "dropouts" brought with it a series of innovations in sexual and child-rearing practices. There seemed to be an increase in the number of single-parent families as well as experimental, communal, and extended families. All of this led to more questions about the "normalcy" of any specified family form.

Although structural functionalists recognize the possibility of dysfunctioning elements in a social system, their actual analysis of such occurrences leads to difficulties. Many functionalists engaged in examining the family began to recognize the existence of dysfunctions and malfunctions, but their explanations of these processes proved less than convincing. In many cases dysfunction was linked to individual problems such as drug use and addiction. Or it was linked to the family's need to adjust to external changes, such as economic dislocation, or to changes in society's views of appropriate roles for males and females. In short, structural functionalists had no systematic theoretical means of explaining the dysfunctionings. What did emerge, however, was a systematic challenge to the entire functionalist approach from those adopting a radically different perspective.

The Neo-Marxist Approach

The Twentieth-Century Marxian Analysis of the Family
Despite Engels's work on the subject, reviewed in Chapter 7, there was little systematic development of a Marxian approach to the family in the period from the turn of the century through the 1960s. This was due, in part, to the fact that Marxism tended to be associated with the Soviet Union and Stalinism, a development that did not particularly foster original and innovative revisions in areas like the analysis of familial relations. During the period since the 1960s the emergence of the women's movement and a renewed interest in Marx and Marxian theory both served to provide an impetus for the re-examination and re-evaluation of the Marxian approach to the analysis of familial relations. In the late 1960s especially, a number of scholars attempted to revise and reformulate the Marxian position regarding the family in capitalist society, carrying the thought beyond Engels's original position.

The Nuclear Family: Serving the Capitalist Class
The initial spate of neo-Marxist writings maintained in essence that the nuclear patriarchal family that characterized advanced capitalist society was perfectly suited to serve the interests of the capitalist or dominant class. Although the neo-Marxists did not dispute the argument that the family performs key functions in the social structure, for them the issue was "In whose interests?" – that is, who or what class benefits from the particular role of the family? How, in particular, does the nuclear patriarchal family benefit capitalists?

Although the neo-Marxist writings cover a range of issues, there are three important arguments we can tease out of them (see, for example, Benston, 1978; Reed, 1978; Seccombe, 1974; Himmelweit and Mohun,

1977; Armstrong and Armstrong, 1984; Armstrong, 1984). These arguments are that the nuclear family serves capital by: producing and reproducing labour power; providing a site for the maintenance of a reserve army of labour; and facilitating the consumption of vast amounts of consumer goods.

Production and Reproduction of Labour Power

One of the essential commodities within the capitalist system is labour power, which is a commodity because, like any other commodity, it is bought and sold on the market, in this case the labour market. If the capitalist system is to function, and if capitalists are to appropriate surplus value and thus gain profits, they must have workers to operate their factories, mills, mines, stores, and offices. These workers sell their capacity to work, their labour power, for a wage or salary. If workers are to stay healthy and come to work for a specified period, say eight hours, day after day, month after month, year after year, those workers must have certain needs met. If they are to be efficient and effective they must be properly nourished and rested. They must, when off work, have an opportunity to "recharge" their physical and emotional batteries, to relax and enjoy life, which often involves producing children.

The process by which workers are prepared physically, emotionally, and mentally for the next day of work and by which workers, by having children, reproduce future generations of workers is called the production and reproduction of labour power. The central questions for this mode of analysis are: where is this done, and who performs the work?

The answer to the first question is in the family. The family in capitalist society, especially the working-class family, is in essence a social factory in which the commodity of labour power is produced and reproduced. The work that goes on in the family – work called *domestic labour* – is geared to both maintaining the life and fitness to work of the current generation of workers and caring for and preparing future generations of workers. In providing a worker with meals, emotional and physical support, and a place to rest and relax and generally to get ready to go forth to work the next day, the domestic worker in the family is really producing and reproducing labour power.

Complex debates have developed among neo-Marxists about the exact role of domestic labour in the production and appropriation of surplus value by capital. For instance, does domestic labour actually produce value or just use value? But the essential point here is how neo-Marxist theorists understand the role of the family. In its function of producing and reproducing labour power, they see the family as serving the interests of the capitalist class. It was, after all, the capitalist class that required a steady and reliable supply of labour power; by providing this supply family structures serve the interests of the dominant class.

The task of performing the required domestic labour has overwhelmingly been the domain of women. The question this leads to – how and why women came to be primarily responsible for the sphere of domestic labour – has itself spawned an enormous debate. (See, for example, Oakley, 1974; Reed, 1978; Luxton, Rosenberg, and Arat-Koc, 1990; Armstrong and Armstrong, 1984; Seccombe, 1974; Himmelweit and Mohun, 1977.) But one set of answers involves the role of ideology, the actions of the state, and even the role of biology.

Ideology enters the process in the form of sexism. Neo-Marxists are interested in the historical evolution of sexist ideologies in both the pre-capitalist and capitalist eras. Ideologies of male domination and sexism have been present in Western culture since the time of classical Greek and Roman society. During the period after the fall of Rome, when the Christian church was emerging, some of the tendencies became enshrined in official church teachings and dogmas – teachings that coincided with particular views of men and women that emerged in the codes of chivalry of feudal Europe, for instance. Before the emergence of capitalism, then, there was a long tradition of patriarchal and sexist thought in the West, and those modes of thinking became a part of the social, political, and economic processes of the capitalist system.

Added to these ideological factors is the role of the state. There is significant evidence that the state in various Western capitalist nations has been a decisive factor in the development of the patriarchal nuclear family (Dickinson and Russell, 1986; McIntosh, 1978). Through legislative actions that reinforce the male breadwinner role and the female domestic role, the state has helped to establish and maintain the structures of the nuclear family. These state actions include everything from the restrictions on women's work in the early English factory laws to more modern laws concerning child custody and family support. By limiting women's participation in certain sectors of the labour force, legislative initiatives served a double function. First, by being excluded women were more likely to be at home producing and reproducing labour power. Second, men were placed in a structural position of having others dependent on them. In theory, workers who are conscious of others depending on them tend to be more reliable; they are less likely to quit and move, or even go on strike, and risk the loss of job security and income.

The Nuclear Family: A Reserve Army of Labour

Given the neo-Marxist notion that labour power is a special and essential commodity in the capitalist system and that there is therefore a market for labour power, the people in a position to purchase labour power – the capitalist class – have an interest in a stable and adequate supply in the market. If there are shortages of labour power, the price of the commodity, in this case expressed as wages, can be forced up. Some degree of unemployment – which creates an oversupply of labour power – is thus in the interests of the capitalist class. Marx examined the role of surplus labour pools in the early development of capitalism, and in applying his approach to modern capitalism neo-Marxists have suggested that women in the family can serve as a labour pool to be drawn on during times of acute labour shortage.

A neo-Marxist might argue that women within the nuclear family serve as an ideal reserve army of labour or surplus labour pool. During times of labour shortage brought on by a period of rapid economic expansion or other crises, such as war, various actions can be taken to encourage women to participate in the labour market. For example, ideological campaigns undertaken during the Second World War tried to convince women that it was their patriotic duty to go out and work in factories. Then, when the war was over, "public relations" (or ideological) campaigns carried the opposite intent, encouraging women to return to their homes and unpaid domestic labour.

The Nuclear Family: An Ideal Consumption Unit

Another neo-Marxist argument concerning how the traditional nuclear family functions in the interests of the dominant class takes up the question of commodity consumption. Capitalism, neo-Marxists would argue, is a system based on the production and sale of material commodities, and one of its inherent problems is overproduction, which could also be termed a problem of underconsumption. The problem arises because in their never-ending pursuit of profits corporations develop levels of technology and productivity that are capable of producing more commodities than can be sold. In modern capitalist society oversupply is a constant problem, and corporations must continually attempt to increase their business, to sell as many consumer goods as they can. What better system to promote sales than one based on a nuclear family?

Picture in your mind a typical Western suburban neighbourhood composed of middle-class and working-class houses. In each of these homes there are several radios, perhaps several televisions, a washing machine, a dryer, a lawnmower, and other products. Given how many hours a week some of these items, such as the lawnmower or even the washing machine, are actually used, wouldn't it make sense for two or more families to share the items? The answer to that question, in capitalist society at least, is no. For Western families, part of the accepted social definition of success and the enjoyment of the "good life" is having their own consumer durables. Indeed, as a result of massive advertising campaigns supported by the corporate sector, the possession of consumer durables has come to be equated with the meaning of life. The more stuff we have, the better off we are in every respect. Consume, consume, consume: this becomes the doctrine that drives our lives, and we can never have enough of the material goodies. If you are a producer of consumer commodities, what better system than one composed of hundreds of thousands of small-sized consumption units in the form of isolated nuclear families, which all compete with each other to have the latest and best of every possible household and personal consumer item?

The neo-Marxist tradition, then, understands the nuclear family within capitalist society as an institutional order or arrangement that functions primarily in the interests of the capitalist class. To be sure, the family looks after the individual and personal needs of its members, but to the extent that the family unit is a part of the process of producing and reproducing the capacity of the working class to sell its labour power, those activities also benefit capital. Neo-Marxists would argue that there are important class dimensions to this process, in that the structures and operations of working-class families will be different from those of the capitalist and middle-class or petty-bourgeois families. Among the essential differences will be the likelihood of the presence of paid domestic workers in upper-class families, a situation that changes the role of family members in terms of domestic work. In addition, the role of the upper-class family, and domestic labour therein, as regards the supply and provision of labour power for the capitalist system is different than it is for the working-class family.

The Feminist Challenge to Sociological Thought

Most of the important new directions in sociological thinking and analysis during the past two decades have been stimulated and informed by feminism. In the case of sociological analysis of familial relations, there has been an explosion of new ideas, arguments, theories, and empirical studies, and most of them have challenged both the structural functionalist and neo-Marxist positions.

In recent years both the Marxist and functionalist approaches have been criticized for failing to address numerous central issues in familial relations. Among those issues are the history of familial relations, especially patriarchal relations, the nature of household organization, sex and gender relations in the family, the extent and causes of domestic violence, and the role of the state in structuring familial relations and reproductive relations.

Although feminist scholars have not completed the task of developing the basis for systematic analyses of these issues, there are several excellent collections of readings that illustrate the new directions in family studies. In *Family Matters* (1988), Karen Anderson, Hugh Armstrong, Pat Armstrong, and other authors present a series of essays that deal with issues ranging from defining family to theories of the family, state policy, and domestic violence. Another significant collection, edited by Nancy Mandell and Ann Duffy, is *Reconstructing the Canadian Family: Feminist Perspectives* (1988). Essays in this collection deal with mothers and mothering, fathers and fathering, children, different family forms, women, family and work, issues surrounding reproductive technologies, and the role of the state. Barrie Thorne and Marilyn Yalorm have edited a collection of equally broad-ranging papers under the title *Rethinking the Family: Some Feminist Questions* (1982).

A central concern in feminist studies is the subordination and oppression of women (see, for instance, Barrett, 1980). Functionalism and Marxism both recognize and acknowledge that men and women tend to occupy different roles and positions in many institutions and that as a result men tend to have higher incomes, more power, and greater status. However, as Patricia Lengermann and Jill Niebrugge-Brantley (1988) argue, it is possible for an analytical approach to acknowledge that there are differences between people's income and their positions in terms of power without acknowledging that these conditions involve relations of subordination and oppression. The functionalist approach clearly sees inequality in this problematic way, and it can also be argued that the neo-Marxist approach fails to address the oppression of women because it concentrates on the issue of class.

In their analyses of domestic work and the relations typical of the traditional nuclear family, feminists have pointed out in detail the existing relations of subordination and oppression. They argue, for instance, that male members of a nuclear family benefit when women are in a structural situation of having to provide meals, undertake child care, do laundry and housecleaning, and engage in a whole range of domestic work that is necessary to produce and reproduce labour power (Hartmann, 1986). As the work of Meg Luxton (1980, 1988) indicates, even when women are employed full-time outside the household, they still tend to do the vast majority of domestic and household labour.

In addition to researching and analysing domestic labour and familial relations, feminist scholars have also developed a compelling picture of the role of the state in the development and perpetuation of patriarchal family forms. Writers such as Jane Ursel (1986, 1992), Varda Burstyn (1985), and Norene Pupo (1988) have provided convincing arguments and evidence that the state in Canada has systematically acted in a way that promotes and bolsters patriarchy. Drawing on historical data, they show how a range of different state actions and acts dealing with issues from family allowances and support to employment measures all serve to maintain patriarchy and thus the oppression of women.

The important issue of reproductive relations has also emerged as central in recent feminist-inspired attempts to understand familial relations. Although many feminists deny that there is a biological basis to the oppression of women, some have suggested that the biological differences between women and men must be addressed in our efforts to understand the dynamics of patriarchal families. Mary O'Brien's *The Politics of Reproduction* (1981) has become a key source for those thinking about the role of biological differences in male and female relations.

Many sociologists who have been influenced by feminism have found that the concept of ideology is also a necessary tool for examining familial relations. Luxton notes that it is necessary and important "to differentiate between *ideology* and the actual ways in which people interact, co-reside, have sexual relations, have babies, marry, divorce, raise children and so on" (1988: 238). She points out, as does Barrett, that the ideology of family tends to involve powerful notions of traditional "oughts" in the views of the nuclear family. As Luxton argues, these ideological frames of reference or belief systems have an impact because they influence how people think things ought to be done and how they should go about organizing their lives, as well as influencing government policy and action.

Feminist theorists have also looked at domestic and family violence, incest and sexual abuse, the role of familial relations in constructing gender identities, different and changing family forms, and the precise historical patterns of family form development – illustrating graphically how new approaches in sociology can offer alternative or extended perspectives. These new approaches are necessary, because it is clear that women have long been excluded from the corridors of power – excluded from positions of power and leadership not just in politics, but in the home and workplace as well, including academia. In the past women were not often included in the making of the sociological imagination – where men and male theory have long held sway. In the current day, new approaches to theory must play their part in dealing with this history of oppression and exclusion.

Terms and Concepts

Family – a concept virtually impossible to define, in part because of its loaded ideological history. Conventional sociological definitions usually include references to "basic kinship unit," or to people related by blood or adoption living together in some kind of recognized social unit. We may be well advised to use the concept only in reference to specific forms of family, as in nuclear family. Familial relations are those related to biological reproduction and extended child care.

Nuclear family – an arrangement or set of established social relationships between female and male biological or adoptive parents and their dependent children (biological or adopted).

Instrumental and expressive roles – relates to the traditional functionalist approach to the family, which argued that there were two essential roles within the typical nuclear family. Instrumental roles are those associated with goal-directed behaviour, more external in orientation, involving authority, achievement, and leadership. Expressive roles are related to a family's more internal emotional matters dealing with nurturing, emotional support, or family integration. The classical functionalist work of Parsons and others suggested that men tend to occupy instrumental roles and women expressive roles.

Functions of the family – in structural functionalism, relates to the view of the family as a universal institution, found in every society because it performs several vital social functions, meeting basic system prerequisites including the regulation of sexual behaviour, facilitating biological reproduction, and providing early child care and socialization of the young, as well as providing a site for the provision of basic material and emotional support for its members.

Functions of the family – in Marxian theory, the assumption that the family tends, like all other social institutions, to operate in the interests of the ruling or dominant class. It has been argued that the traditional nuclear family serves the interests of the capitalist class by functioning to produce and reproduce labour power, by providing a site where a reserve army of labour (a labour pool) can be maintained at no cost to capital, and by being an ideal consumption unit for the commodities produced by capitalists. Although there are variations in the Marxian analyses of the role women play in the overall system, there is acceptance of the position that the nuclear family itself is well suited to meet the needs of the capitalist class and the capitalist system.

THE SOCIOLOGICAL IMAGINATION REVISITED AND NEW DIRECTIONS IN SOCIAL THEORY

Beyond the Existing Approaches

As sociology students first encounter basic sociological concepts and the different theoretical perspectives, two important questions often emerge. The first has to do with what these abstract debates and discussions have to do with the development of the sociological imagination – that is, with the student's capacity to understand everyday social existence. The second question has to do with the fact that students often find themselves agreeing with key points from each perspective, and so they begin to ask if it is possible to synthesize the positions in order to arrive at a more adequate approach.

First, how indeed does seemingly abstract social theory relate to our understanding of everyday social existence? To begin with, theory is an essential part of the scientific project: it is the basis of the intellectual process of explaining why and how things happen. Description and explanation are quite different. There are people, it is true, who are not interested in explaining and understanding their world and who are therefore not interested in theory. Sociologists, by definition, do not fall into this category, because they have accepted the importance of attempting to understand and explain the social world. As a result of our commitment to the development of a sociological imagination, we accept the necessity of understanding and using social theory. We understand that without the study and use of theory we cannot come fully to understand ourselves and our society.

If we accept this argument – that understanding and using social theory are necessary parts of developing the promise of the sociological imagination – we must still confront the issue of which theory is most adequate or most appropriate. Because each of the major

279

approaches undoubtedly has its strengths and weaknesses, we are not likely to accept any of them in its entirety. Perhaps it is possible to formulate an eclectic approach that adopts key elements of the major existing approaches.

Structuration Theory and an Alternative Framework

In recent years the British sociologist Anthony Giddens has developed a series of critiques of the existing sociological theories, an endeavour that has influenced our efforts to develop an alternative approach. In following Giddens's approach – without taking it up in its entirety – we will attempt to construct a possible alternative framework.

Agency and Structure

The central problem faced by any social theory is to explain the relationship between individuals and their society. As biological creatures with unique physiological features – including our huge and complex brains and prehensile hands, for example – human beings have become active, conscious, intelligent social problem-solvers. Once we have accidentally or deliberately solved a problem or met a need, we have the intellectual capacity to remember what we did, and then by using our communicative capacities we can pass this knowledge on to other individuals and future generations.

The social activities we develop and engage in as we attempt to solve our problems and meet our needs can be referred to as *social practices*. Whether it is the noun "practice" or the verb "practise," we are referring to an action that is habitually performed. Taken together these words suit the idea of human action, because it seems that once humans discover or develop a mode of conduct that solves a problem, we stay with it. Our conduct becomes regularized, routinized, patterned, structured, and habitualized – in other words, institutionalized. When we say human practice becomes institutionalized we mean it has developed into a structured and organized mode or way of doing things.

In dealing with our individual and species needs and problems we also develop stocks of knowledge and modes of understanding "how things work." Such knowledge, ideas, belief systems, and consciousness become a part of the social environment. An integral part of the emergence of this knowledge has been the emergence of modes of communicating and of storing this knowledge, a process we commonly call the development of language. Significantly, all of these human practices occur in the context of a particular geographic location and a particular moment in history.

Human social structures, with their institutions, statuses, roles, value systems, groups, and so on, develop, then, as a result of humans acting socially to solve their individual and species needs, drives, and problems. Without doubt, human beings produce their social structures. Once these structures develop and emerge they in turn become the central determinant of subsequent behaviour. Giddens refers to the fact that we are simultaneously the product and producer of our social structures as the *duality of structure* (1984: ch. 1).

Social Causation

Human society is an enormously complex phenomenon whose shape and character cannot be attributed to any single factor or process. It is clear, however, that the structure and organization of some human practices have a fundamental impact on the nature of the overall social structure.

If human beings are to survive as individuals and as a species, we must deal with two basic problems. First we must provide ourselves with the necessary material basis of our physical existence: food, clothing, and shelter. In addition, if we are to survive as a species we must reproduce in order to ensure that the current generation will not be the last. The future of any species is contingent on biological reproduction. The continuation of most of the activities we associate with being human – activities that might include art, philosophy, or even thinking about God – requires the species to ensure that its material needs are met and that the processes of biological reproduction are facilitated.

Besides being necessary for individual and species survival, these practices also seem to be central factors in influencing the general structures of the entire society. The organization of material production and biological reproduction has a profound impact on the entire range of institutionalized practices and structures that exist in a particular society. These key practices represent a kind of social basis or core around which other activities emerge and revolve.

Once again, the relationship between these practices and the larger social structure is complex. All institutions in a social structure are part of a larger whole or totality, and as such they are connected through a complicated reciprocal set of relationships. The practices we commonly associate with the economic order, the family, the polity, religion, and the educational order are each characterized by sets of ideas, stocks of knowledge, and ideologies. Each of them has its own internal structures, patterns of organization, and relationships with other institutional orders.

Both structural functionalism and neo-Marxist theory suggest that institutions are best understood in terms of their functions for either the society as a whole or the dominant or ruling class. The structural functionalist maintains that society has needs and problems that institutions function to solve. The neo-Marxist maintains that most institutions tend to function in the economic interests of the dominant class. According to the alternative approach, institutions are better understood as emerging out of the social efforts of people to solve their individual and species problems. Society as a whole, as well as particular classes, may very well benefit from how institutions have come to be arranged, but this fact alone does not cause or explain the existence of institutions.

The alternative approach maintains that the point of departure for social analysis must be the organization of biological reproduction and material production. Used in this context, *organization* refers to the patterns of social relations taken up by human actors involved in the practice. In the case of production in a capitalist society, the *organization of production* refers to the class relations; and in the case of biological reproduction it refers to the relationships between the sexes. Included in the organization of social relations are the various stocks of knowledge, ideas, and ideologies that emerge as part of these activities as they occur in time and space. The idea of *time and space* refers to the fact that such activities are always concretely located at a particular geographical location at a particular moment in history.

The Limits of Abstract Theory

In the end, abstract theoretical discussions serve only a limited role in sociology, because the final objective of the discipline is not to build abstract theoretical frameworks. When we study theory, it is always necessary to remember that the ultimate purpose of social theory is to explain a certain aspect of the real world. When we come right down to it, sociologists are interested in the nature of the concrete and real social processes that occur in Canada, Australia, the United States, or some other specific society. Social analysis is about social processes and structures that are by definition located firmly in time and space. Social analysis is in each and every case about a specific society at a specific moment and time; thus, all abstract theory can do is assist sociologists by guiding them in their investigations. Social theory can only suggest points of departure and establish priorities for what should be investigated.

This serves to raise the question of how the approach adopted here relates to concrete social analysis. And we must remember that individual sociologists may be interested in understanding any number of different societies at different points in time. A sociologist could be interested in understanding some aspect of classical Greek society, feudal Europe, England in the 1780s, France in 1850, or Canada in 1996. In each case, if the investigator were to follow what I've called the alternative approach, the point of departure would be an analysis of the organization of material production and biological reproduction.

Point of departure is important. While understanding that the organization of material production and biological reproduction is a necessary condition for studying these societies, that understanding remains just that: a beginning point for sociological analysis. After explaining the workings of these aspects of the society, sociologists will still need to understand the nature of the larger social structure, including the polity, the role of religion, the manner by which culture is enhanced and transmitted (media, education), as well as the impact of geographical factors at a given historical moment.

Sociology is, after all, more than abstract deliberations on the nature of society. Sociology is more than the gathering of descriptive data about the social world. Sociology is the analysis and explanation of concrete and empirical social events. Sociological analysis and explanation become possible through the development of adequate theoretical guidelines, which provide the organizing principles necessary for making sense out of historical and empirical data.

One last issue that warrants comment relates to the possibility of developing a theory applicable to all societies in all places and at all times. Over the centuries various theorists have claimed to have found universal principles upon which an all-encompassing theory of society can be established. While the approach being advocated here does make some claims, such as those relating to the necessity of humans producing and reproducing, which might seem like universal claims, it is clear that a transhistorical theory of human society is not a realistic or desirable goal.

To say that human beings must produce satisfaction for their material needs and engage in reproductive behaviour if they are to survive as individuals and as a species is not to make any claims about how these activities are organized or carried out. To argue that how material production and species reproduction are organized and structured has an impact on other dimensions of a social structure is not to make any claims about the precise nature of that impact. As we know, material production and species reproduction have been organized in a multitude of different ways over the span of human history, and no theoretical approach could possibly address them all. What we may require are, in fact, a multitude of quite specific theories addressing, for example, the structures of Greek society, feudal society, early capitalist society, liberal democratic society, and so on. In each case the task of sociologists is to study how material production and biological reproduction are organized and structured, and to consider what ideas and stocks of knowledge have emerged as a part of this process. How do these practices relate to each other and the other institutional orders that characterize the society at a certain moment in time?

This book is essentially written for those who live in a capitalist society. It seems clear that to understand capitalist society we should begin by looking to those who have attempted to understand and explain material production in capitalist societies. The works of Durkheim, Marx, and Weber are obviously of interest. But sociologists must also direct their attention to the processes of biological reproduction and examine the efforts of social thinkers to understand those processes. In doing this the work of feminist scholars forms an essential tool.

As we begin to engage in social analysis the scope of our investigation will become even more focused as we realize that our concern is not just with material production in general, but with material production in Canada. We are not simply interested in species reproduction in the late twentieth century but with reproductive relations in Canada in the 1990s. The specification of our precise research agenda makes our task more difficult and easier at the same time. It is more difficult because we must deal with the complexities and intricacies of the institutional orders and specific institutions that make up Canada in the 1990s. It is easier because we are dealing with concrete historical and empirical processes that we can actually come to know and that can be invaluable in determining the adequacy of our theoretical thinking.

As sociology moves toward a new century, new and innovative modes of theorizing and thinking will be required. There is good reason to think that an adequate approach must build on the insights of the materialist and feminist approaches. The materialist claim that the manner by which humans produce satisfaction for their material problems has a significant impact on the rest of society is compelling. The insights of feminist theory are even more compelling since it is clear that we must consider the relationships between men and women as a basic element of all our theoretical thinking. These considerations

– of sex and gender relations – should never be simply treated as secondary or as issues that can be somehow "added on."

The Sociological Imagination Revisited

The famous dictum of Socrates that "The unexamined life is not worth living" should remind us of what it means to be a human being as opposed to being just another animal. My cat and dog are incapable of examining their lives, and as a result they just seem to live and exist from day to day, enjoying their existence no doubt, but nevertheless just existing without appreciating and understanding what their existence means. It seems they are not particularly concerned about behaving in a way that will help them leave the world a better place than they found it, or at least temporarily altered. All of this raises a question: is there anything wrong with just existing and enjoying life? Perhaps not, especially if it is all a given species has the potential for or is capable of. In the case of humans, however, merely existing is not at all close to what we are capable of.

Given the enormous and incredible potential and possibilities that each and every human is endowed with, isn't it a waste and a pity if we do not strive to develop that potential and thus attempt to improve and better our condition and that of the entire species? Isn't it a waste and a pity if we don't examine life, analyse it, and think about it with an eye to improving the human condition – for the sake of both ourselves as individuals and our species as a whole? C.W. Mills thought it was, and that is why he advised us to seek to understand not only ourselves, our lives, and our biographies, but also others, their lives, and their biographies. In a fundamental way Mills, like Socrates, was telling us something about what it means to be human.

But how do we begin to examine and analyse our lives and biographies? Again, Mills provides some answers. He says that to understand ourselves we must be capable of answering questions that draw our attention to the impact of the social environment on ourselves and others. Further, he notes, we must be capable of understanding how our society is structured and how it operates. Lastly, we must know something about the processes by which that society has developed and is developing. This introduction to sociology, I hope, provides some initial concepts, arguments, perspectives, and tools that will allow readers to begin to ask and answer these questions.

It is impossible to develop the capacity we are calling the sociological imagination by taking one university or college course or reading one book. Indeed, such a capacity takes at least a lifetime to develop – and most likely will never be entirely satisfied. But we must begin sometime, and there is no time like the present. I hope the studies you are doing and this book will whet your appetite for more systematic and comprehensive sociological analysis; and I hope they will provide some of the tools you need to begin the process of undertaking such an analysis.

REFERENCES

Abercrombie, Nicholas, Stephen Hill, and Bryan S. Turner. 1988. *The Penguin Dictionary of Sociology.* 2nd ed. London: Penguin Books.

Aberle, D.F., A.K. Cohen, A.K. Davis, M.J. Levy, Jr., and F.S. Sutton. 1967. "The Functional Prerequisites of a Society," in Demerath and Peterson eds., *System, Change and Conflict.*

Abrahamson, Mark. 1978. *Functionalism.* Englewood Cliffs, N.J.: Prentice-Hall.

Anderson, Karen L., Hugh Armstrong, Pat Armstrong, Janice Drakich, Margrit Eichler, Connie Guberman, Alison Hayford, Meg Luxton, John F. Peters, Elaine Porter, C. James Richardson, and Geoffrey Tesson. 1988. *Family Matters: Sociology and Contemporary Canadian Families.* Toronto: Nelson Canada.

Andreski, Stanislav, ed. 1974. *The Essential Comte: Selected from Cours de philosophie positive.* New York: Barnes and Noble.

Ardrey, Robert, *African Genesis.* 1961. New York: Atheneum.

Ardrey, Robert, *The Territorial Imperative.* 1969. New York: Atheneum.

Armstrong, Pat. 1984. *Labour Pains: Women's Work in Crisis.* Toronto: Women's Press.

Armstrong, Pat, and Hugh Armstrong. 1983. "Beyond Sexless Class and Classless Sex," *Studies in Political Economy,* 10 (Winter).

Armstrong, Pat, and Hugh Armstrong, 1984. *The Double Ghetto: Canadian Women and Their Segregated Work.* Revised ed. Toronto: McClelland and Stewart.

Armstrong, Pat, and Hugh Armstrong. 1990. *Theorizing Women's Work.* Toronto: Garamond Press.

Aron, Raymond. 1966. "Social Class, Political Class, Ruling Class," in Bendix and Lipset, eds., *Class, Status, and Power.*

Baldwin, John D. 1986. *George Herbert Mead: A Unifying Theory for Sociology.* Beverly Hills, Cal.: Sage Publications.

Baran, Paul A., and Paul M. Sweezy. 1966. *Monopoly Capital: an Essay on the American Economic and Social Order.* New York: Monthly Review Press.

Barber, Bernard. 1957. *Social Stratification: A Comparative Analysis of Structure and Process.* New York: Harcourt Brace.

Barnes, Harry Elmer. 1965. *An Intellectual and Cultural History of the Western World.* New York: Dover Publications.

287

Barrett, Michèle. 1980. *Women's Oppression Today: Problems in Marxist Feminist Analysis.* London: Verso.

Becker, Howard S. 1963. *Outsiders.* New York: The Free Press.

Becker, Howard S., and Blanche Geer. 1980. "The Fate of Idealism in Medical School," in Joel Charon, ed., *The Meaning of Sociology: A Reader.* Sherman Oaks, Cal.: Alfred Publishing Company.

Bem, Sandra L., and Daryl Bem. 1982. "Homogenizing the American Woman: The Power of An Unconscious Ideology," in Cargan and Ballantine, eds., *Sociological Footprints.*

Bendix, Rinehard, and Seymour Martin Lipset, eds. 1966. *Class, Status, and Power: Social Stratification in Comparative Perspective.* 2nd ed. New York: The Free Press.

Benedict, Ruth. 1934. *Patterns of Culture.* New York: Mentor Books.

Benston, Margaret. 1978. "The Political Economy of Women's Liberation," in Jaggar and Rothenberg, eds., *Feminist Frameworks.*

Bilton, Tony, Kevin Bonnett, Philip Jones, Michelle Standworth, Ken Sheard, and Andrew Webster. 1987. *Introductory Sociology.* 2nd ed. London: Macmillan.

Blau, Peter, and Richard C. Scott. 1963. *Formal Organizations: A Comparative Approach.* San Francisco: Chandler.

Blishen, Bernard. 1967. "A Socio-Economic Index for Occupation," *Canadian Review of Sociology and Anthropology,* 4(1).

Blumer, Herbert. 1969. *Symbolic Interactionism: Perspective and Method.* Englewood Cliffs, N.J.: Prentice-Hall.

Blumer, Herbert. 1978. "Society as Symbolic Interaction," in Alan Wells, ed., *Contemporary Sociological Theory.* Santa Monica, Cal.: Goodyear Publishing.

Bourricaud, François. 1981. *The Sociology of Talcott Parsons.* Chicago: University of Chicago Press.

Bredemeier, Harry C., and Richard M. Stephenson. 1962. *The Analysis of Social Systems.* New York: Holt, Rinehart and Winston.

Burstyn, Varda. 1985. "Masculine Dominance and the State," in Varda Burstyn and Dorothy Smith, *Women, Class, Family and the State.*

Burt, Sandra, Lorraine Code, and Lindsay Dorney. 1993. *Changing Patterns: Women in Canada.* 2nd ed. Toronto: McClelland & Stewart.

Calzavara, Liviana. 1988. "Trends and Policy in Employment Opportunities for Women," in Curtis, Grabb, Guppy, and Gilbert, eds., *Social Inequality in Canada.*

Canadian Global Almanac: A Book of Facts. 1992. Toronto: Global Press.

Caplan, Arthur L., ed. 1978. *The Sociobiology Debate: Readings on Ethical and Scientific Issues.* New York: Harper and Row.

Caplan, Paula J., and Jeremy B. Caplan. 1994. *Thinking Critically About Research on Sex and Gender.* New York: HarperCollins.

Cargan, Leonard, and Jeanne H. Ballantine. 1982. *Sociological Footprints: Introductory Readings in Sociology.* Belmont, Cal.: Wadsworth Publishing.

Carnoy, Martin. 1984. *The State and Political Theory.* Princeton, N.J.: Princeton University Press.

Carroll, William, Linda Christiansen-Ruffman, Raymond Currie, and Deborah Harrison, eds. 1992. *Fragile Truths: Twenty-five Years of Sociology and Anthropology in Canada.* Ottawa: Carleton University Press.

Case, James, and Vernon Stiers. 1971. *Biology.* New York: Macmillan.

Cassirer, Ernst. [1944] 1977. "A Clue to the Nature of Man: The Symbol," in Dennis H. Wrong and Harry L. Gracey, eds., *Readings in Introductory Sociology.* New York: Macmillan.

Charon, Joel M. 1979. *Symbolic Interactionism.* Englewood Cliffs, N.J.: Prentice-Hall.

Chomsky, Noam. 1989. *Necessary Illusions.* Montreal: CBC Enterprises.

Clegg, Stewart, Paul Boreham, and Geoff Dow. 1986. *Class, Politics and the Economy.* London: Routledge and Kegan Paul.

Clement, Wallace. 1975. *The Canadian Corporate Elite: An Analysis of Economic Power.* Toronto: McClelland and Stewart.

Clement, Wallace. 1977. *Continental Corporate Power: Economic Linkages Between Canada and the United States.* Toronto: McClelland and Stewart.

Clement, Wallace. 1988. *The Challenge of Class Analysis.* Ottawa: Carleton University Press.

Clough, Shepard B., and Charles W. Cole. 1967. *Economic History of Europe.* Boston: D.C. Heath and Co.

Cohen, Albert. 1959. "The Study of Social Disorganization and Deviant Behavior," in Robert K. Merton, ed., *Sociology Today.* New York: Basic Books.

Cohen, Bruce J., and Terri L. Orbuch. 1990. *Introduction to Sociology.* New York: McGraw-Hill.

Cohen, Percy. 1973. *Modern Social Theory.* London: Heinemann.

Comte, Auguste. 1853. *The Positive Philosophy.* New York: D. Appleton.

Connell, R.W. 1990. "The State, Gender and Sexual Politics," *Theory and Society,* 19.

Conway, John. 1993. *The Canadian Family in Crisis.* Toronto: James Lorimer.

Cook, Joan Marble. 1975. *In Defense of Homo Sapiens.* New York: Dell.

Coole, Diana H. 1988. *Women in Political Theory: From Ancient Misogyny to Contemporary Feminism.* Hempstead, Herts.: Harvester Wheatsheaf/Lynne Rienner Publishers.

Cooley, Charles H. [1909] 1956. *Social Organization: A Study of the Larger Mind.* Glencoe, Ill.: The Free Press.

Cooley, Charles H. [1922] 1956. *Human Nature and the Social Order.* Glencoe, Ill.: The Free Press.

Coser, Lewis. 1956. *The Functions of Social Conflict.* New York: The Free Press.

Coser, Lewis. 1977. *Masters of Sociological Thought: Ideas in Historical and Social Context.* 2nd ed. New York: Harcourt Brace Jovanovich.

Cowan, Philip A. 1978. *Piaget: With Feeling.* New York: Holt, Rinehart and Winston.

Crider, Andrew, George Goethals, Robert Kavanaugh, and Paul R. Solomon. 1989. *Psychology.* 3rd ed. Glenview, Cal.: Scott, Foresman.

Cuneo, Carl J. 1985. "Have Women Become More Proletarianized than Men?" *Canadian Review of Sociology and Anthropology,* 22(4).

Curtis, James E., and William G. Scott, eds. 1979. *Social Stratification: Canada.* Scarborough, Ont.: Prentice-Hall.

Curtis, James, Edward Grabb, Neil Guppy, and Sid Gilbert, eds. 1988. *Social Inequality in Canada: Patterns, Problems, Policies.* Scarborough, Ont.: Prentice-Hall.

Dalla Costa, Mariarosa. 1972. "Women and the Subservience of Community," in Mariarosa Dalla Costa and Selma James, eds., *The Power of Women and the Subservience of Community.* Bristol, England: Falling Wall Press.

Davis, Kingsley. 1949. "Final Note on a Case of Extreme Isolation," in Wilson and Kolb, eds., *Sociological Analysis.*

Davis, Kingsley. [1953] 1974. "Reply to Tumin," in Lopreato and Lewis, eds., *Social Stratification.*

Davis, Kingsley, and Wilbert E. Moore. 1945. "Some Principles of Stratification," *American Sociological Review,* 10(2).

Demerath, N.J., and R.A. Peterson, eds. 1967. *System, Change and Conflict: A Reader on Contemporary Sociological Theory and the Debate over Functionalism.* New York: The Free Press.

Dickinson, James, and Bob Russell, eds. 1986. *Family, Economy and the State: The Social Reproduction Process Under Capitalism.* Toronto: Garamond Press.

Djao, A.W. 1983. *Inequality and Social Policy: The Sociology of Welfare.* Toronto: John Wiley.

Dobriner, William M. 1969. *Social Structures and Systems: A Sociological Overview.* Pacific Palisades, Cal.: Goodyear Publishing.

Donovan, Josephine. 1992. *Feminist Theory: The Intellectual Traditions of American Feminism.* New York: Frederick Ungar/Continuum.

Durkheim, Emile. [1895] 1964. *The Rules of Sociological Method.* New York: The Free Press.

Durkheim, Emile. 1933. *The Division of Labour in Society.* New York: The Free Press.

Durkheim, Emile. [1897] 1995. *Suicide: A Study in Sociology.* New York: The Free Press.

Eisenstein, Zillah. 1981. *The Radical Future of Liberal Feminism.* Boston: Northeastern University Press.

Elshtain, Jean B., ed. 1982. *The Family in Political Thought.* Amherst: University of Massachusetts Press.

Endleman, Robert. 1977. "Reflections on the Human Revolution," in Dennis Wrong and Harry Gracey, eds., *Readings in Introductory Sociology.* New York: Macmillan.

Engels, F. [1884] 1972. *Origin of the Family, Private Property and the State.* Moscow: Progress Publishers.

Epstein, Cynthia Fuchs. 1988. *Deceptive Distinctions: Sex, Gender, and the Social Order.* New Haven: Yale University Press.

Eshleman, J. Ross. 1975. *The Family: An Introduction.* Boston: Allyn and Bacon.

Fausto-Sterling, Anne. 1985. *Myths of Gender: Biological Theories about Women and Men.* New York: Basic Books.

Fine, Ben. 1983. "Contradiction," in Tom Bottomore, ed., *A Dictionary of Marxist Thought.* Cambridge, Mass.: Harvard University Press.

Firestone, Shulamith. 1970. *The Dialectic of Sex: The Case for a Feminist Revolution.* New York: William Morrow.

Forcese, Dennis. 1975. *The Canadian Class Structure.* 3rd ed. Toronto: McGraw-Hill Ryerson.

Frager, Robert, and James Fadiman. 1984. *Personality and Personal Growth.* 2nd ed. New York: Harper and Row.

Freud, Sigmund. [1920] 1955. *Beyond the Pleasure Principle.* In *The Standard Edition,* Vol. 18. London: Hogarth Press.

Freud, Sigmund. [1933] 1965. *New Introductory Lectures on Psychoanalysis.* New York: W.W. Norton.

Freud, Sigmund. [1924] 1970. *A General Introduction to Psychoanalysis.* New York: Pocket Books.

Freud, Sigmund. [1930] 1982. *Civilization and Its Discontents.* London: Hogarth Press.

Gandy, D. Ross. 1979. *Marx and History: From Primitive Society to the Communist Future.* Austin: University of Texas Press.

Gannage, Charlene. 1987. "A World of Difference: The Case of Women Workers in a Canadian Garment Factory," in Maroney and Luxton, eds., *Feminism and Political Economy.*

Gay, Peter. 1988. *Freud: A Life for Our Times.* New York: Anchor Books/Doubleday.

Gerth, Hans, and C. Wright Mills. 1964. *Character and Social Structure: The Psychology of Social Institutions.* New York: Harcourt Brace.

Giddens, Anthony. 1979. *Central Problems in Social Theory: Action, Structure and Contradiction in Social Analysis.* Berkeley: University of California Press.

Giddens, Anthony. 1981. *A Contemporary Critique of Historical Materialism.* Berkeley: University of California Press.

Giddens, Anthony. 1984. *The Constitution of Society: Outline of the Theory of Structuration.* Cambridge: Polity Press.

Giddens, Anthony. 1987. *Social Theory and Modern Sociology.* Stanford, Cal.: Stanford University Press.

Giddens, Anthony. 1990. *The Consequences of Modernity.* Stanford, Cal.: Stanford University Press.

Gilbert, Dennis, and Joseph A. Kahl. 1987. *American Class Structure: A New Synthesis.* Belmont, Cal.: Wadsworth Publishing.

Gleitman, Henry. 1986. *Psychology.* 2nd ed. New York: W.W. Norton.

Gordon, Milton M. 1950. *Social Class in American Sociology.* New York: McGraw-Hill.

Grabb, Edward G. 1990. *Theories of Social Inequality: Classical and Contemporary Perspectives.* Toronto: Holt, Rinehart and Winston.

Gracey, Harry L. 1977. "Learning the Student Role: Kindergarten as Academic Boot Camp," in Dennis Wrong and Harry Gracey, eds., *Readings in Introductory Sociology.* New York: Macmillan.

Hall, Calvin S. 1979. *A Primer of Freudian Psychology.* New York: Mentor Books.

Hall, Calvin S., and Gardner Lindzey. 1970. *Theories of Personality.* New York: John Wiley & Sons.

Hall, Edward, and Mildred Reed Hall. 1982. "The Sounds of Silence," in Cargan and Ballantine, eds., *Sociological Footprints.*

Hamilton, Peter. 1983. *Talcott Parsons.* London: Ellis Horwood and Tavistock.

Hansen, Karen V., and Ilene J. Philipson, eds. 1990. *Women, Class and the Feminist Imagination: A Socialist-Feminist Reader.* Philadelphia: Temple University Press.

Harding, Sandra. 1986. *The Science Question in Feminism.* Ithaca, N.Y.: Cornell University Press.

Harp, John. 1980. "Social Inequalities and the Transmission of Knowledge," in John Harp and John Hofley, eds., *Structured Inequality in Canada.* Scarborough, Ont: Prentice-Hall.

Harris, Marvin. 1980. *Cultural Materialism: The Struggle for a Science of Culture.* New York: Vintage Books.

Hartmann, Heidi. 1981. "The Unhappy Marriage of Marxism and Feminism: Towards a More Progressive Union," in Sargent, ed., *Women and Revolution.*

Heller, Agnes. 1979. *On Instincts.* Assen, Netherlands: Van Gorcum.

Himmelweit, Susan, and Simon Mohun. 1977. "Domestic Labour and Capital," *Cambridge Journal of Economics*, 1.

Hobbes, Thomas. [1651] 1968. *Leviathan.* Harmondsworth, Middx.: Penguin Books.

Hockett, Charles F., and Robert Ascher. 1964. "The Human Revolution," *Current Anthropology*, 5.

Hollingshead, A.B. 1949. *Elmtown's Youth: The Impact of Social Classes on Adolescents.* New York: John Wiley & Sons.

Holmes, Lowell D. 1985. "South Sea Squall," in Whitten and Hunter eds., *Anthropology*.

Hoyenga, Katharine B., and Kermit T. Hoyenga. 1979. *The Question of Sex Differences.* Boston: Little, Brown and Company.

Hunt, Elgin F., and David C. Colander. 1984. *Social Science: An Introduction to the Study of Society.* New York: Macmillan.

Hunter, Alfred A. 1981. *Class Tells: On Social Inequality in Canada.* Toronto: Butterworths.

Jaggar, Alison M., and Paula S. Rothenberg, eds. 1978. *Feminist Frameworks: Alternative Theoretical Accounts of the Relations Between Men and Women.* New York: McGraw-Hill.

Jary, David, and Julia Jary. 1991. *The HarperCollins Dictionary of Sociology.* New York: HarperCollins.

Jenson, Jane. 1992. "Gender and Reproduction, or Babies and the State," in M. Patricia Connelly and Pat Armstrong, eds., *Feminism in Action.* Toronto: Canadian Scholars Press.

Jessop, Bob. 1982. *The Capitalist State.* Oxford: Martin Robertson.

Johnson, Willis. 1969. *Essentials of Biology.* New York: Holt, Rinehart and Winston.

Kerbo, Harold R. 1983. *Social Stratification and Inequality: Class Conflict in the United States.* New York: McGraw-Hill.

Knuttila, K. Murray. 1992. *State Theories: From Liberalism to the Challenge of Feminism.* 2nd ed. Halifax: Fernwood Publishing.

Kuhn, Annette, and AnneMarie Wolpe, eds. 1978. *Feminism and Materialism: Women and Modes of Production.* London: Routledge and Kegan Paul.

Leahey, Thomas H. 1980. *A History of Psychology.* Englewood Cliffs, N.J.: Prentice-Hall.

Leakey, Richard, and Roger Lewin. 1992. *Origins Revisited: In Search of What Makes Us Human.* New York: Anchor Books/Doubleday.

Lengermann, P.M., and J. Niebrugge-Brantley. 1988. "Contemporary Feminist Theory," in Ritzer, ed., *Sociological Theory*.

Leslie, Gerald R., and Sheila K. Korman. 1985. *The Family in Social Context.* New York: Oxford University Press.

Lewontin, R.C. 1991. *Biology as Ideology.* Concord, Ont.: Anansi.

Lewontin, R.C., Steven Rose, and Leon Kamin. 1985. *Not in Our Genes.* Harmondsworth, Middx.: Penguin Books.

Lopreato, Joseph, and Lionel S. Lewis, eds. 1974. *Social Stratification: A Reader.* New York: Harper and Row.

Lowe, Graham. 1988. "Jobs and the Labour Market," in Curtis, Grabb, Guppy, and Gilbert, eds., *Inequality in Canada.*

Lorenz, Konrad. *On Aggression.* 1966. New York: Harcourt Brace.

Lukes, Stephen. 1974. *Power.* London: Macmillan Press.

Luxton, Meg. 1980. *More Than a Labour of Love: Three Generations of Women's Work in the Home.* Toronto: Women's Press.

Luxton, Meg, Harriet Rosenberg, and Sedef Arat-Koc. 1990. *Through the Kitchen Window: The Politics of Home and Family.* Toronto: Garamond Press.

Lynd, Robert S., and Helen M. Lynd. 1929. *Middletown.* New York: Harcourt Brace Jovanovich.

Lynd, Robert S., and Helen M. Lynd. 1937. *Middletown in Transition: A Study in Cultural Conflicts.* New York: Harcourt Brace Jovanovich.

Mackie, Marlene. 1991. *Gender Relations in Canada.* Toronto: Butterworths.

Mackinnon, Catharine. 1989. *Toward a Feminist Theory of the State.* Cambridge, Mass.: Harvard University Press.

Maclean, Charles. 1977. *The Wolf Children.* New York: Hill and Wang.

Macpherson, C.B. 1968. "Introduction," in Hobbes, *Leviathan.*

Macpherson, C.B. 1973. *Democratic Theory.* Oxford: Clarendon Press.

Malson, Lucien. 1972. *Wolf Children and the Problem of Human Nature.* New York: Monthly Review Press.

Mandell, Nancy, and Ann Duffy, eds. 1988. *Reconstructing the Canadian Family: Feminist Perspectives.* Toronto: Butterworths.

Maroney, Heather Jon, and Meg Luxton, eds. 1987. *Feminism and Political Economy: Women's Work, Women's Struggles.* Toronto: Methuen.

Marshall, Gordon, ed. 1994. *The Concise Oxford Dictionary of Sociology.* Oxford: Oxford University Press.

Martin, David, ed. 1976. *50 Key Words: Sociology.* London: Lutterworth Press.

Marx, Karl. 1964. *The Economic and Philosophical Manuscripts of 1844.* New York: International Publishers.

Marx, Karl. [1844] 1970. *Towards a Critique of Hegel's Philosophy of Right.* Ed. Joseph O'Malley. Cambridge: Cambridge University Press.

Marx, Karl. [1852] 1972. *The Eighteenth Brumaire of Louis Bonaparte.* In Robert Tucker, ed., *The Marx-Engels Reader.* New York: W.W. Norton.

Marx, Karl. [1857] 1973. *Grundrisse.* Harmondsworth, Middx.: Penguin.

Marx, Karl. [1859] 1977. *A Contribution to the Critique of Political Economy*. New York: International Publishers.

Marx, Karl. [1867] 1967. *Capital: A Critique of Political Economy*. New York: International Publishers.

Marx, Karl, and Frederick Engels. [1845] 1973. *The German Ideology*. New York: International Publishers.

Marx, Karl, and Frederick Engels. [1848] 1952. *Manifesto of the Communist Party*. Moscow: Progress Publishers.

McGee, Reece. 1975. *Points of Departure: Basic Concepts in Sociology*. 2nd ed. Hinsdale, Ill.: Dryden Press.

McIntosh, Mary. 1978. "The State and the Oppression of Women," in Kuhn and Wolpe, eds., *Feminism and Materialism*.

McLaren, Arlene T., ed. 1988. *Gender and Society*. Toronto: Copp Clark Pitman.

Mead, G.H. [1934] 1962. *Mind, Self and Society*. Chicago: University of Chicago Press.

Mead, Margaret. [1935] 1971. *Sex and Temperament in Three Primitive Societies*. New York: William Morrow and Company.

Merton, Robert K. 1968. *Social Theory and Social Structure*. New York: The Free Press.

Michels, Robert. [1911] 1962. *Political Parties: A Sociological Study of the Oligarchical Tendencies of Modern Democracy*. New York: The Free Press.

Miliband, Ralph. 1973. *The State in Capitalist Society*. London: Quartet Books.

Mills, C.W. 1951. *White Collar: The American Middle Classes*. New York: Oxford University Press.

Mills, C.W. 1956. *The Power Elite*. New York: Oxford University Press.

Mills, C.W. 1959. *The Sociological Imagination*. New York: Oxford University Press.

Miner, Horace. 1985. "Body Ritual Among the Nacirema," in Whitten and Hunter, eds., *Anthropology*.

Moore, Wilbert E. 1963. *Social Change*. Englewood Cliffs, N.J.: Prentice-Hall.

Morris, Charles W. [1934] 1962. "Introduction," in Mead, *Mind, Self and Society*.

Morris, Desmond. 1969. *The Naked Ape*. Toronto: Bantam Books.

Morton, Peggy. 1972. "Women's Work is Never Done," in *Women Unite*. Toronto: Women's Press.

Nagle, James. 1984. *Heredity and Human Affairs*. St. Louis: Times Mirror.

Natanson, Maurice. 1973. *The Social Dynamics of George H. Mead*. The Hague: Martinus Nijhoff.

Nelson, Brian R. 1982. *Western Political Thought: From Socrates to the Age of Ideology.* Englewood Cliffs, N.J.: Prentice-Hall.

Nelson, Joyce. 1987. *The Perfect Machine: TV in the Nuclear Age.* Toronto: Between the Lines.

Nelson, Joyce. 1989. *Sultans of Sleaze: Public Relations and the Media.* Toronto: Between the Lines.

Nye, F. Ivan, and Felix Berardo. 1973. *The Family: Its Structure and Interaction.* New York: Macmillan.

Oakley, Ann. 1974. *The Sociology of Housework.* London: Martin Robertson.

O'Brien, Mary. 1981. *The Politics of Reproduction.* Boston: Routledge and Kegan Paul.

Ogmundson, R. 1990. "Social Inequality," in Robert Hagedorn, ed., *Sociology.* Toronto: Holt, Rinehart and Winston.

Ollman, Bertell. 1968. "Marx's Use of Class," *American Journal of Sociology*, 73(5).

Ollman, Bertell. 1976. *Alienation: Marx's Conception of Man in Capitalist Society.* 2nd ed. London: Cambridge University Press.

Pareto, Vilfredo. 1976. *Sociological Writings.* Oxford: Basil Blackwell.

Parsons, Talcott. 1949. *Essays in Sociological Theory.* New York: The Free Press.

Parsons, Talcott. 1951. *The Social System.* New York: The Free Press.

Parsons, Talcott. 1955. "The American Family: Its Relations to Personality and the Social Structure," in Parsons and Bales, eds., *Family, Socialization and Interaction Process.*

Parsons, Talcott. 1965. "The Normal American Family," in Bert Adams and Thomas Weirath, eds., *Readings in the Sociology of the Family.* Chicago: Markham Publishing Company.

Parsons, Talcott. 1966. *Societies: Evolutionary and Comparative Perspectives.* Englewood Cliffs, N.J.: Prentice-Hall.

Parsons, Talcott. 1971. *The System of Modern Societies.* Englewood Cliffs, N.J.: Prentice-Hall.

Parsons, Talcott, and R.F. Bales, eds. 1955. *Family, Socialization and Interaction Process.* Glencoe, Ill.: The Free Press.

Parsons, Talcott, and Edward Shils, eds. 1952. *Toward a General Theory of Action.* Cambridge, Mass.: Harvard University Press.

Peterson, Christopher. 1988. *Personality.* New York: Harcourt Brace Jovanovich.

Piaget, Jean, and Barbel Inhelder. 1969. *Psychology of the Child.* New York: Basic Books.

Pineo, Peter. 1980. "The Social Standing of Ethnic and Racial Groupings," in J. Goldstein and R. Bienvenu, eds., *Ethnicity and Ethnic Relations in Canada: A Book of Readings.* Toronto: Butterworths.

Pineo, Peter, and John Porter. 1967. "Occupational Prestige in Canada," *Canadian Review of Sociology and Anthropology*, 4(1).

Pines, Maya. 1981. "The Civilization of Genie," *Psychology Today*, 15 (September).

Porter, John. 1965. *The Vertical Mosaic: An Analysis of Social Class and Power in Canada*. Toronto: University of Toronto Press.

Poulantzas, Nicos. 1972. "The Problem of the Capitalist State," in Robin Blackburn, ed., *Ideology in Social Science: Readings in Critical Social Theory*. London: Fontana/Collins.

Poulantzas, Nicos. 1973. *Political Power and Social Classes*. London: NLB and Sheed and Ward.

Poulantzas, Nicos. 1975. *Classes in Contemporary Capitalism*. London: NLB.

Pupo, Norene. 1988. "Preserving Patriarchy: Women, the Family and the State," in Mandell and Duffy, eds., *Reconstructing the Canadian Family*.

Randall, J.H. 1940. *The Making of the Modern Mind: A Survey of the Intellectual Background of the Present Age*. New York: Houghton Mifflin.

Reed, Evelyn. 1978. "Women: Caste, Class or Oppressed Sex?" in Jaggar and Rothenberg, eds., *Feminist Frameworks*.

Renzetti, Claire M., and Daniel J. Curran. 1992. *Women, Men, and Society*. Boston: Allyn and Bacon.

Rex, John. 1961. *Key Problems of Sociological Theory*. London: Routledge and Kegan Paul.

Ritzer, George. 1988. *Sociological Theory*. 2nd ed. New York: Alfred A. Knopf.

Ritzer, George. 1990. *Frontiers of Social Theory: The New Synthesis*. New York: Columbia University Press.

Robertson, Ian. 1981. *Sociology*. New York: Worth Publishers.

Rose, Arnold M. 1956. *Sociology: The Study of Human Relations*. New York: Alfred A. Knopf.

Rossides, Daniel. 1968. *Society as a Functional Process*. Toronto: McGraw-Hill.

Rossides, Daniel. 1976. *The American Class System*. Atlanta: Houghton Mifflin.

Rossides, Daniel. 1978. *The History and Nature of Sociological Theory*. Boston: Houghton Mifflin.

Rymer, Russ. 1992. "The Annals of Science: A Silent Childhood – I" and "A Silent Childhood – II," *New Yorker*, April 13 and April 20.

Salkind, Neil J., and Sueann Robinson Ambron. 1987. *Child Development*. 5th ed. New York: Holt, Rinehart and Winston.

Sanderson, Stephen K. 1988. *Macrosociology*. New York: Harper and Row.

Sargent, Lydia, ed. 1981. *Women and Revolution: A Discussion of the Unhappy Marriage of Marxism and Feminism.* London: Pluto Press.

Sayers, Janet, Mary Evans, and Nanneke Redclift, eds. 1987. *Engels Revisited: New Feminist Essays.* London: Tavistock.

Schaefer, Richard. 1989. *Sociology.* New York: McGraw-Hill.

Schultz, Duane. 1975. *A History of Modern Psychology.* 2nd ed. New York: Academic Press.

Schur, Edwin M. 1979. *Interpreting Deviance: A Sociological Introduction.* New York: Harper and Row.

Schusky, Ernest L., and Patrick T. Culbert. 1967. *Introducing Culture.* Englewood Cliffs, N.J.: Prentice-Hall.

Seccombe, Wally. 1974. "The Housewife and Her Labour Under Capitalism," *New Left Review*, 83 (January-February).

Shapiro, Martin. 1979. *Getting Doctored: Critical Reflections on Becoming a Physician.* Kitchener, Ont.: Between the Lines.

Shepard, Jon M. 1990. *Sociology.* 4th ed. St. Paul: West Publishing Company.

Simpson, Richard. 1956. "A Modification of the Functional Theory of Social Stratification," *Social Forces*, 35 (December).

Skidmore, William. 1979. *Theoretical Thinking in Sociology.* 2nd ed. London: Cambridge University Press.

Skocpol, Theda. 1979. *States and Social Revolutions.* Cambridge: Cambridge University Press.

Skocpol, Theda. 1980. "Political Response to Capitalist Crisis: Neo-Marxist Theories of the State and the Case of the New Deal," *Politics and Society*, 10(2).

Skocpol, Theda. 1985. "Bringing the State Back In: Strategies of Analysis in Current Research," in Peter B. Evans, Dietrich Rueschemeyer, and Theda Skocpol, eds., *Bringing the State Back In.* Cambridge: Cambridge University Press.

Smith, Anthony D. 1973. *The Concept of Social Change: A Critique of the Functionalist Theory of Social Change.* London: Routledge and Kegan Paul.

Smith, Dorothy. 1981. "Women's Inequality and the Family," in Allan Moscovitch and Glenn Drover, eds., *Inequality: Essays on the Political Economy of Social Welfare.* Toronto: University of Toronto Press.

Smith, Dorothy. 1985. "Women, Class and Family," in Varda Burstyn and Dorothy Smith, *Women, Class, Family and the State.* Toronto: Garamond Press.

Smith, Lillian. 1971. "Killers of the Dream: When I was a Child," in Edgar Schuler, Thomas Hoult, Duane Gibson, and Wilbur Brookover, eds., *Readings in Sociology.* New York: Thomas Y. Crowell.

Snyder, Mark. 1982. "Self-Fulfilling Stereotypes," in Cargan and Ballantine, eds., *Sociological Footprints*.

Spitzer, Steven. 1978. "Toward a Marxian Theory of Deviance," in Ronald A. Farrell and Victoria Lynn Swigert, eds., *Social Deviance*. Philadelphia: J.B. Lippincott Company.

Standley, Arline R. 1981. *Auguste Comte*. Boston: Twayne Publishers.

Statt, David. 1990. *Concise Dictionary of Psychology*. London: Routledge.

Stellar, Eliot. 1988. "Instincts," in *Collier's Encyclopedia*. New York: Macmillan.

Strong, Bryan, and Christine DeVault. 1986. *The Marriage and Family Experience*. St. Paul: West Publishing Company.

Stryker, Sheldon. 1980. *Symbolic Interactionism*. Menlo Park, N.J.: Benjamin/Cummings.

Sydie, Rosalind A. 1987. *Natural Women, Cultured Men: A Feminist Perspective on Sociological Theory*. Toronto: Methuen.

Szymanski, Albert. 1978. *The Capitalist State and the Politics of Class*. Cambridge: Winthrop.

Tavris, Carol, and Carole Wade. 1984. *The Longest War: Sex Differences in Perspective*. 2nd ed. San Diego: Harcourt Brace Jovanovich.

Terkel, Studs. 1974. *Working*. New York: Pantheon Books.

Theodorson, George A., and Achilles G. Theodorson. 1969. *A Modern Dictionary of Sociology*. New York: Thomas Y. Crowell.

Thompson, Kenneth. 1976. *Auguste Comte: The Foundations of Sociology*. London: Nelson.

Thorne, Barrie, and Marilyn Yalom, eds. 1982. *Rethinking the Family: Some Feminist Questions*. New York: Longman.

Tiger, Lionel. *Men in Groups*. 1969. New York: Random House.

Tiger, Lionel. *The Imperial Animal*. 1972. New York: Holt Rinehart.

Tinbergen, N. 1951. *The Study of Instincts*. Oxford: Clarendon.

Tong, Rosemarie. 1989. *Feminist Thought: A Comprehensive Introduction*. Boulder, Col.: Westview Press.

Torrance, James. 1979. *Higher Biology*. London: Edward Arnold.

Tumin, Melvin M. 1967. *Social Stratification: The Forms and Functions of Inequality*. Englewood Cliffs, N.J.: Prentice-Hall.

Tumin, Melvin M., ed. 1970. *Readings on Social Inequality*. Englewood Cliffs, N.J.: Prentice-Hall.

Tumin, Melvin M. [1953] 1974. "Some Principles of Stratification: A Critical Analysis," in Lopreato and Lewis, eds., *Social Stratification*.

Turner, Jonathan H., and Leonard Beeghley. 1981. *The Emergence of Sociological Theory*. Homewood, Ill.: Dorsey Press.

Ursel, Jane. 1986. "The State and the Maintenance of Patriarchy: A

Case Study of Family, Labour and Welfare Legislation in Canada," in Dickinson and Russell, eds., *Family, Economy and the State.*

Ursel, Jane. 1992. *Private Lives and Public Policy: One Hundred Years of State Intervention in the Family.* Toronto: Women's Press.

Veltmeyer, Henry. 1986. *Canadian Class Structure.* Toronto: Garamond Press.

Walizer, M.H., and P.L. Wienir. 1978. *Research Methods and Analysis: Searching for Relationships.* New York: Harper and Row.

Wallace, Ruth A., and Alison Wolf. 1986. *Contemporary Sociological Theory.* Englewood Cliffs, N.J.: Prentice-Hall.

Waller, Willard, ed. 1942. *Charles Horton Cooley.* New York: Dryden Press.

Warner, W. Lloyd. 1949. *Social Class in America: A Manual of Procedure for the Measurement of Social Status.* New York: Harper Torchbooks.

Weber, Max. [1930] 1958. *The Protestant Ethic and the Spirit of Capitalism.* New York: Charles Scribner's Sons.

Weber, Max. 1946. *From Max Weber: Essays in Sociology.* Ed. Hans H. Gerth and C.W. Mills. New York: Oxford University Press.

Weber, Max. 1949. *The Methodology of the Social Sciences.* Ed. E. Shils and H. Finch. Glencoe, Ill.: The Free Press.

Weber, Max. 1968. *Economy and Society: An Outline of Interpretative Sociology.* New York: Bedminster Press.

Whitten, Phillip, and David E. Hunter. 1985. *Anthropology: Contemporary Perspectives.* Boston: Little, Brown and Company.

Williams, Raymond. 1976. *Keywords: A Vocabulary of Culture and Society.* London: Fontana Paperbacks.

Williams, Thomas R. 1972. *Introduction to Socialization.* St. Louis: C.V. Mosby.

Wilson, Adrian. 1985. *Family.* New York: Tavistock.

Wilson, John. 1983. *Social Theory.* Englewood Cliffs, N.J.: Prentice-Hall.

Wilson, Logan, and William Kolb. 1949. *Sociological Analysis: An Introductory Text and Casebook.* New York: Harcourt, Brace and World.

Wilson, S.J. 1981. *Women, the Family and the Economy.* Toronto: McGraw-Hill Ryerson.

Wright, Erik Olin. 1978. *Class, Crisis and the State.* London: Verso.

Wright, Erik Olin. 1985. *Classes.* London: Verso.

Wrong, Dennis. 1959. "The Functional Theory of Stratification: Some Neglected Considerations," *American Sociological Review,* 24 (December).

Wrong, D.H. 1961. "The Oversocialized Concept of Man in Modern Society," *American Sociological Review,* 26.

Zeitlin, Irving M. 1990. *Ideology and the Development of Sociological Theory.* Englewood Cliffs, N.J.: Prentice-Hall.

Zelditch, Morris, Jr. 1955. "Role Differentiation in the Nuclear Family: A Comparative Study," in Parsons and Bales, eds., *Family, Socialization and Interaction Process.*

SUBJECT INDEX

NAME INDEX